GETTING THE WORDS RIGHT

Theodore A. Rees Cheney hasn't spent all his time behind a typewriter. At seventeen he went to the Antarctic with Admiral Byrd; later made other excursions to polar regions; earned degrees in geology and geography. His impressive credentials also include author of several published books, video scripts, and articles, a Master of Arts in Communication, senior scientist at a "think tank," and president of an aerial mapping firm. He has taught courses in creative problem-solving and conducted writing workshops at the graduate level. Formerly Associate Dean of the Graduate School of Corporate and Political Communication at Fairfield University in Connecticut, Cheney is now director of the school's *Writing Concentration* Program.

Getting the Words Right:

How to Rewrite, Edit & Revise

Theodore A. Rees Cheney

Writer's Digest Books

CINCINNATI, OHIO

Getting the Words Right: How to Rewrite, Edit & Revise. © Copyright 1983 by Theodore A. Rees Cheney. Printed and bound in the United States of America. All rights reserved. No part of this book may be reproduced in any form or by any electronic or mechanical means including information storage and retrieval systems without permission in writing from the publisher, except by a reviewer, who may quote brief passages in a review. Published by Writer's Digest Books, an imprint of F&W Publications, Inc., 1507 Dana Avenue, Cincinnati, OH 45207. (800) 289-0963. First edition. First paperback printing 1990.

Other fine Writer's Digest Books are available from your local bookstore or direct from the publisher.

Visit our Web site at www.writersdigest.com for information on more resources for writers.

To receive a free weekly E-mail newsletter delivering tips and updates about writing and about Writer's Digest products, send an E-mail with the message "Subscribe Newsletter" to newsletter-request@writersdigest.com or register directly at our Web site at www.writersdigest.com.

04   03   02   01   00   11   10   9   8   7

Library of Congress Cataloging-in-Publication Data

Cheney, Theodore A. Rees (Theodore Albert Rees), 1928-

   Getting the words right.

   Bibliography: p.
   Includes index.
   1. Rhetoric. I. Title.
PN187.C54   1983   808'.042   83-16661
ISBN 0-89879-420-X

Design by Christine Aulicino

DEDICATED TO

E.B. White

He turned my life around

ACKNOWLEDGMENTS

I want first to acknowledge the role played by my students during the past twenty years. I learned a great deal about writing as I tried to analyze why some of their papers worked and some didn't.

The writing of these graduate students of communication is generally so good that one editor commented: "Most teachers would be pleased to have the students whose examples you've used to highlight problems." Because their writing was usually of high calibre, the occasional "trouble spot" stood out, enabling me to concentrate on a single problem without having first to clear up others.

I've used some student efforts, some from consulting clients, and some of my own attempts as examples of the perils and pitfalls we all face as we try to get the words right. Without my students and clients, this book would have been impossible to write. Thank you all.

There is an adage that says, "Everyone needs an editor." This book on editing was written by an editor and yet it benefited immeasurably by being edited by other editors. There are only two people who worked as hard on this book as I did, Carol Cartaino, Editor-in-Chief, and Howard I. Wells III, Editor. My prior experiences with editors at giant publishing houses made me wonder whether what I had read all my life about editors was all a myth. This fine, humane editorial team at Writer's Digest Books seems a welcome throwback to the days when editing words and ideas was seen as a profession as well as a business. They and their editorial associates slaved over multiple drafts of this manuscript in a valiant effort to keep me from embarrassment in the marketplace.

No less essential to the writing process is the manuscript typist. The many revisions of this book about revision were prepared by the women at S.O.S. in Union City, Connecticut, under the unusually capable and always pleasant direction of Janice Ulrichsen.

After all these years, it is time, at last, to acknowledge publicly how much I owe my wife, Dorothy Bates Cheney. Her cheerful willingness to endure hundreds of lonely weekends and thousands of husbandless evenings has made it possible for me to write what I needed to write. Every writer should have such a resourceful, self-sufficient and understanding helpmate.

INTRODUCTION

This is a book about *writing, rewriting, rereading, reviewing, rethinking, rearranging, repairing, restructuring, reevaluating, editing, tightening, sharpening, smoothing, pruning, polishing, punching up, amending, emending, altering, eliminating, transposing, expanding, condensing, connecting, cohering, unifying, perfecting.*

One of my initial problems was to find a single word that would convey all those related and connotative meanings. After much thinking, and reflecting on what others have thought, I realized that the most useful, most inclusive word was *revision*.

Revision is good for my purpose (our purpose) because of its etymological heritage. The idea of re(vision) is clearly there—a writer must periodically re-(look) at what he or she is writing. You can see other etymological clues in the number of words that begin with re in the series above.

When you, the writer, "see again" the words you've written, you'll find something you can revise to make your work *more accurate, more concise, more helpful, more euphonious, more humorous, more serious, more in-keeping-with-the-times, more appropriate, more dramatic, more heart-stopping, more memorable, more . . .* or somehow *better* than the words that had originally arrived to convey to the world the vision your mind had seen. This book deals with finding the more and the better.

Since the initial writing entails a great amount of time and effort, why should a writer subject himself to more than a once-over-lightly edit of the first draft? Shouldn't that be sufficient for an intelligent writer? In fact, the more intelligent (read "wise") a writer is, the more capable she is of spotting needed improvements, and of fixing them.

Revision is seen by some as drudgery, like taking out the garbage. It has to be done, so it might as well be done fast, they reason. Most successful writers do not look upon revision as uncreative drudgery.

Anyone who takes writing seriously remembers the purpose of writing in the first place—to communicate with your reader. There are those who are self-centered, writing "to express themselves," but the people this book seeks to serve are reader-centered. Certainly, they, too, have a drive to express something, but it's not solely a catharsis for their own selves. They almost always want to affect the lives of others in some way. Their writing may have so grand a purpose that it will affect the very soul of the reader, or it may have as practical, as down-to-earth a purpose as helping the reader fix the kitchen sink. Whatever the level, they never lose sight of the person on the other side of the page.

Given a reader-centered philosophy of writing, the writer must revise, revise, and revise yet again to ensure that his meaning will cross that abyss between his mind and those of his many (and unknown) readers. Revision is identical with and inseparable from writing. The reader-centered writer knows that revision of subsequent drafts is as creative and enjoyable as writing the first draft.

Some writers, I must admit straight away, claim to revise as they go, perfecting every paragraph before proceeding. The advice from most writers, however, is to "write in haste, revise at leisure." This book is structured around the principle that one revises, if not exactly "at leisure," then simply after completing the first draft. The beauty of this procedure, and what makes it so much fun, is that you are not rushed by the imperatives of the creative drive. You can concentrate on a comma, a word, a phrase, or a fact, in your search for the more and the better. You are no longer compelled to concentrate on all that's yet to be written; you can concentrate on the here and the now, and play around with possibilities.

Referring to the joy of revision in his masterful work, *Style,* F.L. Lucas writes:

> Later on, when the stage of revision arrives, he can complete his reading of what really must be read; then he can add what he has omitted, and rectify what he has forgotten or failed to grasp, with a memory refreshed, and with spirits raised by a sense that the body of his work is already created and it now remains only to make it better and better.

The purpose of revision is to get the ideas and the words that express them as clear, accurate, and attractive as possible. There is another purpose of, or at least another result from, revision, that I wish to stress heavily here—partly because it receives so little attention in classes and books on writing. During revision, a writer often finds a source of new inspiration. It is serendipity at work again in the mind of the creative person—the notion that when searching for one thing, the alert and receptive mind will often find something not sought, but better.

Now, just a few words about why the book is arranged the way it is. First, the sequence of revision routines is artificial. Professional writers do not revise so methodically. They are more apt to undertake all these routines and subroutines simultaneously, not sequentially. But I felt it would be inhibiting, to say the least, for me to say, "Just go out there like the professional writer-reviser-editor and do everything that this book suggests all at the same time." Instead, I've divided it into a logical progression from major revisions (like scrapping an entire chapter) to less ambitious revisions (like worrying about the sound of a word weighed against the connotative load on the word being considered as a replacement for it—or the rhythmic value of a comma in a particular place.)

I'm suggesting that until you feel up to holding all these revision routines clearly in mind every minute as you work through a draft's revision, you consider following the same sequence of routines that this book does. You will gradually, unknowingly, evolve into more and more simultaneity, but you'll go at it step by step. Here's one minor trick I use when I'm going through a draft looking for one class of problem and spot another kind. I flag it for later work with a marginal comment or a simple question mark. Don't get bogged down trying to come up with a more accurate word when you are trying to decide whether a paragraph is unified, or whether the tone is right, or where you can cut the thousand words that you're over the allowable length. Tend to the business at hand—besides, serendipity may shine on you, and you'll end up eliminating the paragraph with the suspect word anyway.

I hope that you will find through this book that revision can be creative and enjoyable—and that in the process you will be alert to the unanticipated sunbeams of serendipity, and that the process itself will stimulate you to create the more and the better.

Let's end this introduction with an extract from an interview Ernest Hemingway gave to George Plimpton of the *Paris Review*—an extract on the topic of interest to us here: the art of revision.

Paris Review: How much rewriting do you do?

Hemingway: It depends. I rewrote the ending to *A Farewell To Arms,* the last page of it, thirty-nine times before I was satisfied.

Paris Review: Was there some technical problem there? What was it that had stumped you?

Hemingway: GETTING THE WORDS RIGHT.

CONTENTS

GETTING THE WORDS RIGHT

CHAPTER I

Revision by Reduction

axe, cut, compress, condense, decrease, delete, drop, eliminate, eradicate, excise, hone, lop, pare, prune, reduce, remove, revise, rewrite, sharpen, slash, streamline, tighten, trim, whittle. . .

Two dozen words to remind us that we almost always write too many words. Nonprofessional writers are relieved when they've been able to produce an abundance of words—and they try hard to keep them. Professionals, however, are pleased to find how many they can cut in successive revisions. There are undoubtedly more precise ways to separate the professional from the nonprofessional writer, but this difference in attitude toward *quantity* is certainly significant. In subsequent drafts, professionals will attend to the other major difference that makes them truly professional: the *quality* of the words.

Seventy-five percent of all revision is eliminating words already written; the remaining twenty-five percent is improving the words that remain.

Although experienced writers may well do all kinds of revision almost as they write, they are apt first to try reducing the quantity of the words. The Victorian writer Walter Pater said, "All art doth but consist in the removal of surplusage." The secret is in knowing which words are the surplus words.

To make this discussion of reduction easier, I've divided the reduction routine into three subroutines:

- Greater reductions
- Lesser reductions
- Micro-reductions

Greater Reductions

The first reduction subroutine is to search for opportunities to get rid of great chunks of verbiage. I've deliberately used the word *opportunities* rather than *necessities*, because revision should be seen in a positive light. It's too easy to slip into a negative attitude toward it: "I know this passage is wordy, maybe even unnecessary, but it's such a beautiful piece of writing. Why cut it out?" It comes as a jolt to discover that entire chapters can simply be lopped. The newcomer to serious revision will have difficulty recognizing that an entire chapter has to go and, once recognizing the possibility, actually removing it.

This is understandable; no one delights in throwing away something he has created. A chapter of any length represents many hours of planning and writing. That it contains some beautiful words, some important thoughts, and some amount of heart and soul makes tossing it all away seem brutal. But the only thing that counts for professionals (not that they don't agonize a bit) is whether the chapter does what needs doing. Does it move the story along or delay it?

There's always the possibility that such a chapter can be saved and moved to another location. When professionals find themselves trying to reposition a chapter, however, they acknowledge the possibility that this is but a childish desire to keep a favorite toy. The chapter may simply no longer work (no longer do what it is supposed to do); cramming it into a closet of the story may merely postpone the day when it must be sent to the dump.

Of course, an unnecessary chapter doesn't have to be junked immediately; you can save it in a notebook labeled "For Possible Inclusion." I've found this a comforting bit of self-deception. By having a definite place to keep my verbal deadweight, a sort of organized attic, I don't mind deleting it. Down deep, I know that anything stored in the attic "for future use" will probably never again see the light of day—but I haven't thrown it away. And, if I find a place for it, or a section from it, in a future story or article, it will be at my fingertips.

I recall well all these unprofessional emotions in connection with my first novel. The first chapter was a beauty. I had researched wide and deep, located maps of a particular river in China, talked with a Chinese man who had escaped from the Communists, and polished the result to a fine glow. After all, this was the leading chapter, the one that would hook the reader. By objective standards, it was well written. The trouble, as a professional writer pointed out (how I hated and didn't believe him at the time), was that it did nothing for the story. He then sprinkled salt into the wound by adding that the story really began with

Chapter Three. An entire year later, I recognized clearly how right he was, and I unceremoniously excised Chapter One. Chapter Three (revised to include information lost in the excision of Chapter One) was moved to the opening position; Chapter Two was saved to become part of a flashback within Chapter Five.

When I threw out those one and a half chapters, I realized that I had crossed over. I was now a professional—at least my attitude was professional. If I could throw away six thousand words and feel good about it, something must have changed.

When I submitted what I considered the final manuscript for my first nonfiction book for young adults, it ran to fifty thousand words. My editor said it would be acceptable and that my final advance would be forthcoming, provided I cut it down to twenty-five thousand words. My immediate reaction was that of the classic amateur: How could I possibly say what needed saying if I, in effect, dropped every other word?

Following revision routines now described in this book, I managed to do it and meet the deadline. I was surprised that I could do it, but what surprised me most (of course, the editor had known it all along) was that in the twenty-five thousand words excised from fifty thousand, nothing was lost. In fact, something was gained through reduction: clarity and ease of reading. Reviewers stressed how clear the writing was, and I'm sure now that they would never have given such positive reviews if the editor had not been so professional—and had not forced me to behave like one.

In shorter pieces of writing, it's unlikely that you'll be faced with cutting out entire chapters, but it's not at all unlikely that you'll find it necessary to delete whole sections. A section is impossible to define, but let's take an article that you're writing for *Writer's Digest*, say, on the art of revision. In your original outline was a section under *Style* labeled "Obscenity." The editor has just asked you to cut five hundred words from the article, and you're desperate for opportunities to find five hundred words—five hundred that won't ruin the entire piece by their absence. Finally recalling that the piece is about writing nonfiction for corporate magazines, you realize that the entire section on obscenity can be eliminated—no one in his right mind would include a blatant obscenity in a corporate publication.

Having dropped that three-hundred-word section on obscenity, you find opportunities to get rid of the remaining two hundred simply by eliminating one anecdote that wasn't too germane in the first place and crossing out a few adjectives that weren't pulling their weight. Five hundred gone and the reader doesn't miss them. The editor is happy because your piece now fits the space allotted, and you're happy because the editor's happy.

Keep in mind always that readers do not usually know what you planned to include; they'll never miss a deleted minor point, or even a minor section. Naturally, you have to consider carefully which words or ideas will be least missed. Even if your editor knows your original outline in advance, he or she is aware of how things can, and sometimes must, change in the doing—especially in the process of meeting length limitations. Keep an open mind about what "must" be retained.

If you are looking for ways to shorten a fictional piece, look for whole scenes that can be eliminated or shortened drastically. Suppose you have written a story about political intrigue in Washington, D.C. One scene focuses on a taxi driver sitting on a park bench, feeding the pigeons and listening with one ear to his cab radio a few feet away. It's a well-written scene that gives us insights into the driver and the city, and you like it particularly because it grew out of notes you took several years ago while eating your lunch in a small park near your office.

After further reflection, however, you realize that this little scene does nothing to move the story forward. The taxi and the taxi driver are never mentioned again and the main character leaves this cleverly described city never to return. You realize, as much as it hurts, that you included the scene primarily to show off your ability to write description.

Recognize it, instead, as an opportunity to save a hundred words that you may use to bolster a weak scene later on that moves the story significantly forward.

Does it move the piece forward? is one of the questions most often asked in the writing profession. You might think that a professional writer would know enough not to have written in the first place something that doesn't move the story forward. The problem is that it may well have seemed significant at the time. It is only later, in the context of the final work, that even a professional can judge the significance of each component of that work. Significance is always relative; you have to wait until all the facts are in the scales. Hindsight wins again—and revision is hindsight harnessed.

This is all a matter of scope. If your planning of a nonfiction piece has been thorough and thoughtful enough, you've decided just how much of a subject you're going to treat. Sometimes this will take the form, "What am I *not* going to cover?" After deciding on the scope of the piece and estimating how many words might be allotted to each subsection, you should not have to face the problem of cutting out whole sections. Even with the best planning, however, things do change with the actual writing, so you must be emotionally prepared to wade in, hatchet in hand.

After you've dropped the section or sections that are inappropriate, it's time to slash out the underbrush. The reader will get lost in the tangle of words and won't see the beauty of your forest if you don't go in with brush hook and machete. A first draft almost always suffers from the tangles. In the throes of creation, we tend (in fact *in*tend) to let it all hang out — to *see* what we have to say. Many writers would agree with E.M. Forster: "How do I know what I think, until I see what I say?" Then, to make it clear for the innocent reader, we must clear out the deadwood.

Often it's a case of having gone on and on, well after the point's been made. Perhaps paragraphs one, three, and five make the point perfectly clear. Diagonal lines with arrows through paragraphs two and four save us a hundred or more words and at the same time clarify the matter. Recognizing that greater clarity sometimes requires more words, not fewer, we watch for opportunities to get more for less.

Paragraphs, even pages, may sometimes be slashed because you find you've written disproportionately. You may know more about a minor point than you do about the primary and secondary points, so you write a great deal more about it. Understandably, the reader may attribute more importance to it than you intended. A careful writer would introduce this minor point with a phrase such as, "We now come to a less significant point, but one worth mentioning nevertheless." After a statement like that, it would be inappropriate to have two or three times the number of words dedicated to that point than to the more important points. (You, too, would be reminded of this simply by introducing it that way, and would keep the word count down.) The relative emphasis or significance of a point is inferred from the attention paid it.

Fiction writers, faced with an absolute necessity to cut way back in total length, have another means of saving words, but one that requires greater thought: eliminating a character entirely. The character will probably be rather insignificant, but nonetheless one you've created and perhaps come to love. The trouble with pruning this kind of growth is that its vines and roots are intimately entangled with the entire story. It's not simply a matter of screwing up courage and deleting every reference to the person's name. Whatever relationships this character has with any of the other characters must also be taken out.

Such severely revised sections and subsections must be reviewed and revised so that the reader is never aware that such drastic surgery has occurred. As great chunks of words and paragraphs fall to the machete, new words must be found to repair the damage done. The goal is that when all the patches are in place, the length will have been reduced significantly—without damage to the whole.

A final note about this reduction process: As you stand at a distance from your creation searching for places to reduce verbiage in major amounts, you're going to spot all kinds of opportunities for lesser and micro-reductions, not to mention examples of poor style, spelling, and grammar. Don't lose forward momentum by trying to deal with everything at once. Simply flag candidates for revision with symbols—stars, asterisks, squares, checkmarks, or verbal marginalia—that remind you to take a closer look later. (Don't presume that the same things will pop out at you the next time through—flag them now. It may be weeks before you get back to revising at that level.)

Another reason not to complete minor reductions and revisions at this point is that your great swings of the reduction machete may eliminate an entire page, section, or chapter in which minor problems exist, thus making lesser revision work wasted effort.

It should be emphasized that although I'm describing these revision routines as though they were discrete, nonoverlapping activities, they are not. The experienced reviser engages in all these activities, but not so sequentially as implied here.

Although editors of nonfiction often encourage an abundance of anecdotes and quotes, there are times when writers can still reduce length by: cutting out weaker examples; cutting out the too-cute anecdote that wasn't very illustrative anyway; cutting down on the number of quotes; shortening quotations by substituting ellipses for the nonworking words.

Fiction writers can search for opportunities to eliminate or shorten flashback scenes (too much flashback can create a flopback) and the cleverly conceived but overlong internal monologue.

The hatchet can likewise be applied to the lengthy descriptive passage. Description can give the feel of a place or a person, but have we gone overboard? An objective scan of a descriptive passage may reveal one particular sentence that is so telling, so right, that it could achieve the effect all by itself. If one, or a few such sentences stand out in a paragraph, give serious consideration to excising the rest. A merely good piece of description can be transformed into a memorable one by cutting away what disguises it.

Although dialogue is usually crucial to fiction, we must always ask ourselves: Is all of it accomplishing its purpose, or could some be lopped off, never to be missed; does it move the story along (or do some other narrative work for the writer), or is some of it just interesting filler?

Long passages, even entire scenes, of dialogue can sometimes be reduced considerably by summary. The story loses immediacy when we switch from scene to summary, but sometimes it takes entirely too many lines or pages of dialogue to accomplish a small amount of narrative work. The only solution is to turn to summary. The following dialogue appeared on page 107 in my *Day of Fate*, but it could have been rendered as summary:

As Scene:

> "D.L.—"
>
> "I messed that one up good, didn't I?" He barked a laugh. "Funny, when he suggested I was cabin-crazy, it hardly affected me. But when he as much as called you a liar—I was ready to go over the desk at him."
>
> "Don't you know yet I'm big enough to fight my own battles?" she said, but her tone took all the sting out of it. "Thank you, D.L."
>
> He turned, and his face was bleak. "Three others took copies of the photographs. Maybe one of them will—"
>
> "No, D.L., you might as well face it. They might have been polite, but they'll do the same as Eldon with the pictures. The trash basket or the nut-case file."
>
> "Damn it, can't they see? The launchers are plain as day in those pictures."
>
> "They're plain if you've seen the launchers. If not—those pictures could be a kid's erector set in a bathtub. That camera just wasn't made for underwater work." She took a deep breath and plunged ahead. "D.L., we're going to have to give up on your government."
>
> "But. . ."
>
> "If I get in touch with my magazine, this story could be in next Monday's issue. I have enough credibility with the editor that he'll buy it, with you, and Simon, and the pictures."

As Summary:

> Samantha made it clear to D.L. that the underwater photographs did not show the missile launchers as clearly as D.L. was convinced they did. She told him to face the fact that his government was not going to help—they were going to have to go directly to her editor with the photographs, Simon, and him.

Although the summary lacks impact, character development, immediacy, emotion, it leaves out none of the essential facts and offers fourfold reduction in the number of words (from 223 to 54). The writer has to decide whether it's worth it. If the characters have been developed fully before or after, then this minor bit of character development might be dropped. If the emotional impact developed by the scene is crucial to the story, however, the writer may decide to keep the dialogue—or perhaps summarize to 100 words instead of 54. The point here is that this summarizing technique is available to the reviser, to be used at his or her discretion.

Whenever you can shorten a sentence, do. And one always can. The best sentence? The shortest.

—GUSTAVE FLAUBERT

Lesser Reductions

"Lesser reductions" may be a misnomer. The reductions I'm talking about here may be shorter than a chapter, section, paragraph, or even a sentence, but the cumulative effect of finding and eliminating these lesser transgressors is great.

I've talked about looking first for opportunities to chop out large chunks: paragraphs, sections, even whole chapters. Such large savings can't be accomplished in all cases, of course, but it's almost always possible to excise a sentence here, a sentence there, and perhaps several from a single paragraph.

How did these sentences that you now feel no compunction about eradicating ever get in there in the first place? Everyone has clutter in the closet of his genius. The anxious beginner may even have less clutter than the relaxed professional. The professional lets practically anything come out as a draft, knowing from experience that revision will clear away the embarrassing clutter before anyone important sees it.

The beginner is so accustomed to having a teacher or a supervisor rip his work to shreds that he tries to compose perfect prose, paragraph by paragraph, sentence by sentence. This self-censorship at the moment of conception can result in a boring, unpersuasive, and ineffective piece. It can also lead to a vicious circle: The more you pass immediate, negative judgment on your writing, the more uptight and self-censoring you become—and the worse your prose becomes. Established writers avoid this problem by allowing the words to flow and afterward revising, revising, and revising yet again before sending their work out into the world. If professionals find they must do this, new writers can hardly expect to expose their first drafts to the people who count.

Superfluous words and sentences hide in many camouflage patterns that keep you from seeing them hidden in the tangle of words. Most of them could claim some right to be there—and they will hold on tight as you fight with your ego to hack them out. Taken individually, each may be a fine, well-wrought sentence, relevant to the paragraph in which it's enmeshed. Regarded with the unblinking, objective eye of the professional, however, the excess sentence will be recognized—and excised.

Sometimes you'll find a sentence that repeats what came some time before. If the repetition is intentional—for emphasis, humor, or coherence—perhaps it should stay. If it results from carelessness, it should be deleted. There's nothing wrong with presenting a point several times, first one way and then another. We speak here of those cases where you've gone overboard.

Although this chapter is concerned largely with redundancy, it is good to remind ourselves occasionally that redundancy does not mean that we've used a great number of words; it means, rather, that we have used more words than necessary to express the message clearly and fully. While concision is a worthy goal, it is not synonymous with brevity. If you try to follow the directions of the laconic Vermont farmer whose information is brief beyond belief, you get lost. Had he used a few more words to make it clear how to get around the mountain, he wouldn't have been redundant, simply concise.

There are two popular constructions whose deletion will simultaneously improve style and cut down on excessive words: those using *manner* and *nature*. The trouble, of course, is that these constructions come readily to the tongue, especially if you are an academic or government person caught up in the jargon adhering to these professions. This attitude naturally leads to an attempt to use words that have an aura of importance about them. A doctoral dissertation or a government report is likely strewn with phrases like, "This two-year study, which is to be very comprehensive *in nature. . .*"

What would be lost by cutting out that deadwood, "in nature"? Nothing. A professional writer wading into this swamp would slash away further, probably ending up with, "This comprehensive, two-year study. . ." How much meaning has been lost? None—despite cutting half the words. That's our goal: to make crisp, clear statements using the fewest (but best available) words.

The *manner* construction is also usually wasted wordage. Is a bulldog any more or less dangerous when he growls "in a menacing manner," as opposed to "menacingly"? Actually he sounds a bit *less* frightening when *manner* is tacked on. *Growls* alone is probably sufficient—ask any mail carrier.

Another overused construction that has insidiously inserted itself into our language is the *type* construction: "He was the *type* of soldier who would rather drive a D-8 tractor than an M-1 tank." Beginning this sentence, "He was a soldier who" or "He would rather" would have gotten the message across equally well.

A worse and totally superfluous use of *type* is as a suffix to an adjective: "a Marine-type guy"; "a super-type hero," "a hospital-type atmosphere." Frequently, this can be improved by substituting *-like:* "a hospital-like atmosphere"; "Marine-like in his bearing."

Delete *-type*. No one will miss it, and you'll have saved a word. Don't be a "professional-type" writer; be content to write "like a professional."

Appears to, like a, seems to, as though, seemed like, and *seemed as though* are what dedicated editors and revisers love to prey upon. They present two-for-one opportunities: We can improve style while reducing the word count. Let's take an example:

> I shot him five times in the chest, and the roar of the Beretta in that crowded room was like that of a thunderclap. Women screamed, men cried out in confusion, glasses splintered, and panic took over. As Schneider tilted backward and fell with a crash onto the floor. . .

The phrase, *"was like that of a thunderclap,"* is about as weak as it could be in such a potentially dramatic, thunderously dramatic scene as this. Since you have the poetic license to carry a loaded Beretta, shoot the bloody thing:

> I shot him five times in the chest. The Beretta's thunderclap in that crowded room made women scream and men cry out in confusion.

While we're talking about eliminating weak expressions, look at that final phrase within the original quotation, "fell with a crash onto the floor." How much crashier it would have been as:

> Glasses splintered, and panic took over as Schneider tilted backward and crashed to the floor.

One thing our education has taught us well, perhaps too well, is that we must qualify statements. You must, in the name of truth (accuracy), let the reader know that you know that what you've written is not always true under all situations, or for all time. You must, therefore, "qualify" the statement, then and there, by telling the reader what all the limitations are. This makes for good research, because anyone who reads your work later will know precisely what you meant. The trouble with such qualification-laden writing is that it makes for slow reading—it requires the long attention span of a highly motivated, highly dedicated reader.

When the habit of qualifying is carried over into other kinds of writing, such as fiction, it doesn't work. No one will read more than a few paragraphs before throwing up his hands—and throwing down the book. Infected by the disease of over-qualification, we are afraid to use a strong metaphor or an analogy. The best we can muster is a simile. Fearing to be inaccurate, we won't write, "The plane was a bird of prey." We hedge and write, "The plane was *like* a bird of prey." Not that a simile is wrong; it's just that accuracy-obsessed people will never come right out and say that something is something else. After all (they reason), something cannot be something else. If poets felt so obliged, the world would be the poorer.

Purveyors of precision disguise their efforts behind such innocent-looking constructions as *seem to, apparently, looks as though, looks like,* and *it would appear that.* If you're writing fiction or poetry and find yourself about to write *seem to,* stop to ask yourself whether you can substitute a metaphor.

> In the white shimmer outside, the buildings are sun-sated, gleaming with light and heat. Sometimes at this time of the day the palm trees quiver and seem to hover in the air, rippling hotly.

Why not flip out your poetic license, and come right out and say:

> Sometimes at this time of the day the palm trees quiver and hover in the hot, rippling air.

As so often happens during revision, serendipity raises its lovely head. We find, for example, that once *quiver* and *hover* have been brought closer together, they have an interesting sound, rhythm, and feeling that they were previously too separated to enjoy.

Then, by moving "hot and rippling" forward for some other reason, we serendipitously discover the touch of alliteration inherent in *hover* and *hot.* Now I find I'm tempted also to play with another slight change so that we'll have "quivering and hovering in this hot and rippling air." I might like that; it's an image that moves.

> . . .Sometimes at this time of the day the palm trees are quivering and hovering in the hot and rippling air.

You may not like this change. My point is that you should play around with alternative phrasings, and not feel compelled to retain your first-draft words.

Writers owe more to the genius of serendipity than we care to admit. On the other hand, the same serendipitous possibilities dropped in the lap of someone else might lie there unappreciated—perhaps because of the very fact that they were unsought and came by accident. Perhaps genius is the ability to see in the accidental, potential.

Redundancy

Redundancy doesn't just mean repetitiveness; it's the umbrella term for superfluity and excess. Redundancies are words that can be eliminated from a piece of writing, *without changing the significance of the passage.* Rhetoricians have identified various subspecies of redundancy, and we have all been guilty of them at some point: *tautology, pleonasm, verbosity, prolixity, circumlocution,* and *repetition.*

TAUTOLOGY

The crudest form of redundancy is probably tautology: saying the same thing that's already been said. It is the needless repetition of an idea in a different word, phrase, clause, or sentence:

- He wrote *his own auto*biography.
- He was *popular* with the *people.*
- He *falsely mis*represented the situation.
- Let us *glance briefly* at the facts.

and the ever-popular

- The *reason* was *because. . .*

Recur again, for example, doubles the statement of *recur,* which already means "occur again." We *continue on* when "continue" alone makes the point. We have the troops retreat *to the rear* when it would be difficult to envision them retreating to the front. Then we have the men penetrate *into* the woods and take shelter in a native hut that is circular *in shape* after first circling *around* the field to connect *up* with the commandoes, only to have them disappear *from sight.*

> Levi and Mike were members of a small clique of insiders who fraternized at the Merry Christmas Bar.

"A small group of insiders" defines *clique,* thus making the sentence tautological, i.e., an attempt to define something in terms of itself. There's even the possibility here that *fraternized* is tautologous, since a clique can be thought of as a group of people who fraternize with each other. That may be stretching tautology too taut, but it does help make the point.

There are many tautological phrases, clauses, and words against which we must wage a war of deletion. I don't know what to label them: saboteurs, infiltrators, spies, sleepers, or covert agents. These undercover infiltrators fit right into the environment, quiet and unnoticed. One waves them through the gate because they look perfectly familiar, certainly not dangerous. Innocent as they may appear, they can torture style and kill concision. Be on the lookout for these agents of redundancy:

- The theater manager promised everyone a *free gift.*
- The troops *advanced forward* on the outer Falklands today.
- The *future outlook* seems rosier.
- The Argentinians claimed to present the *true* facts while the British people at home were presented *false* facts.

- The invaders were *few in number,* but highly trained and eager.
- As was their *usual custom,* the commandoes came ashore, shrouded in fog.
- The submarine fired at the cruiser *General Belgrano* at *a distance of* ten thousand meters.
- *In addition to* missile-firing frigates, they *also* had missile-firing destroyers.
- Apparently the two Harrier aircraft hit *head-on* while flying at five hundred miles an hour *straight for each other.*

There is another, frequently unneeded word we should always look askance at: *personal,* at least where it shows up tied intimately to *opinion:* "It is my *personal opinion* that the Red Sox will never make it." What other kind of opinion could you have than a personal one? Say simply, "It's my opinion that the Red Sox. . ." There may be an understandable exception when, for example, a delegate to the United Nations refers to his personal opinion. He is trying to make clear that he is not speaking for his government. Most of us, however, do not have to make such a distinction. In any event, the delegate could make the distinction simply by saying, "In my opinion. . ."

There are some tautologies, however, that may properly be used because their antiquity affords them protection:

- kith and kin
- ways and means
- to all intents and purposes
- bag and baggage
- safe and sound

Because they are clichés, you may wish to eliminate them totally, but you don't need to drop half a couplet just because the two halves, technically speaking, form a tautology; the remaining half would sound ridiculous: e.g., "He went down to Kentucky to visit his kith."

The following writer managed to fall into two traps of tautology in one sentence.

Original:

It was as if the sand pebbles themselves were fighting one with another to gain ascendancy and to suck from the air any of the remaining humidity that yet lingered from the night before.

Revised:

It was as if the sand pebbles were fighting among themselves to gain ascendance and to suck from the air any humidity lingering from the night before.

In the original, it was tautologous to have the pebbles *themselves* fighting *one with another.* I rephrased it as *among themselves.* This got rid of the redundancy and saved two words—another case of getting two for one.

The original is even more clearly tautologous in repeating the idea of *remaining* in the word *lingering.* The revision shown above not only clears up that redundancy, but also saves five more words.

PLEONASM

While tautology is the error of saying essentially the same thing again in the same sentence, pleonasm is the error of having in a sentence extra words that may be deleted without changing either the meaning or the structure of the sentence.

In the sentence, his motive was *more or less* jealousy, the pleonastic phrase, *more or less,* may be omitted with no change of meaning and no change of sentence structure is required.

The italicized pleonasms in the following examples may be (should be) omitted. Notice that the meaning remains clear and no changes are necessary to make the new sentence.

Both the prime minister and the vice admiral agreed that the time for negotiations had passed. (The prime minister and the vice admiral. . .)

Both Levi and Mike were members of a small clique. (Levi and Mike were members of a small clique.)

For severe cases, doctors may give a shot of Cortisone to block *the development of* further spread and to provide relief from the symptoms. (For severe cases, doctors may give a shot of Cortisone to block further spread and to provide relief. . .)

Deep puddles *of water* wrestled against the direction of the tires plunging into one water-filled pothole after another. (Deep puddles wrestled against the direction of. . .)

Pleonasms often occur in pairings beloved by attorneys: *if and when, unless and until, in any shape or form.* We also see pleonasms when we find *more prefera-*

ble, more especially, continue to remain, predict in advance, and *perpetuate for all time.*

It's not important to remember words like tautology and pleonasm; it is important to remember how readily we all slip into redundancy (he said *once again*).

It's amazing how wordy we can all be when we let our guard down. In the next section I discuss all kinds of verbosities, but let's remind ourselves here at the end of this section on lesser reductions that we can always find a few words to eliminate and, by so doing, clarify. Why use the redundant expressions on the left when the ones on the right are available:

the reason is because	because
based on the fact that	because
due to the fact that	because
inasmuch as	because
in light of the fact that	because
on account of the fact that	because
on the grounds that	because
in the matter of	about
in the neighborhood of	about
a number of	about
in the approximate amount of	about
concerning the nature of	about
in regard to	about
with reference to	about
in re	about
of the order of magnitude of	about

Such a list could go on and on, but this should be enough to remind us that we must stay alert. It's discouragingly easy to fall into the tangled thicket of tautology, pleonasm, and verbosity. Naturally, we wouldn't want to limit ourselves always to the simple words *because* and *about,* but neither should we be wordy.

I can't resist offering a handful more from a list of hundreds that we all backslide into occasionally. If you read these and begin to hear echoes from your own letters, memos, reports, stories, and articles, take heed:

despite the fact that	although
in the not-too-distant future	soon
in the very near future	soon
neat in appearance	neat
at this time	now
at this point in time	now
at the present writing	now

actual experience	experience
at your earliest convenience	as soon as you can
cancel out	cancel
disappear from sight	disappear
following after	after
contains within	contains
for the purpose of providing	to provide
effectualize	effect
recoil back	recoil
in my opinion I think	I think
hexagonal in shape	hexagonal
it would not be unreasonable to assume	it is reasonable to assume
perform an analysis of	analyze
plan ahead for the future	plan
for the purpose of	for
on a local basis	locally
study in depth	study (or scrutinize)
horizontally level	level (or horizontal)
uniformly consistent	consistent
etc., etc.	etc.

VERBOSITY

Verbosity is perhaps the most objectionable form of redundancy, because it is the most difficult to cure. Verbosity is like a Virginia creeper that so thoroughly invades the rose arbor that no amount of clipping does the trick. If you try instead to pull it out, you find the rose coming with it. The original idea is destroyed in the attempt to clear it up. A minor tautology or pleonasm can be neatly snipped out, but a severe case of verbosity may mean pulling everything up by the roots and starting the sentence or paragraph afresh.

Prolixity

A form of verbosity, prolixity is the mention of things not worth mentioning. Probably the most familiar perpetrator of prolixity is the storyteller who insists on informing his listeners of the precise time, date, weather, and other irrelevant details of the story's setting—the equivalent of someone who shows home movies unedited. By the time he springs his punch line, everyone has already anticipated it, discounted it, and gone to freshen their drinks. A public speaker who gives incidental items the same prominence as essential elements will lose the audience's attention long before the final, significant points are put forth. Here's an example:

Original:
He says the college's dream is one day to open the colonnade with special guides dressed in clothing in the style worn about the time of the historic hall's members.

Revised: **Original: 30 words**
*He says the college's dream is one   **Revised: 19 words**
day to open the colonnade with special guides dressed in period clothing.*

Circumlocution

Circumlocution, another variety of verbosity, is saying things the long way 'round. Literally, it means *to talk around* the subject.

Original:
Should any client require behavioral science capability that is not at present available among the staff of our companies, we stand ready to assemble a task force of responsible, capable consultants to provide the necessary consultation and service.

Revised: **Original: 38 words**
*Should any client require behavioral   **Revised: 22 words**
science capability not available within our own companies, we can readily assemble a group of appropriate consultants.*

The revised version is clearer and more direct—and sixteen words shorter. Such editing is the mark of the pro. The revised version still sounds terribly "corporate," but it is easier to understand.

Another example of going around Robin Hood's barn (or in this case, his boat) to get something said should make you shun circumlocution:

> *We spent all of the entire morning caulking the boat for the purpose of making it watertight. That was the first time I had ever done that job in my whole life. (32 words)*

This could be strengthened by making it shorter:

We spent all morning caulking the boat, a new experience for me.
(12 words)

Again we've created clarity through reductions eliminating sixty percent of the rambling original.

Here's another example of reducing circumlocution, this time by fifty percent. Was any meaning lost by this severe cutting?

Original:

Her brother, who is a student at law school, loves to bring up controversial topics that everyone has a different opinion about.

Revised:

Her brother, a law student, loves to bring up controversial topics.

Repetition

Although repetition can be a useful device to achieve emphasis (see the next chapter), make more easily remembered something difficult, or establish a mood, it can also be redundant. In this section, of course, we're looking at repetition gone bad—unwarranted repetition.

Unwarranted repetition creeps in quietly during early stages of writing, when the mind is hurrying ahead more than glancing behind. It is easily remedied during any of the revision routines.

The Trident submarine is the largest and most dangerous class of submarine ever seen at Groton.

You can easily see how you might write that sentence in a first draft, but notice how much better it reads if you sink that first submarine during revision. One mention, probably the second one, would be sufficient to keep the reader on track:

The Trident is the largest and most dangerous class of submarine ever seen at Groton. The Trident has a number of missile launchers aboard. Each launcher is capable of launching a MIRV.

Under thoughtful revision, the second and third sentences might emerge as:

Aboard the Trident are a number of missile launchers capable of firing a MIRV.

Only the second *launcher* was truly a superfluous repetition, but a careful reviser would probably also worry about the repetitive sound of *launch* in *launching,* and might substitute *firing.* He might finally decide to leave it in, satisfied that he had deep-sixed the most offensive *launcher,* but he would have to give it at least a moment's consideration.

Unwarranted repetition can also result from the several meanings a word may have. In the throes of composition, the writer is thinking of the meaning he intends right then, not of all the other possible meanings the word may have. He may therefore unintentionally repeat himself:

Margaret Thatcher had to fight the pacifist Lord Pym in order to wage war on the Argentinian invaders.

Repetition here comes in the form of a *repeated idea* implicit in another word— in this case, the notion of fighting in the words *wage war.* If the author is trying to achieve some level of irony by deliberately setting these words against each other in the same sentence (as the British are apt to do), then this is not superfluous repetition but stylistic repetition.

Let's look for a moment at the sentence you just read. I could have written, "is not superfluous, but stylistic, repetition." I felt, however, that I would gain more in style by leaving it in than I would have improved it by getting rid of a little superfluity. Another day I might feel different. That's what makes style such an individual matter. Not only does it vary between people; it varies within the person from moment to moment. That's also what makes writing and revising partly art. (See section on Style)

Exercises in Reducing Redundancy

Now, without worrying about identifying the exact form of redundancy (or, if you prefer, windiness), let's run through a few examples. Knowing the names doesn't help; recognizing that repair is needed, does.

Original:

It is always the case that in the fall of every year I get homesick for the state of Connecticut.

Revised:

I get homesick for Connecticut every fall.

Original: 20 words
Revised: 7 words
Reduction: 65%

Original:
Somehow, she sensed the man was still staring at her. She glanced casually in his direction. As she suspected, he was staring at her. Her stomach tightened.

Revised:
Sensing that the man was still staring at her, she glanced casually in his direction. Her stomach tightened. He was staring at her.

Original: 27 words
Revised: 23 words
Reduction: 15%
Doesn't his staring become even more ominous with the now staccato rhythm of the final two sentences?

Original:
This time the man picked up his glass of wine. He raised it off the table, toasted Margie with his glass, then gulped the rest of his wine.

Revised:
This time the man raised his wineglass, toasted her with his eyebrow, and drained the glass.

Original: 28 words
Revised: 16 words
Reduction 35%
The addition of a raised eyebrow was a revision for style that couldn't be resisted— an example of how the attempt to reduce verbiage may have serendipitous effects on style.

Original:
Now, like the people he's written about, Pitt, too, has become an individual fighting against odds that most would find too overwhelming.

Revised:
Like the people he's written about, Pitt is fighting odds that most would find overwhelming.

Original: 22 words
Revised: 15 words
Reduction: 30%

Original:
The instruments radiated a soft green glow against the tired, burning eyes which were struggling to retain some soothing protection of moistness against the ever-present currents of hot, dry air driven at them from the hardworking defroster.

Revised:
The instruments radiated a soft green glow against the tired, burning eyes struggling to retain some soothing moistness against the defroster's continuous currents of hot, dry air.

Original: 38 words
Revised: 28 words
Reduction: 25%
A good idea hopelessly entangled in verbiage, but revitalized by diligent pruning. A further revision might also drop out "continuous," shortening the sentence even more without any great loss.

Original:
Very few people can work as closely as fishermen do and remain friends after work, but they were now not working and still enjoying each other's company.

Revised:
Very few people can work as close as fishermen do and remain friends after work, but here they were, still enjoying each other's company.

Original: 27 words
Revised: 24 words
Reduction: 22%
(Note also that they don't work closely; they work close.)

Original:
They say the Maplewood Cafe's been standing for nearly forty years. Most of the younger townspeople often wondered how the Maplewood got her name. The older folks talked of great maples and oak trees that once lined the town's main street across from where the cafe stands.

Revised:
It's not so strange that there's not a maple in sight of the Maplewood Cafe. She was named nearly forty years ago, when great maples lined the town's main street.

Original: 47 words
Revised: 30 words
Reduction: 36%

Original:
The bitter cold and knifing winds forced Joshua to dress in the outrageous manner in which he now appeared.

Revised:
The bitter cold and knifing winds forced Joshua to dress outrageously.

Original: 19 words
Revised: 14 words
Reduction: 25%

Tangents, Digressions, and Irrelevancies

Some writers, like S.J. Perelman, are famous for their humorous tangents and successful digressions, but we are talking here of digression as the enemy of coherence.

In most modern writing we expect the writer to stick to the topic from beginning to end. When he digresses, even though the digression may be fascinating in itself, we are upset. We professors are notorious for lectures that digress. Some professors develop reputations for lectures described by students as beads of digression on a string of irrelevance. If our writing is not to resemble those lectures, we must be forever alert to irrelevance.

The common advice to let your first draft ferment for a while in the bottom drawer before revising it is based on the need to get far enough away from the writing to gain (somewhat) the perspective of the reader. After ceremoniously removing the manuscript from the drawer, or calling it up on your word processor's screen, sit back and read it from the beginning; try your best to be critical of the writing (forgetting who wrote it). As you scrutinize the many facets of this gem, watch for paragraphs of tangency. Don't be fooled—they're often cleverly camouflaged. Relevance is relative, so your question should be, "Is this paragraph sufficiently related to my point to be included?" In some cases, it may very well be relevant and may merely be in the wrong location. Flag it for subsequent consideration, and move on. Perhaps a second reading will make its inclusion here seem absolutely reasonable. Or you may find yourself asking why in the world you ever thought it relevant in the first place.

You must engage in these internal dialogues all the time, and you must let yourself lose the arguments gracefully. Writing may be solitary, but it isn't a game of solitaire at which you can cheat.

There are no simple examples of digression and irrelevance. To show the sins clearly, examples would run so long that this section itself could become a book. These particular forms of verbiage come closest to proving my belief that writing is thinking on paper. Writing that is full of tangents and digressions is the product of a mind unsure of its thoughts.

Authorial Intrusion

I am dead against art's being self-expression. I see an inherent failure in any story which fails to detach itself from its author.

—ELIZABETH BOWEN

The author, in his work, ought to be like God in the universe, present everywhere and visible nowhere.

—GUSTAVE FLAUBERT

Closely allied with the sin just described is a special case of tangential, digressionary verbiage called authorial intrusion. This sin is widespread and found in different garb in fiction and nonfiction. Whenever there's an author around, there's the risk that he will commit the crime of intrusion.

The following paragraph, taken from a student's fictional story about a leftist group meeting, is fine until the author intrudes with a parenthetical comment:

> I noted a very few girls on our side, a slightly larger group opposite. Most of the "right" side (Heaven forgive me such a pun) was occupied by college students, looking fully as grim and determined as I felt.

The writer knew she was intruding—else why the parentheses?—but she went right on and intruded. If part of the style of a particular piece is frequent parenthetical intrusions, it might be acceptable, but why ruin the impression that we're participating in the event by suddenly reminding us that we're actually being told a story by someone? Worse yet, we're being told a story by someone more concerned about a poor pun than about the action going on. The illusion of fiction is shattered by reminders that the author is present.

There were two windows in the church, each with its inevitable Mason jar of zinnias, long wilted.

And yes, wasn't that yet another sun scowling from behind his left shoulder and every bit as penetrating as the one from behind his right? And what's this? Redmond was delirious . . . "Up ahead . . . coming toward me . . . a being of some kind . . . sent to destroy me no doubt . . . made up to look human."

Everything was fine, dear writer, until you walked down the aisle to tell us that Mason jars are *inevitably* found there with their long-wilted zinnias.

Why, dear author, did you think it necessary to intrude into our world of fantasy to tell us that Redmond was delirious! Part of the fun of reading is to discover things for ourselves. We'd figure out soon enough that he was delirious—trust us.

A more subtle form of authorial intrusion in fiction occurs when the author inserts—cleverly perhaps, but nonetheless intrusively—the "mini-lecture." I recall a short story I was writing in which the hero uses a canoe. It may have been because I was also writing at the time a nonfiction book on camping and canoeing, but I found myself writing several long paragraphs about how he got into the canoe, how he shoved off, what paddle stroke he used, and so forth.

Good sense returned during revision, and I eliminated the mini-lecture on correct canoeing. This simple act of reduction not only moved the story along better; it reserved space to use later on when I desperately needed it to finish the story within the length limit imposed.

Some authors remind me of the woman who loves dogs to excess and thinks that everyone else should be made to see what joys a dog can bring to one's life. To make her point, she takes her ugly dog to every social affair she attends. No one minds when she takes it along to Boy Scout dinners, hunt club meetings, and the races, but she ostentatiously takes it along to the opera, formal weddings, and diplomatic receptions. Authorial intrusion, like canine intrusion, has its place.

Some authors can't stay their feet from climbing onto the soapbox. Our stories and articles offer what every soapbox orator dreams of—a captive audience.

If we're serious, professional writers, we won't take surreptitious advantage of the captives. It's certainly all right to shout from the dizzying heights of a soapbox when we're writing an opinion piece; it's not all right, in my opinion, to sneak opinions into the narrative of a fiction piece.

If an opinion the author holds happens also to be part of the belief structure of a fictive character, it's all right to work the opinion in as part of the story, but the reader must be prepared for it. An opinion must not be dragged in by its rhetorical heels; it must belong there.

Excess Modifiers

About some superfluous words it cannot be said that they add nothing to a sentence; rather, they add a bit much. I think particularly of the overuse of adjectives and adverbs. They may be perfectly accurate, grammatical, and apt, yet excessive.

Beginning writers, especially while still under the influence of litterateurs in school and college, fall easily into the habit of excessive modification. Many of the classics written a couple of centuries ago overflow with modifiers, for it was then the style.

Today's writers select their nouns and verbs carefully to avoid the need to "explain" them with adjectives and adverbs. A piece of writing stripped of adjectives and adverbs can be lifeless, though. So, as with almost everything in life, moderation may be the best policy. The general rule should be moderation in modification. Superfluity of modification can be harmful to the health of your prose.

Early sunlight peeked through the apple-blossomed tree outdoors, making playful designs on the yellow-checked kitchen curtains and tablecloth outdoors. While sitting in her shiny chair, Amy noticed the bouncing little shadows sprinkled high and low in the pleasant room.

There may be nothing wrong with any single modifier here; it's the cumulative effect of paragraph upon paragraph full of superfluous flowers of stylistic elegance that finally drives the reader back to the tube. We'll talk more about this in a later chapter, when we consider the careful selection of the perfect verb and the just-right noun.

Idle, Nonworking Words

During revisions, always question your use of *essentially, basically, ultimately,* and *inevitably.* We all use these words too frequently because we use them too loosely. These words should be reserved for more important matters than, say: "Babe Ruth was *essentially* a hitter"; "*Ultimately,* we'll find that Merv Griffin was one of the best"; "*Basically,* I'm in love"; "*Inevitably,* she wore that same old hat." These should not be deleted for being too idle; they should be deleted for doing more than is called for.

Another word used too frequently, particularly in fiction, is *suddenly:* "Suddenly a shot rang out." Can you imagine a shot ringing out slowly? *(Slowly a shot rang out.)* The inexperienced writer often tries to make things more exciting and faster-paced by having everything happen *suddenly.* There are better ways to build pace, create tension, and generate excitement. The right verbs, the right words in general, and a series of sentences that get progressively shorter will establish a feeling of suddenness better than the sudden insertion of the word. (see Diction page 133)

And is one of the more useful words, but it's used far too frequently by lazy writers:

> The ships were huge *and* gray, *and* they stood out to sea at 0600 hours. The admiral was pleased to hear this, *and* went immediately to the flying bridge *and* watched. *And* the captain who was also impressed, came up to the bridge, too, *and* took up his position.

There are no grammar faults here; the overuse of *and* just makes boring reading. The problem is that it takes some thought to get rid of an infestation of *and's.* It's like getting rid of an idle brother-in-law: It's far too easy simply to let him hang around. It would be worth the effort, however, to make the first sentence read: "The ships, huge and gray, stood out to sea at 0600 hours." Perhaps it's me, but the ships sound even grayer and huger in this revised version. It takes a little more thought, but wouldn't the second sentence read better as: "Pleased to hear this, the admiral went immediately to the flying bridge to watch." The final sentence would be better as: "The captain, similarly impressed, came to the bridge and took up his position."

We didn't eliminate all the *and's,* but we did drop four out of six from that short paragraph—along with several other words.

Not that we should arbitrarily delete all, or even four out of six, *and*'s; we should simply be wary of them, lest our readers weary of them. An artistic writer, of course, can use a string of *and's* to create an effect. Ernest Hemingway, in *A Farewell to Arms,* shows *and* in the hands of a master:

> There was much traffic at night and many mules on the roads with boxes of ammunition on each side of their pack-saddles and gray motor trucks that carried men, and other trucks with loads covered with canvas that moved slower in the traffic.

Of is another short, useful, but sometimes idle and in-the-way word: "Outside [of] the house, he was happy"; "Inside [of] the woods, she was helpless"; "He told her to get down off [of] the horse"; "She laughed and told him that one doesn't get down off a horse but from [off of] a duck." If you were writing dialogue between two uneducated people, you might decide not to delete the *of's,* in the service of verisimilitude. In general, however, such use of *of* is unwarranted.

There is another idle word that clutters—the word *there.* The insidiousness of *there* was first made clear to me by Lucile Vaughan Payne in her extremely lively, useful series of books, *The Lively Art of Writing.* She recommends, and I agree, that we should simply "rip out," "ban," "delete," "eliminate" from writing vocabularies the idler *there.*

There itself is not bad; it's the company it keeps that gets it in trouble. *There* usually hangs out innocently on the corner with other idlers, verbs like *is, was, are, have been, had been,* and other weak verbs of being. These colorless verbs merely indicate that something exists, nothing about how it exists, how it behaves, what it smells like—nothing to pique our interest:

> "There will be a discussion of the weakness in forms of *be* later in this book."

If we drop *there* because it's weak, we find we must drop *will be* too. We end up with a much stronger sentence:

> "We'll discuss later in this book the weakness in forms of *be.*"

Take another example:

> There is something frightening going on!

Compare this with:

> Something frightening is going on!

Isn't the second version a little more frightening? It gains by hitting the situation head-on.

Sometimes you need make only a slight change in word order to accommodate the dropping of *there,* as in the revised version above. Sometimes, however, you'll be forced to work a bit harder to get rid of the idler *there:*

> There was a battle.

Obviously, you can't simply drop *there,* ending up with, "was a battle." Even a change in word order won't do it: "A battle was." The verb *was* now presents a problem. It doesn't tell us much about the battle—only that it existed.

Let's think about it. What do battles do, other than exist? Battles break out. Battles start up. Battles ensue. Battles explode. Any one of those verbs would begin to give us a feeling for battle. Anything would be more attention-getting and more informative than that four-word sentence encumbered by the two idlers, *there was.*

Nothing is grammatically wrong with the following, but let's see whether we can improve on it:

Suddenly there was the sound of guns.

Remembering that *suddenly* can also clutter, can we improve this sentence by deleting the first three words?

- The sound of guns. (No, that won't do it.)

- The roar of heavy naval guns broke the stillness of night.

- Heavy naval guns cracked the stillness of night.

- Heavy naval guns roared and flashed into the pink of dawn.

You might now be saying to yourself that I haven't merely stopped at getting rid of the three idlers; I've added material. That's the point! By forcing myself to find suitable replacements for those weak words *(suddenly, there,* and *was),*

I've forced myself to think. When you begin to think about what *exactly* you're trying to say, you become a writer. The nonwriter believes he's said what he wanted to say with "Suddenly there was the sound of guns." That merely *expresses* the thought; a professional writer wants to *impress* something on us. He wants to leave an impression.

As a form of self-discipline that can lead serendipitously to better writing, try never to use *there,* at least not without a lot of heavy thinking.

There was an old lady who lived in a shoe. . .

After a lot of heavy thinking, I've decided I can't improve on that one by dropping out *there*—proving once again that you can't win 'em all.

Which *Which* Is *That?*

I've saved for last the one you've been waiting for so impatiently; how to tell when to use *which* and when to use *that.* This is not an easy matter to understand or explain, so I approach it with trepidation. H. W. Fowler, in *Modern English Usage,* devotes some six thousand words to the uses of *which.* He uses another three thousand for *that*—just as a relative pronoun! I don't pretend to such erudition, but I will try to distill Fowler's wisdom and other writers' thoughts into rules of reasonable length and utility.

Compilers of *The Harper Dictionary of Contemporary Usage,* using a panel of professional writers to argue out the more difficult entries, found that sixty-two percent of the panel agreed that the distinction between *which* and *that* was worth preserving. As I read their comments, however, I could see that even these experts were not themselves too clear on the distinctions. In other words, if you aren't too sure about distinctions, you're in distinguished company. That's a lame excuse for not trying, however, so let's dig in and examine these two, disarmingly simple-sounding, pronouns.

Everyone has pronoun problems. Pronouns are problems because it is often difficult for the reader to figure out what a pronoun refers back to, yet that is the purpose of a pronoun: to stand in for some person, thing, or idea previously (and recently) mentioned. There's always the possibility that the reader will not refer himself back to the same person, thing, or idea the writer intended. It's best for the writer to presume that if the reader can find a way to refer back to the unintended, he will.

Pronoun difficulty reaches its peak with the pronouns *which* and *that.* The rule of thumb is to do everything you can to avoid *which,* especially when you find another *which* nearby. Not only will one or more *which's* probably cause the reference problem mentioned, it is simply an ugly word. Few other English words scratch at the tympani the way *which* will.

Always play around with a sentence to find whether a *which* can be burned without great loss. If you can't think of a way to restructure the sentence, ask yourself whether you can substitute *that* for *which*. You'll frequently find that it will work:

You may have to trust your ear, which is usually a good judge.

For example, let's try substituting *that* for *which* in the sentence you just read:

You may have to trust your ear that is usually a good judge.

The latter version will be correct only if you have but one good ear and were making the point that you could trust *that* ear because it has proven itself usually to be a good judge.

That was surely not the meaning of the original sentence. The original deliberately uses a comma before *which* to give the reader a signal that the upcoming clause ("which is usually a good judge") is not intended to limit our thinking to a particular ear; it's just a comment that your ability to judge correctness by sound is usually good.

By the way, Irving, the experiment that I want you to see will take place here tomorrow morning shortly after six.

The use of *that* rather than *which* means that there are several experiments, but the particular one that I want you to see, Irving, is the one being conducted here tomorrow. If this had been worded, "By the way, Irving, the experiment, which I want you to see," it would have implied that there is only one experiment, and I want Irving to see it.

President Reagan spoke about the Berlin Wall, which divided the city.

Left this way, the sentence means that the president divided the city by speaking about the wall. It would have been correct as:

President Reagan spoke about the wall that divided Berlin.

Your ear can be a fairly reliable guide. When you are confused, read the passage aloud and listen for breaks in delivery that you make naturally. If you find yourself making two breaks, one before the clause under consideration and one after it, then you probably need a *which*, not a *that*. Otherwise, your ear is telling you to use a *that*.

Another rule of the thumb to follow is to eliminate *that* as often as you can. Here again, you may have to trust your ear. Say aloud the sentence in question, and decide whether it sounds all right to drop *that*. If it does, do so.

Are the two *that's* in the following sentence essential to meaning?

> Remember, then, *that* words are the only tools *that* you will be given.

Read the following that-less version; have we lost anything of value?

> Remember, then, words are the only tools you will be given.

My ear says that that that-less sentence sounds better. (Try to top that.) I have no grammatical reason, or any reason other than ear. But if a sentence can be heard and understood without the superfluous pronoun, get rid of it.

Micro-Reductions

In our continuing search for ways to reduce verbiage, we should not overlook the savings possible even by single words, which I've named micro-reductions.

Short for Long

The most productive micro-reduction is to replace a longer word with a shorter one—where reasonable. We'll discuss "reasonableness" at length in the section on style (p. 129). If we become slaves of reduction to the point of absurdity, we'll produce sentences that are shorter, but don't say what we intend; that's false economy. For the moment, however, let's just make the point that it's frequently better to use the shorter synonym than the fancier, *perhaps* more precise, polysyllabic word.

Robert Gunning's justly famous book, *The Technique of Clear Writing*, lists the more familiar, usually shorter, equivalents for hundreds of words. I recommend that book and that list (pp. 302-315). Here's a sampling to whet your appetite:

abandon	*give up, desert*
abatement	*decrease*

abbreviate	*shorten*
abdicate	*give up, resign*
abdomen	*belly*
abduct	*kidnap* (not shorter, but simpler)
abeyance	*waiting*
abhorrent	*disgusting, hateful*

Gunning's list goes on to end with these equivalents:

ventilate	*air*
venturous	*bold*
visualize	*picture*
vitreous	*glassy*
vociferate	*shout*
voluminous	*bulky*

Admittedly, the shorter word may not be synonymous enough for your purpose, in which case you have to decide whether it's better to err on the side of precision or of ease. Nevertheless, you should always consider the possibility that a shorter word may do for the purpose at hand.

Add this to your self-discipline kit: Force yourself to ask whether a shorter word may serve; you are thereby forcing yourself to think. This process called thinking will sometimes find lurking within a polysyllabic monstrosity a lack of precise thought. It's so easy to hide fuzziness within a long word. Since it's your own fuzziness, there's also a human tendency to believe that the polysyllable you've come up with is the just-right word. To believe otherwise would be to admit that you don't know exactly what you want to say. The rule is to use the simplest words that will make the point.

Contractions

Micro-reductions include *contractions,* tiny reductions smaller than those I've described earlier. They may be small, but they can be significant. In the sentence above, I managed to save only two letters by contracting *I have* to *I've,* but I gained something much more important than the two letters; I achieved a tone of informality.

Certainly, there are places where that level of informality would be inappropriate, but the tone of this book is sufficiently informal that I can use a contraction with equanimity. You've read grammar books in which a contraction never shows up, even in the section where the author recommends using contractions to establish a friendly rapport with the reader. In his chapter on other topics, such as verbs, he won't be caught using rapport-building contractions—his rigid training won't let'm do it.

As a consequence of the intellectuals' attitude toward contractions, company letters and memoranda bounce back and forth without a contraction in a carload. Colleagues who share jokes, intimate secrets, and lunch will write letters and memos to each other that begin, "It has come to my attention that. . ." Why couldn't they start the way a lunch conversation on the same matter might: "Jim, I've been noticing that. . ."

This is partly the fault of the English-teaching profession, and partly of the establishment's habit of having a "distribution list" for letters and memos. The corporate writer finds it intimidating to see that copies of what he writes to Jim, his lunch buddy, are going also to several managers and a vice-president. Out go the friendly contractions and in comes the stilted, serious language of the important, memo-writing executive.

Nano-Reductions

Perhaps the next form of micro-reduction should be called nano-reduction. There are a few words that have two acceptable forms, one shorter than the other by only one letter. Most American dictionaries and style books recommend always using the shorter of: towards/toward, forwards/forward, backwards/backward, upwards/upward, inwards/inward, aesthetic/esthetic. British dictionaries usually prefer the longer form.

I refuse, however, to shorten *employee* by one letter, to *employe*. One Fortune 500 company has set a policy for all its publications that a person in their employ shall be referred to as an *employe,* and that personnel the company employs are *employes*. Employees writing for that trend-setting company may, for survival, have to call themselves "employes," but the rest of us may continue to write according to standard English.

Reduction Rules Reduced

Professional writers admit that they almost always write too many words in their first drafts. They also admit that they deliberately "let it all come out" in the early stages, knowing that it is easier to revise by cutting than by adding.

I recognize that the professional writer does not necessarily proceed in the step-by-step sequence suggested here. He or she will usually employ all the methods of reduction discussed in this chapter, but probably in a different sequence or, more likely, simultaneously. For the beginner, or for the long-timer

who wishes to proceed in a more systematic way, this suggested routine of reduction will work well:

- Stand back from the manuscript and look objectively at the major
  chunks. Do they all belong?

- Move in a little closer. Are there paragraphs or sentences the manuscript could live without?

- Lean over the pages still closer. Are there idle, cluttering phrases or
  words?

- Finally, get out your magnifying glass. Could shorter words express
  the thought as clearly; could some words be shortened, even by a letter; and would contractions here and there be appropriate to the
  tone?

Now that you've reduced the bulk and hacked out the underbrush, you can see
what you've said. Typically, you'll find that what you've said is either not precisely what you intended or could have been expressed more clearly, more attractively, more logically. These kinds of changes call for another routine of
revision: You need to rethink and then rearrange.

Before moving to that next major revision routine, rearranging, let's apply
what we've learned to a beginning writer's manuscript. Rather than have you
read the entire piece first, I've interrupted it every once in a while to show some
possible revisions. There are more ways to revise this, but I've limited my revisions largely to those of reduction.

Original:

> The restaurant was set back from the road approximately 100 feet.
> There was parking on both sides of the restaurant and the area set
> aside for parking was separated by an area of well-kept grass.

Revised:

> The restaurant was set back about 100 feet, with parking on both
> sides of the well-kept lawn.

Original:

> I entered the restaurant and directly in front of me was the cashier.
> To my right was the area of the restaurant where patrons were
> served at the counter. I saw more service people than customers.

Located on my right was a self-service ice cream freezer. The dining room was to my left and as I turned in that direction I looked for the hostess, but she was not in sight.

Revised:

I entered and found the cashier directly ahead, a counter and self-service ice cream freezer to the right, the main dining room to the left, the hostess nowhere in sight.

Original:

I envisioned a long wait, but to my surprise she appeared. She led me through one part of the dining room that was composed of only booths. We walked to the end of the room and turned right and walked into another room which contained tables and chairs rather than booths. She seated me at a small table against the wall.

Revised:

The hostess appeared immediately, leading me through a room of booths and into a room of tables and chairs. She seated me at one of the small tables against the wall.

Original:

I was disappointed when she seated me with my back to the main dining area, but then I discovered I could unobtrusively observe in one of two large mirrors bounding the picture window all that occurred in that room.

Revised:

I sat with my back to the main part of the dining area, but directly in front of me was a large mirror, one of the two that were on each side of a picture window. I was able to see all that occurred in that room.

Originals: 214 words
Revised: 113 words
Total Reduction: 53%

CHAPTER II

Rethink and Rearrange

1. *Unity*

2. *Coherence*

3. *Emphasis*

The revision processes described in Chapter I involve *reducing* the number of words. Now we'll concentrate on *rethinking:* adding words, reducing the number of words further, dropping some words and replacing them with better ones, or simply rearranging the existing words. The piece of writing, whether shorter or longer after this additional revision, will come closer to saying what is intended.

A nonwriter may think it strange that a writer would have to rethink at this late stage. After all, in school few of us revised our essays; one felt relieved simply to have churned out the required number of pages—with precise margins and proper footnotes. The teacher may (or may not) have returned the paper with marginal comments about what was wrong; rewriting was rarely required, so a person graduated from high school, even college, thinking that that's all there is to writing: churning out the words.

One also left school under the impression that writers are somehow superhuman—that words must flow from their pens just as they appear in the finished product. It never occurred to me in school that Joseph Conrad, E. B. White, or John Steinbeck had to write and rewrite more than I was ever required to do to get my *A* in English. Imagine President Roosevelt revising up to the last minute his declaration of war on Japan. Impossible. In fact, of course, we kids never thought about it. Presidents, writers, and other famous people were "up there" somewhere, far beyond the comprehension of us ordinary folk.

Any of these famous writers would willingly admit to rewriting their work a number of times to get it right—the way we mortals would finally see it. The second major routine of revision derives from the statement quoted in Chapter One: *after you've got it down on paper, you can see more clearly what it is you're thinking.* You may discover, however, that you're still unsure of what you think. This requires some further thinking. Then some rewriting. Then some rethinking. Finally, you know what it is you want to say.

The next step is to find the best possible way to express that thought to someone else. Frequently a great difference exists between the words you need in order to understand yourself and the words you need to make the same thought clear to someone else. The originating mind has the advantage of knowing all the peripheral thinking that has gone on in the process. The ability to walk in the shoes of the reader is essential. This requires empathy, and that cannot be taught. What can be taught, however, is how to put down the right words with the right emphasis in a logical sequence, and with the most effective transitions.

This chapter will show you how to rethink and then to rearrange words, sentences, paragraphs, sections, and chapters to help the reader over the high hurdles of comprehension. Writers generally agree that at least these three principles must be adhered to if the reader is to go away with anything resembling what is intended: *unity, coherence, and emphasis.* These three principles are so central to writing that they necessarily overlap, but treating them as though they were totally distinct entities makes the core easier to talk about.

Unity

Unity is not an abstraction of interest only to academic rhetoricians; it is an absolutely essential property of good writing. It might be better to refer to *unities,* however, since there are a number of subunities. If all these minor unities are achieved, the entire piece of writing is unified.

Unity of Subject

Let's start at the macro end of this continuum of unities: unity of subject matter. If a book's title is *Baseball,* the reader has a right to expect the author to discuss that one, single topic. If football, basketball, and other ball games are taken up at length in a book called *Baseball,* the book is not unified. If the title is *Games of Ball,* however, it might claim unity. It is unified in that it discusses most major ball games, excluding other games (such as chess, hockey, or PacMan).

You'd think it a given that a writer would stick to what he says (or indicates in the title) he is going to write about, yet editors the world over bemoan writers' failure to adhere to this fundamental, obvious principle of good writing. Furthermore, editors say that writers, even those who do stick to their promised topic, develop their subtopics unevenly. I found this out for myself, the hard way.

My novel *Day of Fate* is about the Chinese communists setting up underwater missile launchers in the Canadian and Russian sub-Arctic. Their dastardly scheme is uncovered and the world saved from World War III by a doctor and his Inuit and Cree Indian parishioners. In preparing to write this book, I visited its Canadian locales and spent years doing part-time reading and map research.

When I sent the original draft of 100,000 words off to the first publisher to read, I was proud of the book. I was especially, not to say inordinately, proud of how authentic I had made my story sound by including so much excellent geographic, climatic, and ethnographic information.

My sails slacked when the editor wrote back that he loved the plot but felt that my information got in the way, obstructing the story's movement. "After all," he said, "this is supposed to be a tale of high adventure, not a textbook on Inuit and Cree culture."

It took some months before I admitted to myself that he was absolutely right. In my zeal to add authenticity and verisimilitude, I had lost sight of my subject. It took a lot of rethinking and rearranging, but I managed to cut out thousands of words that dealt with interesting but peripheral matters. I left in enough research-derived information to establish authenticity, but I kept to the main subject.

I had, in effect, promised my readers a riveting tale of international intrigue in the Arctic; I had not prepared them for a socio-economic treatise on the modern Inuit. I would not be breaching that promise, however, by mentioning, here and there, an interesting fact about the life of the Inuit—provided it connected directly with the yarn I was spinning. A paragraph telling how today's Inuit hunts with a high-powered rifle, not a harpoon, would make credible the eventual capture of the Chinese submarine by rifle-bearing Inuit and Cree. If, on the other hand, I were to discuss how the Inuit women used to place a tub full of warm female urine above a woman in labor, I would be going beyond the subject.

Unity of Scope

If, in the book *Games of Ball,* the chapter about baseball discusses history of the game, rules of the game, famous players of the past, and statistics for 1983, whereas the football chapter discusses history, rules, and famous players, but mentions nothing about 1983's statistics, the book does not have unity of scope—one sport is covered in greater breadth than another. Another chapter might leave out the history of the sport or discuss only currently famous players. Such a chapter would be unified in subject but not in scope.

If you had written the first draft of such a sports book and were new to the revision process, you would now have to do a lot of *rethinking:* pushing your chair back from the desk, staring out the window or up at the ceiling, and asking yourself just what it is you're doing.

In some cases you can simply do some more work to bring the scope of the short-changed chapter into line with the scope of the others. Depending on circumstances (such as contractual obligations), you may decide to narrow the scope of some chapters to conform to the narrower scope of the others.

In nonfiction, unity of subject and scope can be ensured by working from an outline, even a sketchy one. For example, here's one for *Games of Ball:*

    I.   *Baseball*
        A. history
        B. rules of the game
        C. famous players
        D. statistics for 1983

   II.   *Football*
        A. history
        B. rules of the game
        C. famous players
        D. statistics for 1983

  III.   *Basketball*
        A. history
        B. rules of the game
        C. famous players
        D. statistics for 1983

Working from an outline should prevent your leaving out an important subsection. If you find you must leave out a subsection, you should explain to the reader the reason: e.g., lengthy strikes in the baseball leagues made statistics for 1983 meaningless. In such a situation, one might substitute 1982 statistics to approximate unity of scope (after making the substitution and the reason for it clear to the reader, of course).

Unity of Tone

Tone in writing is as close to tone of voice in speaking as metaphor will allow. Whether in writing or in speaking, tone helps us discern the originator's true meaning; tone *modifies* meaning. A written transcript of speech will not always tell us what a speaker means, because the speaker's manipulation of his voice gives us the clues we need to "read between the lines." In conversation, nonverbal techniques like eyebrow arching, shoulder shrugging, and hand wringing supplement words and tone of voice. Since the writer has only words to work with, they must be thoughtfully selected to produce the desired tone.

A single word may give a clue about the writer's attitude, but it is usually the cumulative effect of many precisely chosen words, and even the rhythms employed, that results in the piece's tone. Because of this cumulative effect, unity of tone requires consistency. A careless writer will use words that create different tones within the same piece. This inconsistency of tone can cause misinterpretation. Even if the overall tone comes through by the end, inconsistent word choice may create interim confusion.

Beginning writers not yet in command of their diction will sometimes set the wrong tone early in a piece. In the very first sentence they may establish (unintentionally and inappropriately) an informal tone for what is going to be a serious piece: "The nurse came in with a cheerful 'Time for our shot' and stabbed him in the butt." Later in the piece, we find that the patient is a fine young man who dies in his hospital bed. The initial lighthearted tone was established because the writer didn't stop to think that *butt* is a very informal word and one frequently used in jokes. The misled reader does not discover that the intended tone is one of serious concern until he has read a number of subsequent paragraphs. The reader would have a right to be upset with the writer for such lack of sensitivity. A writer, therefore, must always be alert to not only the denotations but also the connotations of words. A sense of humor, or a sense of the absurd, is a useful tool in the writer's kit, since a good deal of humor grows out of the multiple connotations of words.

Often a writer will display an attitude he does not wish to convey: pompous, arrogant, obsequious, phony, patronizing, or too, too sophisticated. This happens when the writer either doesn't care or doesn't understand the power of words to create tone—the kind that's not desired, as well as what is desired.

I seem to have concentrated on the negative aspects of tone, probably because they're easier to spot in their exaggerated forms. It is difficult to conceive of an exaggeratedly "good" tone. A good tone is one that has its desired effect but does not wave flags. It is so appropriate, so right, so sincere that it slips quietly past the attention and neatly effects the intention. The best tone to adopt is one that is called *plain*. An unaffected, undecorated, plain tone has the power of clarity.

It is my hope that if readers of this book conscientiously follow its recommendations, they will achieve a plain but nevertheless unique style. E. B. White, Lewis Thomas, and William Zinsser write in plain styles. Each renders a plain tone—one that neither yields easily to the temptations of contemporary speech nor sticks doggedly to the language of the past. Each man's style is plain but identifiably his own. E. B. White, by the way, offers an excellent, short commentary, "Prefer the Standard to the Offbeat," in *The Elements of Style*. Jacques Barzun has written an equally useful discussion of tone in his *Simple & Direct*.

Tone begins to sound like style, but style is the overall effect of a piece, *including* tone. We'll discuss style more thoroughly in the next chapter. For now, simply bear in mind that a writer may create many tones while using just one style.

Tone is important to any form of writing, including everyday writing for organizations. The wrong tone (patronizing, autocratic, condescending, bureaucratic) in a memo from the boss can make employees, out of spite, do exactly the opposite of what the boss intended. Any memo from a supervisory person stands a good chance of being misinterpreted, simply because of its source. A boss should recognize that many subordinates delight in misinterpreting executive memos even when clearly written. He can intensify the problem by careless and insensitive selection of words. Employees are quick to sense the tone of a memo, so it's source had best create the tone that will encourage employees to cooperate with the memo's directives. It never occurs to some bosses (and who dares tell them?) that their words as they trip from their tongues into the dictating machine are not perfect. Even a highly educated boss, who should know better, is unlikely to ask someone to read over the draft of a memo and say what tone comes across. A boss is apt to be insulted by any suggestion from the subordinate who reports that the tone is inflammatory, patronizing, or "picky." An experienced writer, on the other hand, would not be at all surprised to learn that he or she has created such an unintended tone, and would be grateful that someone had noticed the tone and brought it to light in time.

Unity of Style

Somehow I have to advise you here to maintain a unity of style when my full treatment of style doesn't appear until the next chapter. Fortunately, however, a complete understanding of all that is meant by style is not necessary to appreciate the need for maintaining a consistent, unified style throughout a piece.

To give you an idea of what I mean by style, I've selected paragraphs by two of my favorite authors, writing here about cabins. Let's not worry about naming their styles; that arcane business is for literary critics, not writers. Simply decide whether their styles are somehow different:

> (1) This was an airy and unplastered cabin fit to entertain a travelling god, and where a goddess might trail her garments. The winds which passed over my dwelling were such as sweep over the ridges of the mountains, bearing the broken strains, or celestial parts only, of terrestrial music. The morning wind forever blows, the poem of creation is interrupted; but few are the ears that hear it. Olympus is but the outside of the earth everywhere.

> (2) "Thank Heaven Lars is so good with wood. Poor Elsie—it's all Pierce Kercher can do to split cord wood, let alone whomp up a settee like Lars did right after we got here." She looked with renewed appreciation at the settee she had since covered with the big black bear's skin. Lars had also fashioned a comfortable chair by cutting a section out of a great flour barrel. She had then fancied it up with a seat cushion stuffed with dried caribou moss and covered with rabbit skins. She couldn't help but pity Elsie Kercher, who was still using the wooden packing crates for chairs around the table in their cabin.

The point is that a writer about cabins today should not write in Cheney's style (2) that uses the vernacular sound of real people working hard at survival along an Alaskan river, if he's then going to write in the same piece in Thoreau's style (1) of philosophical musings with allusions to Greek gods and goddesses.

The incompatibility of styles is obvious here because of the length, but beginners will occasionally allow a Thoreauvian sentence or two to slip in among their more modern, unadorned sentences. Sometimes it's done in a vain attempt to appear deep, symbolic, important. It doesn't work.

Unified Point of View

The narrator—the person telling the story—must be either an *observer* of the action or a *participant* in it. There are only two fundamental points of view, first person (participant) and third person (observer), but many gradations and variations exist: Omniscient (personal), Omniscient (impersonal), Limited Omniscient, Single Character, Multiple Character, Dramatic (External), Narrator (Observer), Narrator (Participant), etc. Treatments of these variations can be found in books on how to write and in books analyzing literature. I recommend most highly the fifty pages of instruction in *Techniques of Fiction Writing: Measure and Madness,* by Leon Surmelian (Doubleday).

Unity of Character

Developing believable characters is one of the most essential and difficult tasks a fiction writer faces. In some stories plot is more important than character development, but even in those, the characters must be credible. A good writer has many techniques for making characters live, but this book is concerned only with revising what's already been written about the story's characters. Among the first questions the reviser asks about characterization is, "Is each character consistently drawn?" Does the character sound stupid here (where it suits the author's need) and intelligent there (where highly developed intellectual faculties are called for)? Is she a wallflower in Chapter 1 and in Chapter 10 a professional belly dancer? If she has become extroverted, has the reader been prepared for this change?

In that rare instance in which the character is meant to be totally inconsistent (perhaps schizophrenic), the author must be careful to make clear the consistency of the inconsistency, lest the reader attribute the inconsistency to the author's inability to create a unified character.

Unity of Scene

If a scene is properly drawn, it is unified. *Scene,* as used here, means a unified piece of action, not simply a pretty country setting. It is a single episode or situation and remains a scene only so long as there is no break in time and no major change of place.

All we have to concern ourselves with in the revision process is that each scene is reasonably pure, or unified. A pure scene is all action with minimal distraction. The narrator, for example, should not be forever poking his omniscient head into the scene to provide background information. He's allowed in there to describe the movement, the smashed vase, and the rumpled rug; he should not give us a lot of data about the vase. He might properly refer to it as a *Ming* vase, even as a *priceless* Ming vase, but he violates the unity of scene if he elaborates on the history of the Ming Dynasty, or how much it might bring at a Sotheby auction. Only the narrative points necessary to make the scene alive and dynamic are allowed.

Although I've just said that a scene is less than unified if a lot of attention is paid to nonessential elements, it's not difficult to imagine a scene that is unified despite attention to seeming nonessentials. A scene, for example, in which a husband and wife are in the midst of a divorce-portending argument might include narrative descriptions of family photographs and memorabilia scattered about the room. Such description increases the scene's emotional impact. The husband, for example, might well be saying hateful things to her in the heat of battle, yet he might be thinking, in a momentary flashback triggered by the sight of his dead son's fishing tackle in the corner, what a loving family they had been before the drowning. Frequent flashbacks like this, of course, would make it difficult to keep the battle scene hot, ruining the unity of this scene.

The decision whether to include such a flashback would depend on the writer's objectives for the scene. He may have invented The Big Argument Scene simply as a literary device to launch a series of long, important flashback scenes. In that case, the battle business would not be a scene so much as a thread connecting the flashbacks.

The style and tone of the entire piece will help determine what narrative details can legitimately be included in a scene. James Thurber, for example, might in the midst of a fight scene, go off on a long, hilarious tangent about Chinese dynasties, and no critic would fault the apparent lapse in unity.

In general, a scene should be clear, unencumbered by extraneous matter, pure—unified. The modern reader, brought up on movies and television, wants highly visual stories, not narrative summaries. Life itself, which art is supposed to mimic, is a series of events, actions—scenes. The creator of life must have been a dramatist, not a narrator. The closer our writing comes to putting our readers plunk in the center of one scene after another, the closer we come to making them believe they are living the lives of the characters—and that is our professional goal in writing fiction.

Although what has just been said about life being dramatic is largely valid, we should not forget in our writing and revising that people do have meditative moments between, and even during, events. When it serves his purpose, a good writer will let us share those reflective times by means of internal monologues and narrative summaries.

The writing of internal monologues, covered well in many books on writing techniques, is an art worth studying and using because it comes closest, when done well, to real life. Less realistic is the technique of having the narrator *tell* the reader what a character is thinking and feeling. Such narrative summaries are certainly acceptable and definitely efficient: It's more efficient (uses fewer words) to tell the reader that Harry feels sick, physically and mentally, about losing his job than to lead us through a carefully wrought internal monologue that weaves in details about his psychological problems, his thoughts about tomorrow, his current relationship with his wife, the effect of his unemployment on that relationship, and so forth.

The question the writer-reviser must always ask when dealing with a specific passage is whether it is more important to tell his story *efficiently* or *effectively*. There can be no generalizing about that; it all depends on the total situation: Is this woman a minor or major character? In either case, should the reader be made to care deeply? Have I (the author) been using too much of one technique already? Am I better at one technique than the other? Is the scene too long or too short for the objectives set?

Writers of the past sometimes used great amounts of narrative summary and few scenes. Many nineteenth-century novels, for instance, are totally or largely narrative summary. It was largely during this century that the internal or interior monologue became common in fiction. Made famous by James Joyce. in *Ulysses,* internal monologue has enlivened modern writing.

The problem for writers in the television age is that TV-nurtured readers will not stick with long pages of descriptive narration, and they'll tolerate even less an internal monologue that goes on and on. The message for modern writers is not that we should stop conveying a character's thoughts, but that we should do so in moderation. Whether we employ summary, scene, or internal monolgoue, we must strive to render the unspoken thought concisely—in fewer, better-selected words.

If we believe we're writing for a small audience of intellectuals, of course, the advice is not so pertinent. Nevertheless, we shouldn't lose sight of the fact that all of us have been affected by the increasing pace of life in general (not just life on television); our willingness to read long, reflective passages that require intense concentration is decreasing as time flies by—time itself seems to *fugit* even faster these days.

Although I've emphasized fictive scenes, it's just as important that real scenes in nonfiction articles and books be unified. The more we're able to tell nonfiction "stories" through a series of scenes rather than narrative summaries, the closer we'll come to capturing life. In the following excerpt from a journalistic story, the writer gives us a feel for life at that moment through dramatic factual scenes. He could have used the technique of narrative summary and written something like, "When I flew from Ushuaia to Rio Grande and Rio Gallegos I was viewed with great suspicion by the Argentinian army officers on board." Instead, he chose to tell us the same thing through scenic writing:

> At daybreak in Ushuaia I was put on a 44-seat air force Fokker turboprop for a mail flight to the coastal bases of Rio Grande and Rio Gallegos. It was the first leg of a three-flight, twelve-hour journey in custody. It was also an edgy and unpleasant experience. My bags were "searched" twice, that being the kindest term for the hostile way in which personal contents can be scornfully tossed, spilled, and made to seem like bits of compromising evidence all their own. Why was a "distinguished" American journalist carrying a duffel bag? Why were his shirts rumpled? One army officer found a bottle of shampoo to be suspicious. Another officer confiscated an as-

sortment of old notes, then asked me to number each page with a forwarding address. That was so I could not later claim anything had been stolen, he explained. "How old are you?" asked an officer. "You've lived a good life. You ought to be shot."

At Rio Gallegos I was put aboard a six-seat air force Turbo Commander bound for Comodoro Rivadavia. It was jammed with commuting army officers. There were no "buenos dias," no smiles. Just two hours of their staring impassively at the American passenger. Their looks said they assumed I was there because I had done something wrong, something against them and their country.

The first paragraph is unified in scene: all the events it lists occur at the airport in Ushuaia before the narrator *(Time* correspondent William McWhirter) gets aboard the turboprop. The second paragraph opens by telling us that the scene has shifted to the interior of a six-seat Turbo Commander. The paragraph break serves to separate the two scenes.

Another example of fine scenic writing comes from an article in the *Christian Science Monitor* by the newspaper's Latin American correspondent, James Nelson Goodsell.

SALVADOR WAR: WHY ONE YOUNG MAN JOINS THE GUERILLAS
AROPA, EL SALVADOR

[1] The night air was cool. The stillness was broken only by an occasional song of a bird. Overhead a few stars blinked.

[2] We entered a makeshift compound of several ramshackle buildings—a guerrilla lair.

[3] Its exact location is hard to pinpoint. But it's somewhere near the small town of Apopa, a scant 30-minute drive north of San Salvador, the Salvadoran capital.

[4] There was virtually no noise as shadowy figures darted quickly from one hut to another. One of the huts served as a command post. Its walls were partially eroded away by time and its roof covered only part of the one room inside.

[5] "We don't have much time to talk," a voice from the corner said. "We have word the Army is headed this way and we need to move on to a better location."

[6] But we had 20 minutes to talk before the guerrillas moved on.

The setting here, a makeshift compound, is a little wider in scope than the cramped quarters of a six-seat plane, but it still qualifies as a single scene. After the fourth paragraph the scene shifts into the command post hut. Thinking in television terms, one can imagine the camera panning around the compound for the first four paragraphs of narration, then stopping with a still shot of the command post. The scene is the same until the camera zooms to the guard at the door. When the television image cuts to the interior of the hut and we hear that voice from the corner, we're in a new scene.

If the writer is going to squeeze the most out of the scenic approach, he must keep the scene as pure and unified as he can. If Goodsell, for example, had led us scenically into the guerrilla lair and then shifted to summary to tell us about how things were going in San Salvador, Managua, and Brasilia (even if the summary had been about the worldwide guerrilla movement), the emotional effectiveness of that scene would have been jeopardized—the scene would have lacked unity.

Writers should aim for unity of scene while recognizing that absolute purity or unity is usually impossible to attain. In a pure scene, only the characters would talk and move, as on a stage; no narrator would be in evidence. Since no literal stage exists in a written work, we need the narrator to poke in periodically to tell us about the characters' moves. To achieve the purest unity possible, however, the narrator must confine himself to interjecting only immediately relevant information. As soon as the narrator imposes himself on the scene at length, the reader's level of belief begins to decline.

Unity of Tense

There's not much we need say about this, unless we want to go into a grammatical study of verbs and their tenses—and we don't. This book presumes a basic knowledge of tense; the concern here is only that tenses be kept in the proper sequence.

The tense of the initial verb tells the reader when the main action takes place. The tenses of other verbs in the sentence or paragraph express time *relative to* the main verb. If the action in a subordinate clause takes place at the same time as the main action, then the verb must be in the same tense as the main verb (present with present, past with past, and so on). If, however, the subordinate action took place before the main action, the subordinate verb must be in a past tense. Then, even though the two verbs are in different tenses, there is unity of tense; i.e., they correctly express the *sequence* of happenings.

Past/Past

When the fleet *returned* to England, Prime Minister Thatcher *waved* from the quay.

Present/Present

As the jet fighter *climbs* steeply, it *leaves* a sonic boom behind that *forces* the crowd to hunch their backs.

Present/Past

I *understand* that the Prime Minister *has promised* British rule for the Falklands.

Past/Prior Past

Mrs. Thatcher *learned* that the islanders *had known* trouble before.

The next paragraph seems to make sense until you try to learn just what was happening when:

> As Harry knew all along, he goes where she goes. He had known it for years, but now it was clear; he was addicted to her. She didn't feel the same about him; she couldn't care less about how he had felt toward her. It all depends, of course, on how others felt toward them now as a couple. Some felt one way; others feel different. Some are indifferent. If that was the situation, then Harry would worry about it. Oh, if only he knew. He knew it clear enough back then. Had she only known, things might be different in the future from now.

Tense confusion is insidious because the writer has his own mental picture of the chronological layers involved in a story. The reader's mind is a clean slate: he can comprehend the chronology of events only by understanding the writer's use of tense. If the author is careless, confusion results. The confusing use of tense in a business memo, a military order, or a legal brief can create chaos. In fiction, it can't cause chaos in the real world, but it can lose you a reader.

One point rarely made clear in books on grammar and writing is that it's not necessary to continue using the prior past (past perfect) tense after the chronological layering has been established. The writer can then use the simple past tense. In effect, the writer has put the reader in a time machine and dropped him into the period when the action, now completed, was still going on.

If the reader then wants to refer to some action completed at an even earlier time, he lets the reader know by again using the prior past tense. The following displays these uses of tense:

> The old man *was talking* about his exploits in the big war. He *spoke* of how he *had shot* many enemy soldiers in their sleep. Apparently

he *had not wanted to* do it, but *had been forced to* by his officer. They *had been on* Guadalcanal for some weeks when the incident *occurred*. The officer *told* him to creep forward and infiltrate the enemy camp at midnight. He *did* as ordered and *killed* them as they *slept*.

I showed that the initial scene was some time in the past by using a simple past tense: *was talking* and *spoke*. Then, to establish that the action the old man was talking about had occurred further back in time, I used prior past verb forms: *had shot, had not wanted, had been forced to, had been on*. Feeling then that I had moved the reader back in time sufficiently, I switched to simple past tense forms: *occurred, told, did, killed, slept*.

I have to admit that I believed for years that to be perfectly correct a writer had to use the prior past tense throughout. My writing was suffocating under an overload of *hads, had beens,* and *had hads.* I find that today's students make the opposite mistake. They never indicate to the reader that an action they're describing has been completed some time in the dim past. They use the simple past to convey actions that occurred an hour ago and those that Caesar completed some time ago:

- He told me yesterday that he was a sailor.
- He told me yesterday that he had been a sailor.

Do we come away from the first sentence believing that he was a sailor *yesterday?* We're not certain, if we know we're dealing with a careless writer. With the *had been* of the second sentence, we can be fairly certain that he was *not* a sailor yesterday.

Unity of Sentence and Paragraph

A group of words does not a sentence make. Even when the words satisfy the grammarian (they include a subject and predicate and provide a complete thought), if the sequence of words could be revised to make the thought clearer, I would not consider it a sentence. In other words, a group of words can be a sentence without being an effective sentence. Since the sentence is the basic unit of writing, it must be unified if the whole piece is to be unified. If a sentence takes up several distinctly separate ideas, it is not unified.

It may seem unusual to find this discussion of sentence and paragraph unity at the end of this section on unity. I deliberately organized the section this way to provide a logical bridge to the following discussion of coherence. How well we make sentences and paragraphs cohere is determined to some degree by how unified is each sentence and paragraph. Unity does not ensure coherence, but it helps. A paragraph, for example, might be unified in its subject, scope, tone, style, point of view, character, scene, and tense, but unless all the logical connections between sentences within a paragraph and all the logical connections between paragraphs are clear, the total piece is not coherent.

I'll end this discussion of unity with a homegrown example (from my story *Matanuska)* that exhibits all the unities we've been thinking about in this section:

> [1] Minnie had gone to bed that night tired and reasonably happy, but sleep eluded her. It may have been the extreme brightness of the Alaskan moon forcing its beams through the glass bottles that served as the window. It may have been her husband's incessant snoring, but that didn't usually bother her too much. It was the dog's thumping that had brought her out of her initial nodding.
>
> [2]She could see him in the moonlight scratching his right ear industriously with his left rear paw. She laughed quietly as she told him to hush. The scratching brought such a blissful, simple-minded grin to his face as he drummed away on the wide-plank flooring.
>
> [3] His persistent drumming may have started things off, but now she heard everything, each sound triggering another poorly connected series of thoughts. She could hear the thick ice on the Matanuska River booming as it expanded to relieve its tension. She remembered the river in the spring when she could hear the soft roar of the melt waters. Now, at midnight on the longest night of the year, she could hear the wind building.
>
> [4] It was beginning to whistle through the spruce outside the cabin, and she recalled how hard it had blown recently, enough to sweep the valley entirely clear of snow. It had now begun to work on the river's exposed, dry silts and alluvial sands. The light silt sifted daily through the little open spaces around the door and the window. No matter how diligently she tried, she couldn't keep them all plugged tight, even with the spruce gum Lars had brought her.

Let's look at each numbered paragraph and see why I consider it unified:

(1) The entire paragraph is unified in that all of it has to do with what caused sleep to elude Minnie. The writer does not wander from this subject to tell us why she went to bed happy; he does not tell us what a fine, or terrible, husband she has—just that he keeps her awake with his snoring. The writer does not develop the details of the dog's scratching; rather he saves them for their own paragraph.

(2) The second paragraph deals only with the principle cause of Minnie's wakefulness, the dog's scratching and thumping. The writer does not describe the dog, the characteristics of his breed, or his ability to tree coons. The first sentence promises scratching and delivers scratching, nothing more.

(3) The first sentence of this paragraph promises that it will be about the sounds that trigger Minnie's thought associations, and the writer limits himself to just that. He does not go off on a tangent to tell us how beautiful ice on the Matanuska is in the winter, or how lovely is the spring.

(4) This paragraph does not stray from the subject of windblown silts and sands.

The entire quotation is a unified scene in that the *subject* is unified: it's all about Minnie having difficulty falling asleep in her room. It's unified in *scope* in that we don't learn about her daylight hours or her childhood. The *tone* and *style* are unified because they are consistently plain throughout these four paragraphs. The *point of view* is unified because it remains third person (omniscient-personal) throughout. *Character* is unified because it is consistent (although this is too short a segment by which to judge accurately). The *scene* is unified since it all happens in a single time period in one room. Finally, the *tense,* while not the same throughout, does not jump around through time: the *had* at the beginning lets us know that the action was completed some time in the past; the tense switches gradually, through the simple past in the second paragraph, to make us feel part of the scene, allowing the present tense to be used in the third paragraph; and the final paragraph returns us properly to the past.

As a timely introduction to the next major section (coherence) I'll point out here how I made the four paragraphs from *Matanuska,* each with a slightly different subject, cohere as a unified piece of writing.

The final sentence of paragraph [1] introduces you to the dog and his thumping, which bridges the white space between paragraphs [1] and [2]. I make clear the relationship between [1] and [2] by referring right away to "him," which can only mean the dog of paragraph [1]. Any possible ambiguity as to "him" is immediately resolved by mentioning that he is scratching with a paw—and that he's doing it industriously, explaining somewhat the "thumping" in [1].

Paragraph [2] ends by referring to the dog's drumming on the plank flooring, which enables you to leap without difficulty into [3], where I pick up with a "drumming" early in the first sentence of that paragraph.

Paragraph [3] introduces you to the discussion of windblown silt in [4] by mentioning last in the list of sounds bothering Minnie, the "wind building." If I had mentioned the wind somewhere farther back in the list of other sounds, it would not have provided so clear a bridge to [4].

Although you don't see a paragraph 5 here, you can be sure that it will be about either the wondrous properties of spruce gum or Lars.

I elected to analyze my own writing not because of its perfection, but because I knew why I did what I did. Had I used another writer's work, my analysis would have been speculation—and I could easily have done him or her disservice by speculating incorrectly.

Analyzing paragraphs in such detail may make writing seem mechanical and contrived, but if it's done well, the reader doesn't feel it; he just moves along easily from sentence to sentence, paragraph to paragraph. The reader is disturbed when the writer *fails* to contrive for coherence.

Coherence

Coherence is half a matter of logic and half of form—half and half because a sentence can meet all requirements of grammar and still fail the test for simple logic: *He got out of bed as early as the sunrise*. The sunrise, of course, never got out of bed at all.

Grammar is also satisfied by the following sentence, but logic demands revision:

> John Smith is in critical condition at General Hospital from a chest wound following surgery.

Revised as follows, it satisfies both grammar and logic, and it restores my faith in surgeons and hospitals.

> Following surgery for a chest wound, John Smith is in critical condition at General Hospital.

Unity and coherence are closely allied, but we must keep them distinct, at least for the purpose of discussion. *Unity* is a matter of keeping all elements of a piece of writing, whether a paragraph or a book, centered on the primary topic. *Coherence* has to do with the *order* in which the various elements are presented and the devices used to make clear the *relationships* between those elements. Several real-life examples should clarify the principles of coherence.

STUDENT'S FIRST DRAFT
(I've numbered her sentences for your convenience.)

> [1] The room projects coziness. [2] A white woolly animal has had its winter coat sheared in order that my feet can bury themselves in the warmth of a rug. [3] An orange tree was flown all the way from

the Philippines to decorate the corner of my room. [4] A colorful crewel scene depicting animals in the forest contrasts with the sometimes seen buck's head mounted on the walls of restaurants and hunters' homes. [5] A cheery plain covers the couch.

MY COMMENTS TO STUDENT

Your assignment was to write a short piece that would give the reader a "feel for place" It's hard to express, in a few words, what bothers me about this first paragraph, but let me try.

I had the impression as I got into sentence #2 that you were setting me up for some kind of moral statement about the poor sheep sheared for your feet— but you didn't do anything more with it. You set up false expectations in your reader.

In sentence #3 I thought you were going to expand your scope and talk about how many people, animals, ships, etc. were involved in the task of decorating your room (and I was getting interested), but then you didn't. Again, false expectations—a writing sin.

In sentence #4 you are apparently trying to make the point that you are more "crewel" than cruel—and I thought again that you were about to make some point about the killing of animals (well, the shearing of them) for frivolous purposes, but you didn't.

There are some other problems of craft here, but I'll take them up with you in a conference.

Everything else in your paper felt warm and cozy—so, when you think of it, why bring up the deaths of animals? This caused a *lack of unity* in *subject, scope,* and *tone.* Three strikes. You're lucky that in this game of writing, you can revise your errors and go on to win!

Your paragraph is not coherent because you do not show us a *meaningful relationship between or among your sentences.* If your purpose was to tell us how you had always loved your room until, with mounting horror, you realized how many lovely animals had been killed to give your room its style, you should have connected the sentences in various ways to portray your mounting horror. Coherence is the glue that sticks sentences and paragraphs together and promotes unity.

CLIENT'S FIRST DRAFT AND MY SUGGESTED CHANGES

(1) **distinct from the**   (2)

This Business Area Plan is ~~of necessity,~~ **distinct from the** ~~different than the~~ other

~~Business Area Plan, as it deals~~ *in that this one deals* with two new business opportunities

(3) ~~that are~~ still being evaluated. ~~For this reason, it is a plan outline that~~ (4) *This plan presents the outline*

~~indicates the steps that should be followed in order to create~~ *of a procedure* a sound *developing*

basis for ~~evaluation~~ *evaluating* (5) of the new ~~areas.~~ (6) *opportunities.*

MY COMMENTS TO CLIENT

(1)   Just to cut down on verbosity.

(2)   It would logically refer back to *other,* but the intent was to have *it* refer all the way back to "This Business Area Plan." The single word "Plan" seemed sufficient to carry the meaning. To achieve maximum coherence, all references must be unambiguous.

(3)   Nothing lost by deleting this form of the verb *to be* and its accompanying *that.*

(4)   This sentence is what gave verbosity a bad name.

(5)   Changing this ending enabled me to get rid of an awkward *of.*

(6)   *Areas* is one of those vague words like *situations,* so try to avoid it unless you mean areas of space—measurable space. Your client is going to prefer the "profitable" tone of *opportunities* to the blah tone of *areas.*

STUDENT'S FIRST DRAFT

(1) *Polyester Fibers are* ~~Synthetics~~ used for clothing and sleeping bags ~~are polyester fibers.~~ *because they* ~~These~~ resist taking on water. Actually, these fibers ~~trap water, but~~ *don't absorb water,* *they trap it.* (2) ~~do not absorb it.~~

MY COMMENTS TO STUDENT

(1)   Coherence is better served by combining the first two sentences. By inserting *because* between them, we make clear to the reader how the two sentences are related. The original version merely gave us

the facts. The new version tells us why polyester fibers are used; i.e., the *significance* of facts.

(2)   This was a matter of getting the emphasis clear. By putting the important point about trapping at the end of the sentence, we emphasized the point.

CONTINUATION OF STUDENT'S FIRST DRAFT

(3)   ~~They,~~ Wrung out like a sponge, fibers   (4) Almost immediately, these
~~They,~~ dry almost ten times faster than down. ~~Wrung out like a~~
                                                        (5) again ready to use
~~sponge,~~ synthetic fibers are ~~operative~~ and will keep you relatively

warm.

CONTINUATION OF MY COMMENTS

(3)   Coherence is damaged here because your logical sequence was off. You needed to inform the reader right off that the fibers need to be wrung out like a sponge *first,* if they are to dry almost ten times faster than natural down.

(4)   By inserting "almost immediately" we promote coherence and add emphasis to the rapidity with which they dry.

(5)   I don't like your governmenteeze use of "operative" here, but the least you could have done to promote coherence was to point out by inserting the word *again* that the fibers have been returned to their original condition. The replacement of *operative* by *ready to use* is for purposes of both accuracy (fibers don't operate; machines do) and tone *(operative* sounds bureaucratic).

The Logics of Order

I've introduced coherence as having largely to do with the logical ordering of elements: words within sentences; sentences within paragraphs, paragraphs within chapters; chapters within a book; and books within a series of volumes. Let's look more closely at this business of ordering by logic. There are several forms of "logic" as we use the word here. The logic selected will vary, of course, with the subject matter.

"CHRONO" LOGIC

A very common logic to impose on your piece is a time logic, or *chronolo-gic*. If you decided to use a chronological approach, you must ask yourself when outlining: Shall I go from past to present, present to future? Might this particular story be told better from the present backward to the past? Or, should I forget the normal sequence of time and instead begin *in medias res* (in the middle of things) and then go back and move forward? Fiction frequently uses the latter approach to great effect. Only with care, however, does this method work in nonfiction articles, science reports, or business studies. If it is used, the writer must be particularly adept at maintaining coherence. Readers have enough trouble keeping track of what's going on when you present matters in a straightforward, past-present-future chronology. In nonfiction, scrambling the order of events is asking for double trouble.

SPATIAL LOGIC

Descriptive passages, whether fictive or real, are most coherent when *spatial* logic is used. The writer is usually best off moving the reader's eye in a consistent, logical pattern—from left to right, right to left, near to far, far to near, up to down, down to up.

Any pattern is all right in fiction, but in writing for science or technology, there may be a logic within the subject that will be obvious to the writer as the only sensible pattern.

A glaciologist, for example, might explain the motion of glacial tongues by writing first about the morphology of the snowflakes that fall high in the mountains; then about how they are gradually converted to ice; then about how the pressure of thousands of feet of snow on top combine with gravity to give the ice its initial shove downhill; and then how that motion causes friction which causes melting which provides lubrication which promotes faster motion which causes more melting, more lubrication, more rapid movement, and so to the sea.

This glaciologist-writer would not be following the more usual forms of logic (chrono, spatial, general-to-specific, etc.) to achieve coherence. She was following a logic (a cause and effect sequence) that she saw within the physics and chemistry of glaciers.

If the same writer were later to describe surface features of glaciers, she might think about it for a while, and then decide to make her discussion cohere by starting with a discussion of *sastrugi* up on the *polar plateau* and then work downhill (like the glacier itself), describing the *ice falls*, *crevasses*, *moraines*, and other features as they typically occur, finally reaching the *wave notch* in the *ice front,* which forces the ice to *calve* into the sea.

FROM GENERAL TO SPECIFIC

In fiction and nonfiction, one of the most common patterns of logic is to move from the general (universal) to the specific, or vice versa. Once decided upon, the same pattern should be used throughout, to achieve coherence and unity.

You might introduce the topic of matter in the universe by discussing first the stars with their orbiting planets and then proceed down to the atom and its orbiting electrons. You might, however, elect to proceed just as logically by working your way out from the electrons, i.e., from the specific to the universal.

In writing about the desert climate, you might elect to discuss first the desert environment as a whole (the scarcity of water, sparseness of vegetation, and so on) before considering specific desert plants, animals, and minerals.

The choice of direction is frequently governed by what is to follow this development. If you planned to then go into a discussion of how life forms adapt differently to this harsh environment, you might decide to go from a discussion of the universal (deserts in general) to a description of the tiniest (specific) grain of sand. It would then be coherent to leap from this grain to the microscopic forms of adsorbed water associated with that seemingly dry grain.

A writer could write a paragraph or series of paragraphs that went in a direction opposite to the logic I've just presented. His paragraphs could be grammatical and they could even be unified, yet not meet the requirements of coherence. Good writing needs a thread of coherent logic along which are strung the beads of thought.

Every writer occasionally fails to follow the coherent outline he originally drew up, or fails to make a coherent outline in the first place. Here, the revision process can save the day. Revision may be simply a matter of reshuffling sentences, paragraphs, sections, or chapters. Reshuffling is not always simple to do, however, for it may require new transitions between sentences, paragraphs, sections, or chapters. Regardless of the effort required, coherence must be achieved.

Once the all-important matter of logical order has been found or established, what other elements of coherence should the reviser evaluate, and how might any errors or lapses be corrected or improved?

Although it's impossible to determine a universally acceptable list of the most important elements of coherence, I'm going to take up four elements of coherence that would be near the top of anyone's list. Since this is a book on the revision process, I've put the elements in the form of questions you should ask yourself about the draft you're working over:

1. Are all references unambiguous?
2. Are all words together that belong together?
3. Are the relationships between sentences (ideas) clear?
4. Are transitions smooth?

Are All References Unambiguous?

We are much more tolerant of poor referencing in conversation than in writing, because in conversation we receive other clues (sometimes subliminally) to the antecedent. However, if a reader is forced to guess at an antecedent, there's a better than even chance he'll guess incorrectly. A careful writer does not want her reader confused, even momentarily, so she watches her pronouns as carefully as she does her briefcase in a restaurant. She is particularly wary of any sentence that begins with a pronoun. A paragraph that begins with a pronoun is immediately suspect. The following example demonstrates how a fine writer got into trouble by writing an ambiguous *they.*

STUDENT'S FIRST DRAFT

Drink after drink was followed by another four, then more drinks, then more. By the time she chased the children to bed, they were all slurring their words and giggling.

MY COMMENTS TO STUDENT

Kids do have a way of slurring after the third martini, don't they? It would have been a lot clearer had you been wary of the problem posed by pronouns (here, *they*) referring back to the nearest noun that agrees in number *(children).* Try, *By the time she chased the children to bed, the adults were all slurring. . .*

STUDENT'S NEXT SENTENCE

She was glad she'd had the foresight to feed the kids before they came.

MY COMMENTS TO STUDENT

This is the same problem, but worse. The reader automatically presumes that the *they* refers back to the nearest agreeing noun—in this case, *kids*. The grammar is correct; the logic, or meaning, is wrong. As it stands, the sentence means that the kids had come from somewhere, and she'd had the foresight to feed them before they came. In fact, the writer intended to say that she had fed the kids before those adults arrived (referred to two sentences ago, before the kids' speech became slurred). One way to revise it, would be to write, . . .*foresight to feed the kids before her guests arrived.*

I presume that you are already familiar with the grammar requirement that a pronoun agree with its antecedent in gender, number, and person. My concern here is to remind the careful reviser to ask whether the pronoun refers *unambiguously* back to its antecedent. Even if the pronoun does agree with its antecedent in gender, number, and person (i.e., meets the rules of grammar), it may still be misread. For example, if the writer intends the reader to interpret *they* as referring back to those heavy-drinking adults, but *they* also agrees in number, gender, and person with *kids* and *kids* is the nearest noun, the reader naturally jumps on *kids* as the antecedent. Of course, the reader would probably figure out that there is no reason for the little ones to slur their words. But the ambiguity has caused him to halt, lose track of his thoughts, and perhaps even give up on a writer who causes more trouble than she's worth.

Keep constantly in mind that the reader will leap like a lion to the noun nearest the pronoun. Don't abandon pronouns simply because they're tricky. Like the man who loves lions, preserve them, but don't take your eyes off them for a second.

Let's try our hands at revising several sentences that lack coherence as the result of poor pronoun referencing:

> The paratroopers found the weapons where they were hidden in the woods.

I suppose it was the weapons that were hidden in the woods, but I can't be absolutely positive that it was not the paratroopers who were hiding in the woods and found some weapons there. Wouldn't the sentence be less ambiguous—more coherent—as follows: "The paratroopers, hidden in the woods, found the weapons." Or, if this meaning was intended: "The paratroopers found the weapons hidden in the woods."

> After he came back from the war, the father disinherited his son.

Perhaps the context would clarify this sentence for us, but right now we can't tell whether it's the son or the father who has returned from war. If it was the son who came back, the writer would better have written, "After his son came back from the war, the father disinherited him." If it was the father who returned from war, it could have been put more clearly as, "After the father came back from the war, he disinherited his son."

> He attacked the man with a smile on his face.

Here we go again. Did *he* gleefully attack some man, or did *he* attack the man who had a smile on his face (as distinct from another man who had a scowl on his face)?

When you begin revising, remember that pronouns are good and useful, but they bear watching. Without them as tools, we'd be forever repeating nouns, and that would be dull—unambiguous, yes, but dull as dishwater.

Are All Words Together That Belong Together?

People who otherwise write coherently seem not to recognize that some words need each other's proximity for absolute clarity of thought. In the following sentence, for instance, three misplaced words can transform the writer's meaning:

> The keypunch operator incorrectly punched in a program, which created a power failure in the building where she worked for two days.

If it is the power failure that lasted for two days (and not the keypunch operator's job), the writer must move closer together the words that belong together:

> . . .which created a power failure for two days in the building where she worked.

That simple revision cleared up two inaccuracies: we now know that the failure lasted two days; and we now realize that she had not been working in that building for just two days.

Sometimes misplacement doesn't lead to such potentially serious consequences, but simply to awkward writing:

> There was little glory to winning this one. It had taken three of his last four cartridges to down whatever it was that lay before him now—and the remainder of his energy.

To complete the thought in that final phrase after the dash, the reader has to backtrack to *It had taken*. A writer should not expect a reader to carry every phrase forward on the off chance that it may be needed to complete a thought at the end of the sentence. If the writer wants the reader to carry something forward, he must warn him, as *not only* does in this revision:

> Not only had it taken three of his four cartridges, it had also taken the remainder of his energy to down whatever it was that lay before him now.

A writer is considerate of his reader in the smallest ways:

> She was sure that once the storm let up, the lights and the heat would come on again. Meanwhile, she piled quilts on the beds and bundled the children in woolen socks and sweaters over their pajamas, talking calmly about spring in the flickering candlelight.

There's nothing absolutely wrong in saying that the concerned mother talked to the children calmly about spring in the flickering candlelight, but there is an incipient ambiguity lurking (it sounds as though the damned power might still be off come spring). It would be better to have the flickering candlelight closer to the mention of lost lights and heat. The point of mentioning the flickering candles was to reinforce the loss of the lights in the storm; the main point was not that she was talking about spring in candlelight. Listen to how much better it sounds this way:

> She was sure that once the storm let up, the lights and the heat would come on again. Meanwhile, in flickering candlelight, she piled quilts on the beds and bundled the children in woolen socks and sweaters over their pajamas. She talked calmly about the spring that would come.

That was an instance in which the separation did not cause terribly serious problems of coherence. Imagine, however, the insurance implications of a report that makes it sound as though a power failure has been caused by an operator who has worked in the building for only two days. In any event, your goal is to achieve maximum coherence and accuracy.

Coherence could be improved in the following safety engineer's report by breaking up the noun string and bringing closer together thoughts that belong together:

Original:

>Recommendation 82-6: Carefully redefine the lockout and electrical hot work procedures.

Revised:

>Recommendation 82-6: Carefully redefine the procedures for lockout and electrical hot work.

The next safety engineer's report could get the reader's attention better by not making him wait until the end to find out that the writer is pointing up a serious safety hazard:

>Low water pressure for eye washes and emergency showers at the Loading Dock and especially at the Barge Dock on Exxon property is one of the more serious problems.

In this case, both emphasis and coherence are better served by moving related elements closer together:

>One of the more serious problems is the low water pressure for eye washes and emergency showers at the Loading Dock and especially at the Barge Dock.

Jumping now to a student's proposed novel about Amazonia:

>When Ethan returns to New York, alone, he discovers he is dying a slow psychological death—from his experience in the jungle.

The significant fact—that Ethan's experience in the jungle is responsible—seems, in that position, but an afterthought. Revised, the significant fact is emphasized:

>Returning to New York, alone, Ethan finds his jungle experience driving him down a slow road to death, psychological death.

Let's move now from the Amazon to the American West and the history of rodeos:

Original:

>These contests gave the cowboy a chance to gain some glory as well as a few dollars. Other events were added to bronc riding that had their roots in ranch work.

Confusion (lack of coherence) is created by those words in the second sentence that fall between *events* and the final phrase, which answers the "So what?" about those events. A simple change brings the related words into closer proximity:
Revised:

> . . .Other events, rooted in ranch work, were added to bronc riding.

In the following original, thirteen words divide the two parts of the compound subject (calf roping and steer wrestling)—and to no end.

Original:

> Calf roping, a necessary part of branding the herd, became a timed event as did steer wrestling.

Revised:

> Calf roping and steer wrestling, necessary parts of the branding operation, became timed events.

The following two sentences present several problems of coherence:
Original:

> In later years, two other official events were added for purely show purposes. Bareback riding and bull riding came about with the desire for more dangerous and exciting competition.

When we begin reading the second sentence, we're not certain that bareback riding and bull riding are the "two other official events" mentioned in the first sentence. Since those two phrases are so closely related, why not bring them closer, this time by getting them into the same sentence:
Revised:

> In later years, two other official events were added for purely show purposes—bareback riding and bull riding.

Now we're still left with the awkward "came about with the desire for," which takes a little more thought to revise with an active verb, *satisfied:*

> —bareback riding and bull riding. These two new events satisfied a growing desire for more dangerous and exciting competition.

Notice how this revision increases coherence by adding the phrase, "These two new events," which makes clear what events are being described.

Because this particular error—failure to keep related words together—shows up in otherwise excellent manuscripts almost as frequently as in otherwise poor manuscripts, I decided to demonstrate its epidemic proportions with a lot of varied examples from many students, clients, and me. I'll wind up this section with one more example from an otherwise excellent paper. I've included the first three sentences to put it in context and to show the caliber of this student's manuscript:

> My mother lowers the slatted wooden shades against the sun; the rooms are dark and cool now. In the white shimmer outside, the buildings are sun-saturated, gleaming with light and heat. Sometimes at this time of day the palms quiver and hover in the hot, rippling air. The streets have been full of activity since dawn, until now—shoppers, cars, donkey carts, camels, Arab men lounging in clusters, kids, and beggars.

Everything is fine until the last sentence, when we trip on an awkward sequence: "since dawn, until now." While searching for a way out of this awkwardness, I noticed that the writer had let some related words get separated. Interestingly, the words that intruded were the words that presented the awkwardness I was trying to correct. My suggested solution follows.

> Since dawn, the streets have been full of activity—shoppers, cars, donkey carts, camels, kids, and Arab men lounging in clusters.

Although it was never an "incoherent" sentence, it is now more coherent because the sources of activity are listed immediately after the statement about how busy the streets are at this hour. *Since dawn* now resides at the dawn of the sentence, giving it a kind of organic coherence. *Until now* has been eliminated and no one mourns its passing, because it was implied anyway by the phrase, *since dawn*. Not that this bit of revision will change the world; it's just that hundreds of minor "saves" like this may make a book or article succeed.

Are the Relationships Between Sentences (or Ideas) Clear?

BETWEEN "EQUALS"

When several ideas in a sentence are of equal importance, this equality must be made clear for the reader by a *parallel* structure. There are many ways to keep the parts parallel. In both elements of a parallel structure, there should be an adjective, a noun, an active verb, a participle, and so on—each finding its counterpart in the other.

In the haste of initial composition, it's very easy to shift constructions in two parts of a sentence. During revision, these shifts are more easily caught and corrected. Several examples should make the idea of parallel construction clear:

Original (about a firehouse):

> As a carrier launches its jets out over the sea, the ancient structure catapulted the rigs into the street.

Revised:

> Then, like a carrier launching ITS jets INTO the sky, the ancient structure catapulted ITS rigs INTO the street.

In the original, the structures of the two parts of the sentence do not match. The revision renders them parallel: "*its* jets. . .*its* rigs"; "*into* the sky. . .*into* the street."

Original:

> She had never gone to a party alone, much less an event like this.

Revised:

> She had never gone alone TO A PARTY much less TO AN EVENT like this.

The error in construction was hidden and made worse by poor placement of the word *alone*. The original leads the reader to anticipate a construction parallel to *alone,* but lets him down. When *alone* is moved closer to the words with which it is associated *(never gone),* the lack of parallelism shows up more clearly; i.e., the parallelism has to do with, *to a party/to an event.* The simple addition of *to* to *an event* solves the problem.

Original:

> Readers appreciate your getting to the heart of a matter in a hurry, rather than being forced to read through paragraphs or pages to find it.

Revised:

> Readers appreciate your GETTING to the heart of a matter in a hurry, rather than FORCING them to read through. . .

Getting to and *being forced* were not parallel.

We find poor coherence through lack of parallelism everywhere, even in a salesman's kit:

Original:

> GE innovations in power-switching technology began with the first SCR. They have included development of the TRIAC, pellet glassivation, heat transfer, and over twenty years' application experience compiled in the GE *SCR Manual and Data Handbook.*

The problem here is the classic one of mixing garters and guitars. The writer has unwittingly listed "twenty years' application" as another innovation, in parallel with true innovations like SCR and TRIAC. This calls for drastic revision:

Revised:

> GE innovations in power switching, beginning with the first SCR, have included TRIAC, pellet glassivation, and heat transfer.

The garters of the original sentence about the handbook belong in a later paragraph, not here with the guitars of innovation.

Original:

> We believe that our consulting firm enhances rather than constricts the professional wisdom and experience of its members.

Revised:

> . . .firm EXPANDS rather than CONSTRICTS the professional wisdom and experience of its members.

Enhances may have been the accurate word for what the firm does for its members' wisdom, but when it is set off against *constricts,* it is not completely parallel. Since the writer obviously wanted a word to contrast dramatically with *constricts, expands* offers a better contrast. Fortunately, *expands* does not do serious damage to the effect the writer hoped to get from *enhance;* thoughtful revision has accomplished everything that seems to have been intended.

Original:

> The Prime Minister's goal was to win the war and bringing an end
> to unrest at home.

Revised:

> The Prime Minister's goal was to WIN the war and BRING an end
> to unrest at home.

Original:

> There is a lower standard of living in Port Stanley than among the
> British in their Buenos Aires enclaves.

Revised:

> The standard of living among the British in Port Stanley is lower
> than among the British in their Buenos Aires enclaves.

Original:

> We can attack at night or we can do it in the light.

Revised:

> We can attack BY NIGHT or BY DAY.

The reviser could make the last example parallel by writing "in the night or in
the day," but the idiomatic expression, *at night,* is too ingrained for us to accept
in the night. When idiom confronts logic, idiom wins. Perhaps it would be better as: "We can attack in the dark or wait for daylight." There may be no "correct" answer. The lesson is that the reviser should go to any length to find the
most parallel construction.

   Some of the most apt parallel constructions in recent history are found in
John F. Kennedy's inaugural address. One reason they will long be remembered
is the rhythm developed by the parallelism.

> Let the word go forth from this time and place, to friend and foe
> alike, that the torch has been passed to a new generation of Ameri-
> cans, *born* in this century, *tempered* by war, *disciplined* by a hard
> and bitter peace, *proud* of our ancient heritage, and *unwilling* to

witness or permit the slow undoing of those human rights *to which this nation has always been committed,* and *to which we are committed today* at home and around the world.

So let us begin anew, remembering on both sides that civility is not a sign of weakness, and that sincerity is always subject to proof. *Let us never negotiate out of fear,* but *let us never fear to negotiate.*

Now the trumpet summons us again—*not as a call to bear arms,* though *arms we need; not as a call to battle,* though *embattled we are;* but *a call to bear the burden* of a long twilight *struggle,* a year in and year out "rejoicing in hope, patient in tribulation," a *struggle* against the common enemies of man: tyranny, poverty, disease, and war itself.

And so, my fellow Americans, *ask not what your country can do for you; ask what you can do for your country.*

BETWEEN "UNEQUALS"

So far, we've been considering parallel constructions among equals. When elements are of unequal importance—when one part of the sentence is subordinate to another part—this must be made clear for the reader, lest the several parts be thought coordinate (equal).

These unequal parts must *not* be set up in parallel, because that gives the incorrect impression that they are of equal weight, as just seen in all the examples of parallelism. When elements are unequal, their inequality must be shown by an unequal construction.

I made clear earlier that a technique for indicating that several ideas are more or less equal (coordinate) is to set them up in as parallel a way as possible. Writers also have a technique to indicate that several ideas are unequal (one is subordinate to the other). The writer puts the more important idea in a clause that could stand alone (if called upon) as a sentence with nothing needed but a period. The less important idea is deliberately put as a clause that could *not* stand alone without some involved change. The grammarian would rather say that the inequality is demonstrated by a subordinate clause modifying the principal clause, and their relationship is shown by the subordinating conjunction that connects the two clauses. The following example should clarify this business.

I wrote about polar regions/after/many trips there. The principal clause, "I wrote about the polar regions," could stand alone with only a period added. The secondary (subordinate) clause, "many trips there," could not stand on its own two feet without adding several words. In this way the reader sees the relationship and relative importance of the two ideas presented.

The beginner is apt to write a series of short, choppy sentences whose relationship might better be shown by combining them into one sentence. Again, coherence is accomplished and the new rhythm may improve the style. Naturally, there are times when a series of choppy sentences promotes the writer's purpose, but the following is more typical of chopitis:

Original:

> I went on several expeditions. They were all into the polar regions.
> I loved being where none have been.

Revised:

> In love with being where none have been, I went on several expeditions into the polar regions.

Here the more important idea, "I went on several expeditions into the polar regions," could stand alone with but the addition of a period. The secondary point (subordinate point) "In love with being where none have been," could not, without some additional effort, stand alone. It is this unequal structure that lets the reader know how the writer viewed the relative significance of the several ideas.

Many problems of poor coordination or subordination would never arise if writers followed an idea's "natural" or logical order more often. The most frequently needed orders are these three:

(1)   the order of time
(2)   the order of relationship
(3)   the order of emphasis

Scrutinize every sentence (and paragraph) during revision to see whether you've used the order most effective for your purpose. Most of the time, you will find yourself using one of the three. The content will usually make it clear which is appropriate.

Original (haphazard order):

> I went below after the storm abated. The damage to the crew's quarters was severe because the porthole had opened during the storm.

Revised (by order of time):

> After the storm abated, I went below. Because the porthole had opened during the storm, damage to the crew's quarters was severe.

The order here is by time, but it turns out also to follow (without my deliberate effort) the order of relationship. Time order is followed in that the revised sentence takes us from the time of the storm into the present. As often happens, time order is apt to reflect also the relationship of cause and effect: "Because the porthole had opened" (cause) "damage. . .was severe" (effect). It also happens that the order of logic puts the most important point, that the damage was severe, at the end of the paragraph, where it gains the desired emphasis.

The "perfect" paragraph might be one that achieves all three orders (time, relationship, emphasis) at once. I suppose there's no such thing as a perfect paragraph—it would all depend on your purpose, wouldn't it? For instance, you might be more intent upon pointing out that the porthole had opened than upon emphasizing the severity of the damage resulting from its being open:

> After the storm, I went down below. The crew's quarters were severely damaged—the porthole had opened during the storm. This, after I had just conducted a storm drill in which Howard had been permanently assigned to dog down that particular porthole.

This paragraph seems "perfect" for its purpose, a purpose different from the one previously posited. Clearly, then, there is no perfect, all-purpose order for a sentence or paragraph. Given a purpose, however, there is a "perfect" order for any sentence or paragraph. If, as an editor, you revise someone's haphazard paragraph and superimpose order on it, you run the risk of selecting the wrong order. The author should not then fault you; it was his fault that his original order did not make his purpose clear.

It may seem to teachers, from the sad evidence they see, that the "natural" order must be haphazard rather than purposeful. In a sense, that is true—our thoughts, as they first tumble out, are typically haphazard. Good writers do not mimic that haphazard order; they strive to impose a logic that will make their thoughts clear to someone who did not originate those thoughts—the reader. The "natural" orders we refer to here are natural for the logical, rational reader.

Are the Transitions Smooth?

A writer's goal is to move from sentence to sentence and paragraph to paragraph without jarring the reader—unless it is his intention to do so. The writer should be considerate enough to lead the reader across a bridge—not force the poor soul to leap across a chasm in the dark. Some writers fool themselves, assuming that such leaps are easy for any reader of intelligence. It's relatively easy to leap to the next thought without a bridge, provided you know where you're going to land, how high to leap, and how much of a running start to take. The writer knows all this in advance; the reader does not.

There are traditional words and phrases for building the bridges of transition, but normally they should be employed only when nothing else can be invented. When going through the various routines of revision, ask yourself whether you have used too many of these prefabricated units. Stand back and look objectively at your piece of writing: Is it pockmarked with *and, but, for, in addition, nonetheless, in conclusion, nevertheless,* and infested with the dreaded *howevers?* Those ready-made, too-easily-available phrases and words are all proper transitional devices, and they exist to be used; the question is, how often?

Like so much else about the writing game, the only rules are rules of thumb. Here the general rule is to try to make the sentences, rather than the transitional phrase, do most of the work. Actually, of course, it's you, the writer, who must do the work—and not leave it to the harried reader. Think ahead.

There I go again, exhorting you to think. Sorry about that, but that's why some writing works and some does not. Anyone can "write" with a minimum of careful thought; sentences will come out and join with others to form blocks of words that resemble paragraphs. But the thoughtful reader will not be moved to do something you've requested, let alone be reduced to tears or lifted to laughter. The chances are that she will read no more than a few paragraphs that require heroic leaps over chasms of confusion. Certainly, the thoughtful reader enjoys a challenge, but success must be seen as achievable. If you make it impossible to win, the reader will give up and wonder whether you are all you're cracked up to be. If a reader gives up on your novel, that is sad enough, but suppose your corporate superior is reading a report you've written and gives up on you as an employee because of your illogical writing.

Think ahead and let the sentence do the work. Easily said. How can it be done? Well, for one thing, your sentences will work together best if you show clearly how one thought flows into (connects with) the next. In other words, you must provide good transitions. How can you improve coherence by good transitions? Let's think first about transitions between sentences, then transitions between paragraphs, and finally the business of getting from one scene to another.

TRANSITIONS BETWEEN SENTENCES

One of the better ways to bridge sentences is to repeat a key word, or a key thought, from the previous sentence. It may not always be possible, but it is better form to use a different word rather than repeat a word appearing in the previous sentence. Don't be as compulsive as your grammar teacher about this rule of thumb; sometimes repeating the same word is better than using a synonym. It may even serve your purpose to repeat a word—for emphasis as well as transition. Unless repetition suits your purpose, however, it's best to avoid it. In the following passage from *Land of the Hibernating Rivers,* for example, I could have repeated the word *birthplace* to make the transition or connection with the second sentence, but I chose instead to use a related word, *beginnings:*

> The Yana River has a different personality because its BIRTH-PLACE is not so far south. It has its BEGINNINGS in the Verkhoy-anski Krebet, where not much snow or rain falls.

In the following several sentences, in which I'm describing bothersome mosquitos in the subarctic, I repeat the word *relief,* rather than seek another, to connect back more clearly to relief in the first sentence:

> The only hope for even temporary RELIEF is a WINDY day. The mosquitos will not venture out of the woods if there is even a light WIND. Since the woods are a wind-break, one must get out into AN OPEN AREA to get the blessed RELIEF of a BREEZE.

Notice, too, that I first used *windy* and shifted slightly to *wind* for the connection in the second sentence. Then, realizing that I might be overdoing it, I switched to *breeze* to make the connection in the third sentence.

As the paragraph continued, I chose to repeat the phrase *an open area* to make the connection with the next sentence:

> Since the woods are a wind-break, one must get out into an OPEN AREA to get the blessed relief of a breeze. This partly explains why the animals also like to live near an OPEN AREA in the taiga. Even an animal so heroic as the moose is driven almost out of his mind by the hordes of mosquitos. Moose will swim to the MIDDLE OF A LAKE to get away from it all; they'll even go into a village if it seems to provide relief from these terrible torturers.

To reinforce the notion of the relief that comes from an open area, I had the moose swim to the middle of a lake—that is, I repeated the key concept, *open area,* without boringly repeating the phrase a second time.

Notice that coherence is also promoted by mentioning for the first time in a while that it's mosquitos I'm talking about. I was able to use *relief* a third time to wrap up the paragraph, because it had been long enough without relief.

Occasionally transition is simply a matter of gently reminding the reader that two sentences are logically connected:

> Sometimes the grizzly will eat well by finding the carcass of a sea mammal washed up on a beach. IN THIS WAY the food web is extended into the usually separate food web of the sea. Scientists working in the area estimate that on any one day there is likely to be one CARCASS of seal, walrus, or whale for every mile of BEACH. One CARCASS of a WHALE could mean up to 50 tons, or 100,000 pounds, of meat, and this can keep a number of GRIZZLY BEARS happy—if an animal with the Latin name of *Ursus horribilis* can ever be HAPPY.

In this way makes clear the logical connection between the first two sentences. *Carcass* carries us through two others; *beach* and *happy* help others flow coherently. Even *grizzly* is repeated in the last sentence, partly to remind us that we are still talking about the grizzly bear last mentioned in the very first sentence, and partly to prepare us for the Latin term for grizzly bear, *Ursus horribilis.*

See how the next paragraph (from Smith and Brouwer's *Performance Appraisal and Human Development)* is made coherent.

> A major purpose of the performance appraisal system is to strengthen the LINKAGE between PERFORMANCE AND REWARD: to ensure, on the one hand, that the HIGH PERFORMERS receive the extrinsic REWARDS they most value and, on the other hand, . . .that these HIGH ACHIEVERS are also experiencing significant intrinsic REWARD. It is vital that organizations make a deliberate and explicit CONNECTION between PERFORMANCE AND REWARD. . .

The key word *reward* is used once and then repeated three times; *high achievers* is used as a variation of *high performers; connection* is used in place of *linkage;* and *performance and reward* is used in the same form in the final sentence to connect back to the first.

Like a piece of fabric, a piece of written material must be woven. Words and ideas are interwoven forward and backward in a paragraph, each thought adding strength that finally makes a unified, coherent paragraph.

Now, let's look into ways to interconnect paragraphs so that the garment itself, not just the cloth, is unified and coherent, i.e., it hangs together solidly and is smooth at the seams. There should be no puckers or bumps where the sleeve paragraphs join the shoulder paragraphs. Our next tailoring lesson, then, is on transitions between paragraphs.

TRANSITION BETWEEN PARAGRAPHS

There is, as mentioned earlier, a rather extensive list of ready-made, pre-fabricated words and phrases one can use as devices of transition, but because they are overused, I'm deliberately holding off repeating that list. This book presumes that you are familiar with these traditional devices, but also that we are jointly interested in revising your writing—writing that may already use many of these well-known, time-honored, almost worn-out words and phrases.

Re-vision enables you to re-look at the transitional devices you've used to see whether there might be smoother, more professional substitutes for some of them—for the sake of variety, if for no other reason. Let's look at an excellent technique for tailoring your garment.

The technique is not too different from that used for transitions between sentences: repeating a word, phrase, or idea from one paragraph in the next paragraph to show that the two are connected. Frequently, you'll find that the best word, phrase, or idea to use is one found in the final sentence of the previous paragraph. If you're able to use it as a lead-in for the first sentence of the next paragraph, there should be little chance that the reader will miss the bridge (to return to my earlier metaphor). If you prefer the garment metaphor, you'll find it best to use the same color or pattern established in the shoulder paragraphs as you stitch on the arm paragraph.

Let's leave the world of abstract analogy for the concrete world of example:

> Before the Yana River ever begins to melt and flow in the spring, the Lena River is already carrying the warmer water of the southern spring into the land of winter. The Lena becomes a scene of spring FLOODS of monstrous character, whereas the Yana never FLOODS.
>
> The FLOODING of the Lena is the result of the difference in water temperature between the place of its birth and the neighborhood where it dies. . .
>
> The Yana River has a different personality because its birthplace is not so far south. It has its beginnings in the Verkhoyanski Krebet, where not much snow or rain falls.

Because the word *floods* is used several times in the final sentence of the first paragraph, I made the second paragraph cohere by using the closely related word *flooding* as soon as possible in the first sentence of the second paragraph. I used *place of its birth* to connect with the previous paragraph, in which the river's origin is referred to once as *birthplace* and once as *its beginnings*. This weaving of similar words, images, and ideas through several paragraphs is good form. I just noticed that in this explanation I've used the phrase *river's origin* to connect the present paragraph with all the previous words about the river's birth, to provide variety for you while promoting coherence in my writing. That's the nice thing about practice. After a while you find yourself doing this almost subconsciously. Meanwhile, you can do it consciously by following the various revision techniques outlined in this book.

The following two paragraphs are stitched together in a classic way—the final two words of the first are picked up and used early in the second paragraph.

> Ellesmere Island, the tenth largest island in the world, is one of the very few arctic lands from whose glaciers icebergs are calved directly into the polar pack. Several of these glaciers on Ellesmere join hands as they reach the sea and float on as a wide ice shelf, still attached by icy apron strings to the mother glaciers. Occasionally a great section of this shelf will break off and float away as a TABULAR BERG.
> Because these TABULAR BERGS may be as large as several hundred square miles in area and several hundred feet thick, they have been mistaken for and mapped as ISLANDS. Recently, these ICE ISLANDS have become rather famous. . .

There is no way that a reader could miss the point that the writer is now going to carry on the discussion of tabular bergs introduced in the previous paragraph. An example of making two sentences cohere by repeating a key word is seen in the final sentence of the foregoing excerpt from *Land of the Hibernating Rivers*. The fact that such tabular bergs are sometimes incorrectly labeled as islands gave me an opportunity to refer to them as ice islands. The next paragraph in the book discusses ice islands and how they are used as floating laboratories. This is the best kind of transition to make—it is actually made in the reader's mind. The author doesn't use a "transitional word" to make the connection; he sets things up in advance so that when the reader comes to the important phrase *ice islands,* his mind makes the transition. Now the writer can go directly into a discussion of ice islands without any awkward transition. The transition is not abrupt or obvious.

In *Camping by Backpack and Canoe,* I wrote these paragraphs about the importance of packing a poncho:

> A poncho is a must. This may be just a personal thing with me, because I am known as the last of the great drought-breakers, but the poncho always comes along with me; and camp is established on the KNOWN FACT THAT IT WILL RAIN.

> I am NEVER SURPRISED when it rains; I am SURPRISED when it holds off long enough to get the tent up and a meal completed.

> THIS FATALISTIC APPROACH gives one a certain advantage. The greenhorn is always SURPRISED when it rains. He mumbles and grumbles as he sees the experienced camper come out of a dry tent, after a wet night, carrying an armload of dry kindling and birch bark tinder. . .

The transition between these two paragraphs is a type we haven't discussed enough: *transition by idea*. In the first paragraph I claimed, with irony, that I establish camp on the known fact that it's going to rain. The first words of the opening sentence in the third paragraph ("this fatalistic approach") refer to that *idea*. None of the same words is used, but the connection is unmistakable.

The paragraphs are also backstitched by my reference to the greenhorn's *surprise* at the rain, in contrast to the earlier statement that I'm *never surprised* when it rains.

> A recreational camper can get along without an axe of any kind most of the time. It is rare that a camper, particularly when backpacking, will need to cut down a tree or chop up a log of any great size.

> The greenhorn, however, is always chopping. He chops great logs for firewood, he cuts down good trees for no good reason, and he chops through logs that should be split. . .

The *general idea* of chopping is carried across from the first paragraph to the second, even though the idea of the first is "not chopping" and that of the second is "chopping." The contrast between the ideas is reinforced by *however*.

The transition between the following paragraphs is a more subtle form of transition by idea:

> Another psychologically based conflict that militates against effective appraisals arises from the simple but dynamic fact that the requirement to appraise someone else's performance may highlight the manager's own inner conflicts.

> If a person is deeply uncertain about his or her own capability, it be-
> comes extremely difficult to maintain objectivity when evaluating
> the strengths of a subordinate. . .

This transition requires an intelligent reader who will have no difficulty making the mental connection (transition) between *inner conflicts* in paragraph one and *uncertain about his or her own capability* in paragraph two. Only the author can know just how subtle he can be with his presumed audience. In this case, he could be reasonably sure that anyone reading a book on performance appraisal and human development could make the mental connection with ease. If he were writing about the same topic for a less specialized audience, his lead sentence in paragraph two would probably repeat some of the words from the final sentence of paragraph one:

> If a manager has his own INNER CONFLICTS about his capabili-
> ty, it becomes extremely difficult to maintain. . .

TRANSITIONAL WORDS AND PHRASES

Before moving on to the somewhat separate matter of transitions between scenes, let's (at last) take up the list of words and phrases most commonly used to provide transition between sentences and between paragraphs. These are the transitions I've suggested you use sparingly. They tend to be over used, simply because they're just too easy to depend on. Their use is justified only when they accurately present the relationship between what precedes and what follows. For example, if what follows will indeed be something *in addition to* what's just been said, then use *furthermore* or *in addition*. If, however, what follows is in *contrast* with what has just been said, use *in contrast, by way of contrast, on the other hand, however,* or something else indicating that whatever follows is to be understood as in contrast with what preceded. They're simple words, but always check their meaning:

admittedly	granted	obviously
also	hence	of course
although	however	on the other hand
and	if	or
as	in addition	rather
assuredly	in fact	since
besides	indeed	so
but	it's true that	still
certainly	moreover	the fact remains that
clearly	needless to say	then

consequently	nevertheless	therefore
even so	no doubt	thus
for	nobody denies	to be sure
furthermore	nor	true
undoubtedly	whether	yet
unless	while	

Then there are the *balanced connectives,* which promote coherence by demonstrating clearly the parallel structure of the several thoughts involved, whether within one sentence, between two sentences, or between two paragraphs. These balanced connectives are particularly useful in reasoned arguments and essays of opinion:

as. . .as	neither. . . nor
both. . .and	not only. . .but also
either. . .or	on the one hand. . .on the other hand
just as. . .so too	on the one side. . .on the other
in general. . .in particular	in that case. . .but in this case

As in life, so too in writing: A careful writer will use these traditional transitions in moderation. More often, he'll use techniques mentioned earlier—repeating a key word or phrase from a preceding sentence or paragraph; carrying forth an idea in different words; and backstitching, using words, and phrases and ideas not only from the preceding paragraph but from ones preceding that. As you revise, note whether the writer (you or someone else) has used an interesting variety of transitional devices.

Notice how the following writers have gone to some lengths to keep their readers aware of the direction their work is taking—how one part of a sentence relates to another and how one paragraph connects with the next. First, Bruce Catton in *A Stillness at Appomattox:*

> Grant and Lee sat at two separate tables, the central figures in one of the *greatest tableaus* of American history.
>
> It was a *great tableau not merely because of* what these two men did *but also because of* what they were. No two Americans could have been in greater contrast.

First, Mr. Catton makes it clear within the first few words of the second paragraph that he is continuing the topic of the first paragraph. He accomplishes this necessary bit of transition by repeating two words from the first: *great tableau.* Then, to let us know that something is to be *added to* something else, he uses the balanced connectives: *not merely because . . . but also because.* He lets us know his attitude toward the relative significance of the two things by slipping in the word *merely.*

A less careful (less accurate) writer might have written the second paragraph something like this:

> This was an important meeting because both men had fought hard for what they believed. It was also significant in view of what they were like. They were quite different in appearance.

This hypothetical writer might claim that his paragraph says exactly the same thing as Bruce Catton's second paragraph. Well, it does—sort of. Apparently this less experienced writer was influenced too much by a sixth-grade teacher who ruled that a word should never be repeated soon after it has been used the first time. He's afraid to write at the opening of his second paragraph *a great tableau,* thereby depriving us of coherence. He might argue that *an important meeting* is an adequate transition. Perhaps so, in other circumstances, but his boringly common sentence structure ("This was an important meeting because. . .") deprives us of the mental image evoked by *tableau*—especially since there is an excellent tableau painting of that meeting between Grant and Lee in a fine country home at Appomattox Court House.

By overlooking the little word *merely,* this writer fails to convey his feeling that what was *more* important was the two men's contrasting appearance. He leaves us with the impression that he thought their appearances were as important as what each had done in the war.

From the same book, let's look at another example of Bruce Catton's careful use of transition words:

> Grant seems to have been almost EMBARRASSED when he and Lee came together in this parlor, YET it was definitely not the EM-BARRASSMENT of an underling ill at ease in a superior's presence. RATHER, it was the diffidence of a sensitive man who had another man in his power and wished to hurt him as little as possible. So Grant made small talk and recalled the old days in the Mexican War. . .

By using the little word *yet,* Catton lets the reader know that he is a little uncomfortable about using the phrase *almost embarrassed.* It's Catton's way of saying something like, "Yes, Grant was embarrassed, but not in the way you may be thinking. What I mean is that he was uncomfortable about being in this parlor with a man of great character, and a man under whom he had served back in the Mexican War." The combination of *yet* and *rather* provides the effect of all these thoughts without their being explained at length.

Because this business of transition and coherence is so central to good writing, let's observe the work of another master, John Knowles, in "Everybody's Sport":*

> In many ways a pool is the best place to do real swimming. Free water tends to be too tempestuous, while in a pool it is tamed and imprisoned; the CHALLENGE has been filtered out of it along with the bacteria.
>
> . . .They [outdoor pools] offered you all you could ask of water, all you could wish for in swimming. No indoor pool could rival them.
>
> NEVERTHELESS, indoor pools excel in one way—in the use of ARTIFICE to enhance the pleasure of swimming. The best ARTIFICIAL effects I have seen are in the Exhibition Pool at Yale University.
>
> . . .I dived in. The light seemed amazingly to increase my buoyancy; the water bore me up as though I were made of cork and could float forever.
>
> IN FIERCE CONTRAST TO such peace and glamour, is the surf, which is charged with CHALLENGE. Surf swimming is better managed NOW, of course; IN THE OLD DAYS people who came near drowning were revived by being hanged from the heels, bled, or rolled over a barrel, or, as sometimes happened, pushed back into the water lest God consider it impious of men to bring back someone so close to eternity. We know better NOW, BUT EVEN SO, the surf's disturbing undercurrent is there for every swimmer to feel and on rough days the warnings go up and the swimmers are restricted to a particular area or kept out of the water altogether.
>
> The SURF at SUCH MOMENTS is not to be trifled with. IN FACT you never TRIFLE with the surf; when it is in a playful mood, the surf TRIFLES with you. That's the joy of swimming in it. . .

I won't point them out and discuss them individually, but each word in UPPER CASE is an example of a coherence device. Each either repeats a key word or phrase from the immediately preceding sentence or paragraph (or one even farther back); repeats the *idea* first appearing previously in different words; or shows the relationship of what is being said to what has gone before (e.g., *in fierce contrast to*). The writer wants to ensure that we don't lose track of what he's said, is saying, or is about to say. By using a variety of linking devices, he

*Copyright John Knowles 1956. Used by permission

vices, he also ensures that we won't be bored with all his backstitching.

I know that one should not generalize, so I'd like to hyperbolize and say that if there is one characteristic technique by which one can spot a good writer, it is the care with which he or she makes thoughts cohere.

TRANSITIONS BETWEEN SCENES

A special form of transition, particularly important in fiction but also used in nonfiction, is the transition to a new scene. The filmmaker's task here is easier than the prose writer's in that when the camera jumps to the next scene, it's immediately clear to the viewer that the scene has changed. The viewer may not know immediately where the scene is, but that is usually soon revealed by the dialogue or by more detailed views, (e.g., a zoom in on the town's name above the post office). The writer and his reader, however, are at a disadvantage. A scene may change, but the words don't look any different.

If the writer has been thoughtful, he or she has set up the scene change in advance. Even if the scene has been anticipated, however, the good writer will want to reinforce the fact that the anticipated change has occurred—and to do it as early as is reasonable.

If the new scene is far enough away that some form of transport must be used, a favorite transition technique is to refer to the voyage, or perhaps just the end of it. This is a natural transition in that it mimics life—the character has moved from one place to another. Show this move and you've made a transition without calling undue attention to the writer's task of providing transition; it simply happens:

> Damn, she muttered to herself. He was erecting the wall between them again. Sooner or later, she knew, she was going to have to find out what was behind it.

> When the Jeep swung to a halt on the gravel drive in front of D.L.'s house, Samantha gasped. Whatever she'd been expecting for a bush doctor's home, this wasn't it.

This move to D.L.'s house was set up about eight paragraphs back in the book, so it was necessary to remind us that we were pulling up in front of his house. The reference to the Jeep reminds us of a line six paragraphs back when Willy says, "I brought the Jeep, doc. Should get everything in one trip."

Nonfiction, too, needs to move smoothly from scene to scene:

> On December 17th, around 5:00 a.m., Mr. and Mrs. Herndon awoke suddenly with a terrifying feeling of being smothered. They

wildly threw off several feet of white stuff from their faces and bodies to find their bedroom jam-packed with snow. Gone from their $30,000 ranch-style house was their entire roof.

Nearby, in her own shattered house, Mrs. Chinnock wandered numbly through her rooms. She was unmindful of bare feet grinding through glass from broken windows, bureau mirrors, and framed photos of the children.

By using the very simple words *nearby* and *her own,* I moved this scene (from *An Alaskan Cornice*) from one house to another. In the first draft, in which I had written simply, "Nearby, Mrs. Chinnock wandered numbly through her rooms," there could be the possible misinterpretation that we were still in the Herndon house; Mrs. Chinnock could have been a boarder living in the house with Mr. and Mrs. Herndon. *Nearby* lets the reader know that the new paragraph is not taking us across town, but that word alone leaves ambiguous whether we are simply nearby in the same house. Therefore the phrase *in her own shattered house* was added for coherence.

One very simple transitional device is to leave an extra amount of white space before the subsequent paragraph. Because this technique is used by writers sometimes to signify the passage of time and sometimes to signify a change of location, there is still the possibility of temporary confusion. It is therefore best to reinforce the transitional white space with appropriate words, in the previous paragraph, the following paragraph, or both.

In this example from my short story, "The Capture Plan," I mentioned Agent Cassiar at the beginning of the second paragraph to show immediately that I am no longer talking about the Constable. Then I set the new scene inside a U-2 aircraft. I also use extra white space to reinforce the transition:

In his ten years of patrolling the vast district, the Constable had never had to cope with anything so dramatic as a plane crash. He began immediately to break camp, throwing gear into his canoe box, kicking the still-burning logs down hissing into the lake, and running down to load his canoe. Taku leaped into her assigned position in the bow and watched impatiently, tail curled and tongue hanging, as the Constable knelt toward the stern and began paddling northward to Tamarack Point.

Agent Cassiar sat hunched up in the cramped man-bay in the bottom of the modified U-2 as it swooped down the final hill and out over the lake. He sat there staring at the yellow warning light, his life flashing before him.

If your revision needs to show a greater passage of time, or if you want the break unmistakable, you can insert a line of asterisks in the white space. It would take a dim reader not to recognize that some form of transition is occurring.

In *An Alaskan Cornice,* I had a fellow sitting in his Juneau hotel room and reading the *Seattle Sun:*

> Why in the world should my deep-down mind have released so much adrenaline on the basis of linens. Linens! Of course! The goddamned linen closet! Their shelves are always lined with old newspapers. I took off over the bed and stumbled into the bathroom.
>
> Before I finally found page seven with the story's continuation, linens were stacked three feet high in the sink and on the seat. What I learned on page seven did not ease my concern.

In this case, I made the transition partly in the first paragraph's final sentence. I could, instead, have waited and had him leap over the bed and stumbled into the bathroom in the lead sentence of the second paragraph, but that would have broken the pace of mounting excitement. Because I had established in the first paragraph that it was the linen closet he was heading for, I didn't feel the need to spell that out fully in paragraph two. Nevertheless, I was still worried about coherence and used the reinforcing connector, *linens,* within the first sentence. I suppose I could have had *towels, sheets,* and *pillow cases* stacked up, but I felt linens would convey the image while making a better connection back to the first paragraph with its *linen closet.*

A transitional device useful only when time is crucial to the plot, is to list the date and time:

> October 3
> 0440 hours
> The engine room repeater rang bells for all stop, and the Pai Te Yun's four propellers stilled. The grainer floated, motionless and all but invisible in the early morning dark, beneath a moonless sky three hundred eighty-seven miles southwest of Coats and Mansel Islands. She was seventeen hours late reporting her presence in Hudson Bay to the Ice Information Office in Churchill.

In my book *Day of Fate,* every major shift of scene is announced by giving the date and precise time as a paragraph heading. In the first sentence quoted above, the reader is also informed that the scene has shifted to the Chinese grain ship. Then the fairly precise location of the ship is given. The reader is even reminded that this is all taking place in Hudson Bay.

It is good writing form to set up the scene change in the last sentence of the paragraph preceding the shift, or at least a hint that there is a direct connection with the subsequent paragraph:

> Notify all members of Implementation Group One. There will be a meeting immediately in the level twenty-seven conference room.

> As Yu expected, he was the first member of the Implementation Group to arrive. Even so, he barely had time to. . .

Transitions into and out of flashback scenes cause the writer special problems. The reviser must see that these crucial transitions occur without ambiguity, yet without awkwardness. The writer may have trouble recognizing an ambiguous, confusing transition, because it's all very clear to him. If you are revising or editing another's work and find yourself deep inside a flashback before you realize what's happening, presume that thousands of other readers will also be thrown off. Some authors seem to feel it's *artistic* to let the reader flounder around inside a flashback scene for a while. Unless ambiguity serves a specific purpose, the writer's goal should not be to confuse but to clarify.

As you revise your work, pay close attention to all the transitions we've discussed. These points of transition are the places to apply the glue that makes sentences stick together, paragraphs cohere, and renders the piece whole, unified. Don't forget your goal: *coherent unity.*

Beginnings, Middles, and Endings

We've been discussing coherence for many pages now, at the basic working level of words, sentences, paragraphs, and transitions of various kinds. Another, broader level of coherence must be considered. If a story, article, or book is to cohere and satisfy the reader, it must flow from the very beginning, maintain the flow through the developmental middle, and come together smoothly by the ending. Let's look now at how *beginnings, middles,* and *endings* contribute to overall coherence.

COHERENCE FROM THE BEGINNING

> She pressed the sleek, cold barrel of her father's revolver against her cheek. It was a pleasant sensation. She held it there until the metal warmed, and then with the awkwardness of those who have never shot a pistol, carefully pressed the breech and peered inside

the chamber. It was loaded. She knew it would be.

This first paragraph of "Going," a story by Joan Johnson, has all the elements of a good opening. When you are revising a piece, read its opening carefully. Coherence should begin with the opening sentences, carry through the middle, and wrap things up toward the end.

It used to be that the opening of a journalistic or other nonfiction piece would not at all resemble the opening of a short story or novel. Today, however, leads in the *New York Times* or *Fortune* are largely indistinguishable from a fictive opening:

> Van Valken strode into the room with two of the peasants whose cause he championed. He was light-haired and tall, physically prepared for the rigors of guerrilla life. An accomplished marksman, he selected for his weapon a Hunsinger .32 automatic rifle.

> Guardian Industries strode into the flat-glass business with all the unruly determination of an uninvited dance guest. Barred in the late 1960's from access to the float technology that has revolutionized glass making, it crashed in by building a factory without a license. . .

The first paragraph is the opening of a short, fictional story by Raoul Bataller; the second is the lead for a nonfiction article by Gwen Kinkead in *Fortune*.

When reviewing leads and openings for revision, ask such questions as:

Have I introduced the main character? In each foregoing example, the main character is introduced in the first words of the paragraph. Not that this is a rule that must never be broken, but for the purpose of coherence the main character should be introduced soon, if not so soon as in the two examples above.

Have I gotten things rolling—is there movement? In the Van Valken paragraph, there is not much that one might call movement, but there is certainly the promise of movement. Van Valken is championing a cause; he's prepared for rigors; and he has selected his weapon. What more could one expect from the first three sentences?

The opening paragraph from *Fortune* gets things rolling as much as can be expected in an article on a glass-making company. The writer manages to create movement by having the company "stride" into the business and "crash" into the revolution.

In the example that opens this section, in which the woman holds her father's revolver against her cheek, the writer practically kicks the story into a roll. The character has deliberately taken the gun and pressed it cold against her cheek, knowing that it is loaded. We want to know why she is caressing a loaded pistol—thus the story rolls.

Have I begun to establish place? If place is of central significance to a story or article, you should attempt to establish the locale early on—if not in the first paragraph, then in the second. Even a hint about where the action is going to occur will help hold the reader's attention and hold the plot together (make it cohere)—and that is what this business of openings and leads is all about. The opening paragraph below does not come right out and say "China," but it does give several clues. The reader enjoys putting the pieces together. The clues, of course, must not be so subtle or vague that the reader cannot solve the puzzle by the end of the first several paragraphs.

Not all stories and articles require immediate mention of locale (for example, the glass-making article). In the following from *Day of Fate*, however, a sense of place is critical.

> September 8
> 2155 hours
> The two submarines floated like whales on the surface of the night waters. The base at Luta was dark, patrolled by more than the usual number of taciturn soldiers in quilted coats. Occasionally, a flight of jets rumbled overhead, fighters from the Chou-Shui-Tzu Air Force Base under orders to report anything that moved from the Gulf to Liaotung to the southern tip of Korea.

It may not be possible to figure out exactly where the subs are, but this opening at least tells the reader that they are somewhere in the Far East and far enough north that the soldiers on patrol must wear quilted coats. Without too much effort, the reader could reason that we are viewing Chinese or Korean soldiers. That's enough for the first paragraph to accomplish.

That paragraph was the first in a novel's first chapter; it's equally important that each successive chapter also have a strong opening. The author is always struggling to keep the reader going and to keep him on the right track (i.e., provide a coherent story line). If the author expects the reader to embark on yet another chapter, its opening had better sound interesting and worth the effort.

The following paragraph is the lead for Chapter 2 of the same novel. Without any prior warning, the scene shifts from submarines in China to a train in Manitoba, Canada.

> September 12
> 1130 hours
> D.L. Childe ignored the Manitoba muskeg slipping past outside the train at a bare thirty-five miles per hour. He'd seen the bogs and

> swamps a thousand times as he travelled from Churchill, and there was never anything new in the chill, green scrub.

The main character is identified right off. The locale is given as Manitoba, and the fact that it's northern rather than southern Manitoba has been established (perhaps too subtly) by mentioning the muskeg.

A writer could open with paragraphs that introduce the main character, get the story rolling, and set the scene—yet still find his reader turning to another story or going out for pizza. If this happens, the writer has probably not gone out of his or her way to demonstrate that the writing itself is going to be worth the effort of reading.

When we revise, as when we write, we must take pains to write interestingly, vividly, movingly. It does not serve the writer's purpose to write well only in the final hundred pages—he must do it right from those first paragraphs.

A short story, *The Stainless Steel Step-bottom Waste Can,* by Ronald E. Gallow, opens with a style that tells us right away that he's going to be easy and enjoyable to follow. He introduces the main character immediately and indicates quickly that this story will have something to do with abortion. The topic itself might discourage some readers, but the intriguing sentence about a stainless steel step-bottom waste can will probably delay the potential quitter for at least another paragraph. That's the trick—keep hooking the reader into at least one more paragraph.

> Johnny Richards could drink a bottle of bourbon and walk by you on the street three years later and still remember your face. Johnny never forgot anything, especially if he tried. So it was with the morning of the abortion. He remembered it all, but most of all he remembered the stainless steel step-bottom waste can. That can burned like a branding iron in his memory.
>
> Johnny talked with me about it one hot autumn evening after we'd roofed the barn. We'd driven down the road to Portageville Bridge to drink some beers and relax while watching the reflection of the sunset on the river below. That evening was the first time Johnny ever mentioned the abortion to me and, unfortunately, it turned out to be the last. Of course Diane had spoken to me about it many times, but she'd never mentioned a stainless steel waste can.

We're intrigued by the statement that this is the first and last time Johnny has mentioned the abortion. Particularly intriguing is the way the writer inserts the word *unfortunately.* Because it's not immediately obvious why this is unfortunate, we're hooked into at least another paragraph.

The writer grabs our lapels again by mentioning Diane in the final sentence. Is she the woman who had the abortion? The nurse who knows about the waste can? Is she a friend of Johnny's? The writer has certainly demonstrated that he can write well and that he's easy to follow, so we're willing to take the time to find out more. He clears up Diane's identity soon after.

Writers frequently open with a piece of dialogue and something that begins to establish the locale, especially if the setting is foreign. The following opening for a short story by Nayana Sanghvi combines these techniques by giving us dialogue in a foreign language (although there's enough English in it for us to have a feel for its meaning). We comprehend right away that the scene is in a restaurant, a foreign restaurant:

> Mutton biryani chicken biryani dal fry aloo puri brain marsala mutton marsala chicken korma. . . . In a single breath, in a single tone like an express train rushing past stopless stations, the waiter of the Asha Lunch Home reels off the menu. Oh well, they'd all taste the same anyway—equally oily, equally hot, equally delicious.

Sanghvi keeps us reading by moving quickly into English—her story will not be all in a foreign tongue; she'll be easy to read. She accomplishes this through the informal, familiar tone of the unknown narrator: "they'd all taste the same anyway."

Sometimes a writer will hook us early on by mentioning something unusual but leaving it a little unclear. The reader, to satisfy his curiosity, must then read the next paragraph. Notice how Charles Luchun, without pausing to explain, refers to something unusual in the first sentence of an unpublished article:

> The brown geese and white swans dipping for their food in the lee of the Count's floating hangar little noticed the regularity with which their patron emerged to study the wind and the sky. It was he who had built the long, cavernous structure whose bottom was now rich with plant life and small lake fish. The old gentleman happily noted the evaporation of the morning mist by the mountain air as it approached the temperature of the lake water, still warm from the previous day.

Any reader with normal curiosity must read into the next paragraph, if only to discover what the long, cavernous, floating hangar is for—and who this count is. As you will see, the next paragraph tells neither what the hangar is for nor who the count is, but we do learn that a lot of people consider the count crazy.

Now we're further intrigued to learn why they think him strange, and we suspect it has to do with that floating hangar. We are further fascinated to find that
the scene is apparently in Germany:

> By noon, newspapermen from Berlin and Frankfurt began to con-
> gregate along the shore, leaning against, or slouching beneath, the
> numerous poplar trees. They were later joined by scientists and
> professors who also wished to witness today's event. The mood of
> the on-lookers ranged from academic curiosity to mild disbelief,
> with the exception of one fraction—the scoffers. This latter group,
> devoid equally of manners and objectivity, openly referred to the
> Count as "crazy."

Who would not be interested, for at least one more paragraph, in a floating
hangar built by a crazy German count? I was going to leave you hanging there,
but I'll reveal that this is the story of Count Zeppelin and his original lighter-
than-air dirigible. We know by the end of this paragraph that Mr. Luchun is going to tell us a fascinating story about something, and we're comfortable in the
knowledge that we're in good hands for the voyage.

Teachers and editors have discovered an interesting fact about most beginning writers: they don't know a beginning when they see one. A new writer will
almost invariably wind up like a baseball pitcher and deliver a few warm-up
sentences before letting the batter come to the plate. The result is that the pitch,
or true beginning, will be found a few paragraphs into the work. It's so obvious,
once discovered, yet the novice writer misses it, really believing he's started the
story with the first word. Sometimes the only revision needed is to delete the
cap tugging, chaw chewing, and first-base checking that precedes the true beginning. If, indeed, a whole series of sentences or even paragraphs can be deleted without their loss being felt, that is all the proof needed that the first words
are not the true beginning.

Writers discovered long ago that readers, especially modern readers, prefer a story, even a nonfiction piece, to begin not at the chronological beginnig
but *in medias res*. After beginning that way, it may be necessary to go back
(flash back) to an earlier point to provide essential background information.
When revising, take a fresh (reader's-eye) view of the transitions into and out of
the flashbacks.

COHERENCE THROUGH THE MIDDLE

The most important advice I can give about coherence in the middle is that
you must carry out what you promised in the beginning. If you are revising a
first draft, you must sit back from the words and ask yourself some tough ques-

tions. Not that the questions are so difficult; they're tough because you may not want to hear the answers. They may mean that you have a great deal of work yet to do—when you thought you were almost done. Ask yourself:

Have I fleshed out my main character(s)?

In your mind, you may know the character inside-out, but is he or she down there on the paper, in words? It is no easy task to reenter a story and add some flesh. It's far easier to go back and edit out excessive character development. Surgery to add character takes a lot of hard, imaginative thinking—even more than the original writing. One typical technique for developing a character is to invent a scene during which a bit of the character's personality is revealed. To insert such a scene between other scenes in a rewrite requires that transitions be invented to get into the the the new scene, and then to get out of it smoothly and into the subsequent (already existing) scene. In a first draft, the writer is not so constrained by scenes on both sides. In thinking about revision, the very human temptation is to convince oneself that the character is adequately developed and there is no need to insert new scenes, new dialogue, or new minor characters.

Sometimes you can flesh out a character in revision simply by extending the existing dialogue. It takes some clever work, but the topic of conversation can be gradually changed to enable the writer to insert bits of character development through what the character says, what others say, what the character and others do *not* say, and how they say or do not say it.

Is the plot thickening, yet remaining clear?

The plot is usually only hinted at in the beginning, but in the middle it unfolds in all its complexity. Conflict between characters or between characters and natural elements intensifies to the point of crisis. Whenever the character sticks a finger in the dike, a new leak develops ten feet away.

In revision you must look objectively at what's happening. Analyze the story as though someone else wrote it. Criticize it. Has the writer remembered to foreshadow, here and there, the major crisis, so that when the ending arrives it will be seen as a reasonable outcome, given the circumstances? If the ending does not grow logically out of the middle (and the middle out of the beginning), the story is not coherent. An incoherent story will not be satisfying to the reader. He must not feel cheated. He'll accept a *surprise* ending, but he must never feel cheated.

In a nonfiction piece, has the middle been used for logical development?

The beginning has laid out the "problem" to be discussed and given the essential background information. The middle's job is to develop points or arguments that "solve" the problem. These should be logically developed in a linear series of thoughts (see the section in this chapter on order). Little place here for *in medias res*. The development must proceed from A toward Z, and each move must be explained. Verify the facts and the logic of the development during revision.

Ask the twin questions: Have I developed the argument or thought enough? Have I unwisely dragged in by the heels evey possible piece of evidence, thus opening to question the best evidence—or should I eliminate the weaker points now, before the reader attributes equal weakness to the entire argument?

Ask also whether the middle is answering the questions posed at the beginning. Surprisingly, you may find that in the middle you are making some excellent points about topics you never said you were going to discuss. Either go back and introduce these questions at the beginning (provided they really need asking and answering in this particular piece), or eliminate them from the middle. You can always write another paper using these already written thoughts. Don't yield to the temptation to stick them in just because they're good, well-developed ideas.

COHERENCE BY THE ENDING

The ending of any piece provides the last chance the writer has to make the whole coherent. The general idea of the work may already be clear, the theme apparent, and the characters well drawn, but the average reader will not be satisfied unless things are wrapped up in a neat package.

In a nonfiction work, such as a persuasive essay, the reader will benefit from a short, sharp summary, even though earlier the arguments may have been made very well. The careful writer will not summarize by simply repeating what already has been said perhaps several times. As you read for revision, look closely at the wrap-up. Have you used a memorable statement or phrase that the reader can retain long after the details of the middle, with its careful development, have faded? Have you saved one new, possibly powerful piece of evidence or argument to slip in near the end? Even one small bit of new information will keep the reader from feeling that he's just reading "the same old stuff" he's read in the beginning and through the middle. Rephrasing the points that are being repeated and adding one or two good, new points will stave off boredom, promote coherence, and establish unity.

Important as it is, the end of a piece of fiction must nevertheless be brief. Though brief, it must tie up a lot of loose strings. Scrutinize in revision as though you were a first-time reader. Have you by the end tied up all the plot elements? Or have you left an entire contingent out in the desert searching for the hero long after he's been found? Are aircraft still heading with their bombs toward London long after the threat has been resolved?

Once the crisis has passed, the blood cooled down, and the excitement subsided, the reader doesn't want to go on much longer. The reader does not, however, want the story to end right at the resolution of the problem. Writers discovered long ago that readers want the plot pieces pulled together in a relatively short section after the end of action, a section called the *denouement*. The challenge, then, is to write a satisfying denouement in a few words. Take another look at your denouement. Does it run on and on explaining too much?

Has the theme been restated in new words, but not with a heavy hand? If it's reasonable to do so, have you found a way to connect the final paragraph(s) with the opening? This is particularly important in short pieces, since the reader might reasonably be expected to remember the opening words or ideas. Is it apparent that the main character has grown during the story? Depending on the story, this growth can be stated explicitly by the narrator, or the character may state it implicitly by his words or actions in the final scenes. While the point must be clear, the reader must not feel he's being lectured at.

Finally, do the last sentences leave us feeling that life goes on, that the characters are out there somewhere continuing their lives? Their lives may well be different as the result of what they've just lived through, but their lives do go on. Allow our imaginations to toy with that thought.

Don't be surprised to find yourself revising, throwing the revision away, rewriting, revising the rewrite, and revising the revision of the ending. For different reasons, the ending and the opening are equally important, and both therefore deserve great attention. Most writers find the ending the more difficult. Aside from the writer's dilemma of wanting to be through with the piece, yet not wanting it to end, satisfying endings are hard to write.

Just as you will often find the "true beginning" several paragraphs into the first draft, you'll be surprised how often in revision you'll find that the best ending point was several paragraphs back from the end. It's easier, admittedly, to see this in someone else's piece, but force yourself to rummage around in the final few paragraphs—you may be surprised and delighted to find the perfect ending (or the makings of one) hiding there. ~~somewhere near the end, but not where you first wrote the ending~~. (See how well it works! My ending is now after *hiding there*—much better ending point.)

Emphasis

Emphasis has not received enough emphasis in books about writing, so I'd like to emphasize that it is no less important than unity and coherence. I sometimes wonder whether *emphasis* is the best word to express this principle, but I've found no adequate substitute. In general, it connotes intensity, stress, or force. In the context of writing, it concerns specifically *relative importance*.

Conveying relative importance (of the thoughts, ideas, and issues that bear on the subject of your writing) is really a matter of communicating accurately. As the eminent scholar and writer Jacques Barzun wrote in his *Simple & Direct,* "Emphasis in speaking and writing is nothing else than pointing to the object you want your audience to attend to." When pointing at something you want someone else to see, you must point in the right direction—you must be accurate.

Writing accurately is no easy task. The audience is forever in danger of misreading your signals; their focus may be long, short, or wide of the mark. It is the job of a serious writer to refine the coordinates until the audience's focus is sharp—until their aim is on target, accurate. Proper emphasis is central to that accuracy.

If you are going to write accurately, you must always make clear to your reader which point is telling; which is not so telling; which is of central significance; which is peripheral or trivial. In this section on emphasis I describe how to indicate the relative importance of written thoughts. Unless you make clear the relative importance of your thoughts, whether in fiction or nonfiction, the reader will react to them in ways you did not intend.

The Emphasizers

Like coherence, emphasis can be instilled into spoken, face-to-face communication through myriad devices (tone of voice, gesture, facial expression, and so on) that are not available to the writer, whose only tool is the printed word. The writer does have recourse, however, to communication strategies on which the speaker may not need to depend—and some to which the speaker has no access:

- proportion
- position
- repetition
- diction
- sentence, paragraph, and chapter length
- word order
- pauses
- humor
- irony
- typography
- layout

PROPORTION

As you review a piece prior to revision, notice the relative proportion given to the various points. The reader is going to sense emphasis of a particular point simply on the basis of how much space (how many words) you have devoted to it. The reader will not consciously analyze how many lines or paragraphs were used to make this point versus another, but the length of the discussion will affect him. Things you write on and on and on about will be interpreted as deliberately emphasized. Sometimes, of couse, that interpretation will be accurate; you have said a lot because you are emphasizing a significant point.

The problem comes when we write a great deal about something of only secondary, tertiary, or even quaternary importance. We write page after page about it simply because we're happy to have the opportunity to discuss at length a subject we know a lot about. Misplaced emphasis is often the result of having just spent great amounts of money or time on research. We are bursting with information, and here's an outlet. That we've blundered into error is easier to see during the revision process than during the creative throes of writing immediately after the research effort. It's also much easier to spot this trouble in someone else's writing than in our own.

There's another common cause of unintended emphasis: we write on and on when we don't yet know our attitude toward the topic. We write every thought that comes along in our search for focus. There's nothing wrong with that for finding out what we're thinking, provided we're willing to be ruthless in the revision process. The reader doesn't want to read about all the grown-over side roads we've spun our wheels on—the reader wants to know where we are headed.

Since the reader is consciously or unconsciously weighing the proportion of time you spend on each topic, help him out either by using reasonable proportions or by coming right out and telling him why you are not using appropriate proportions. If you find yourself straining to think why you are going on and on, sit back and ask yourself the tough question: *Why am I running off at the typewriter like this?* If you can't come up with valid reasons, take heed.

POSITION

The most effective way to achieve emphasis is to position the idea (its words) properly. Fortunately, this effective technique is also easy to use. It is simply a matter of positioning the most important words near the end, whether the end of a phrase, sentence, paragraph, or section. The next best position is at the beginning of any of those same segments of writing. Words and the ideas they express, if positioned somewhere in the middle, stand little chance of being emphasized in the mind of the reader. Not that those in-between words and ideas are of no value—their value lies in their ability to set up, support, and develop those ideas you *most* want emphasized and remembered.

In my early English classes I was forever being told about the transcendent significance of THE TOPIC SENTENCE—usually the first sentence of a paragraph. It was mentioned so frequently and with such reverence that it seemed—and for some became—the object of cult worship in a Church of the Topic Sentence. Not that my teachers were totally wrong in their religion—they were simply worshipping at a sub-altar. We should certainly pay close attention to the first sentence of any paragraph, but we should pay particular attention to a paragraph's final sentence. I don't recall my teacher-preachers even mentioning this all-important position. The New Church of Professional Writing, of which I am a member, preaches that the significant goal in a writer's life (in this world) is to achieve proper emphasis. Before we can believe in this new cult, we need proof, scientific proof.

Emphasis: a Matter of Chemistry

Total scientific proof is not yet available, but brain research has revealed fascinating evidence supporting our modern belief that the receiver's brain gives emphasis to those words positioned toward the ends of sentences, paragraphs, and sections.

It is only recently that brain researchers have come to believe that the brain operates both electrically and chemically. Electrical activity in the brain has been recorded for many years, but only lately has it been realized that the electrical activity sparks chemical activity that is probably the stuff memories are made of. If thinking and memory are indeed chemical, that is an extremely significant finding for writers, who are forever trying to affect their readers' thoughts and memories through mere words.

Our words are not so mere, after all. Our words actually change the chemistry of our reader's brain. Those changes are filed away as bits of memory. The longevity of each bit of memory depends upon the vividness of the experience being recorded. If it's a physical happening, it may be extremely vivid (as in a parachute jump). To the extent the event also had emotional content, it'll be that much more vivid—and more lasting as a chemical memory.

If the life expectancy of a memory depends upon vividness, and if vividness depends partly on the emotional content of a physical experience, how can a second-hand experience (a story) ever hope to stay long in the memory? "Mere" words that only "tell" about an experience would seem at a disadvantage compared to living through the experience. That is the physiological basis for the writer's expression, "show, don't tell." "Showing leads the reader through the experience, vicariously, to be sure, but it's more likely (than would "telling") to evoke emotions in the mind of the reader that approximate those experienced by the real person (in the case of nonfiction) or the emotion experienced in the mind of the fiction writer.

Because chemicals take time to change, our words must be so used and so timed that those we want remembered longest will be. One technique to ensure this is to position the most "showing" words where the reader's brain chemicals will have the most time to react before the writer continues to add new thoughts that must be dealt with.

First of all, your brain cells don't immediately understand the electrical signals from your optical system as you read. The brain thinks only by association. It can understand new data only by associating them with the old data it has stored. As you think about thinking, it's helpful to bear in mind that the brain can work only with what it already knows. If you keep this perspective, you'll understand why other people's brains and minds have trouble understanding anything new that you have written for them. You must present your ideas in ways that promote easy access to associations—memories. Let's look at how you can promote efficient thinking through effective positioning—and how positioning equals time, which equals chemical action.

A word or idea gains emphasis (and is therefore remembered) if it is positioned right before the period that ends the sentence—for the simple reason that the reader's eye-brain system has time to process the last few words as soon as it scans ahead and sees that period and the following double space before the first capitalized word of the next sentence. You might think that so little white space would not provide enough time to be helpful, but when you realize that thoughts "move" at about 200 miles per hour, and since the distances involved are extremely short, the brain can make very effective use of fractions of seconds.

The reader's eyes do something else to gain time for the brain: they do not move steadily from left to right. Instead, they scan rapidly ahead and back, involuntarily and continuously. This helps the brain make quick sense of the squiggles on the page—to "see" a string of words at a time so that it can understand the meaning of the words on which the eyes are focused at the moment. For example, seeing the word *bridge* in the context of words like *New York* or *San Francisco* enables the eye-brain system to tell early on that the discussion is about a particular bridge over water, not about a card game or a bridge of friendship between two peoples.

Involuntary scanning not only promotes rapid comphrehension through context, it also provides the brain some extra operating time—perhaps even a full second—to search for associated thoughts from the past. This enables the brain-mind to understand the incoming data, and to figure out where best to store it for short-term use in understanding the material currently being read. The brain needs a great deal more time to decide what and where to store for long-term memory.

What we've said about the period and its following white space is true for shorter whistle stops at commas, semicolons, and colons. Since these are followed by only a single white space, there's not quite so much time for the brain and its chemistry, but then again, the ideas associated with them are not intended to receive as much emphasis as those positioned at the very end. The dash (or double hyphen in manuscripts) provides a lot of space before the words that follow it, but the space is partly filled by the dash, reminding the reader to hold onto the preceding thought because what's upcoming is so intimately related to it that a full-period stop is not appropriate.

So far, we've been looking at how the punctuation and white space within paragraphs work with the brain to impart emphasis. Imagine, then, the emphasis signaled by the period and white space at the end of a paragraph—like this.

Since the idea in the previous sentence is so central to this discussion of positioning for emphasis, I assigned it a position at the end of a short paragraph. If my theory works, you'll remember for a long time that just about the most emphatic position is at the end of a sentence that is itself at the end of a paragraph.

There, I did it again.

Moreover, I did it from a remote location (in my study) and remote time through the simple mechanism of empty, blank, white space. Truly magic.

The use of subheads and other such breaks surrounded by white space serves the dual purpose of headlining what's about to be treated and giving the brain time to process the preceding matter. Occasionally a writer will leave double the normal amount of space between two sections, without providing a subhead. In nonfiction, this serves mainly as a quiet indication that an entirely new topic is about to be addressed, rather than a new aspect of the same topic (which would be indicated by a simple switch to a new paragraph). Such white space, of course, serves the purpose of emphasis. In fiction, extra white space after a paragraph indicates a switch in scene—perhaps a jump forward or backward in time—and provides chemistry time.

The end of a chapter frequently is followed by a great amount of white space, since a new chapter normally begins on a new page. Editors and publishers should see this not merely as a typographic tradition. They should make a deliberate effort to provide the reader time to "absorb" the chapter—to allow the reader's brain chemistry adequate time to associate, comprehend, and cross-file for future reference.

The greatest amount of white space, of course, follows the final word of the final sentence of the final paragraph of the final chapter. In effect, the reader's brain has the rest of his life to process what was transmitted to it by the book as a whole. This is why writers typically have difficulty with endings. The writer knows that the last few words will be emphasized in the reader's mind, whether the writer wants it or not, simply because of their prime position—at the end.

The experienced writer almost automatically takes all these points into account when writing a first draft, but an inexperienced writer (or an experienced one rushing deliberately through a first draft) will want to consider all these chemical matters during revision.

Revising to achieve proper emphasis through position is so important to good writing that I've provided a number of examples with explanations:

Original:

> I had noticed that some of my ex-tennis partners were beginning to take notice of our game. To rub it in a little, I started to yell the set and game scores enthusiastically, and loud enough that my mother, who lives in Arkansas, could hear me.

Revised:

> . . .loud enough that my mother could hear me back in Arkansas.

Why waste emphasis on *could hear me* in the final position? Your punchline is that she is way *back in Arkansas*.

Original:

> People who played on the courts after me were able to identify my style. Deep gouges in the courts exposing sewer pipes or prehistoric fossils were not uncommon.

Revised:

> People who played on the courts after me could identify my style by the deep gouges, newly exposed sewer pipes, and prehistoric fossils facing for the first time the light of day.

The writer wanted to make the crazy point that his gouges were so deep they unearthed fossils, so why waste emphasis on *were not uncommon*.

Original:

> She was very doubtful that such a handsome man would ever be interested in her. She saw herself as a negative image of him. She was

too short and fat. Her long, frizzy hair was almost blond, as she preferred to describe it.

Revised:

. . .She saw herself as a negative image of him, too short, too fat. Her long frizzy hair was, as she preferred to describe it, almost blond.

The punch line here is that she referred to her own hair as *almost blond.* To give it the punch it needs, put it at the end of the sentence after holding it back with the deliberately interruptive clause, *as she preferred to describe it.*

Original:

Levi and Mike were content with each other's company. Mike's slower, more stoic attitude combined with Levi's expansive and perceptive behavior to create a partnership as valid ashore as at sea. Each personality accented the other and made their individuality all the more evident.

Revised:

. . .Each personality accented the other, making all the more evident their individuality.

The *individuality* of each man is the main point, and it was weak in the middle of the sentence. How strongly it comes over as the last word in the sentence.

Original:

There are hundreds of thousands of square miles of this dull forest composed of larch trees with moss underfoot. It is so silent in the taiga forest that a Russian poet has said that to tread there is to know fear. People who have been alone in it have described it as gloomy, mournful, silent, and forbidding.

Revised:

. . . People who have been alone in it have described it as gloomy, mournful, and forbidding. It is so silent in the taiga forest that a

Russian poet has said that to tread there is to know fear.

There has been no change of wording here, just a change of position. The statement by a Russian poet is so dramatic that it should never have been left in the undramatic middle of a paragraph. Put at the emphatic end, the word *fear* lingers ominously, echoing through the silent forest. Likewise, it is followed by white space that enables it to echo through the reader's mind—and that is the writer's goal.

Original:

> In one corner of that room there is a strikingly beautiful wooden chest, proud and domineering, easily the most attractive piece in the room.

Revised:

> In one corner of that room there is a strikingly beautiful wooden chest. Proud and domineering, it is easily the most attractive piece in the room.

The key words *proud and domineering* are so right, so unanticipated, that I hated to see them embedded in such a nonemphatic position. The writer was aware that they call for emphasis, since he set them off with commas. Just to make the point, however, that the front end of a sentence also lends emphasis, I've put them there.

You might feel that *proud and domineering* had more power in mid-sentence than in the more traditional position at the beginning of the sentence I've suggested. It is up to the writer. It is my job here to point out that there are possibilities beyond those often found in first drafts. Play around with the options as you review sentences for possible revision. Here are several more examples:

Original:

> These two new events [bareback riding and bull riding] satisfied a growing desire for more dangerous and exciting competition. If it all started as a true contest between animal and man, it became a show with the addition of an audience.

Revised:

> . . . If it all started as a true contest between animal and man, the addition of an audience turned it into show business.

The key point to be emphasized and remembered is that the rodeo, once an audience was added, turned into show business. Why waste the emphatic final position on the phrase *with the addition of an audience?* The writer could have achieved an even more accurate Hollywood ring had she ended the paragraph with *an audience turned it into show biz.* A decision to use the latter revision would depend on the overall tone of the piece.

Original:

> Later on we provide assistance to the entrepreneur himself in selecting and molding a management team that builds on his or her strengths and complements weaknesses.

Revised:

> Later on we provide assistance to the entrepreneur himself in selecting and molding a management team that complements his or her weaknesses and builds on inherent strengths.

The sentence benefits from moving the thought about strengths to the emphatic end position. Why leave the notion of weakness in the location that sets off all kinds of electro-chemical activities in the reader's brain—in this case, a client's.

Original:

> She fingered the purple scarf around the neck. Suddenly, she flung it over her shoulder, in an attempt at sophistication.

Revised:

> . . . Suddenly, in an attempt at sophistication, she flung it over her shoulder.

The vividness of the woman throwing her purple scarf over her shoulder is diluted if the abstract *attempt at sophistication* is allowed to linger in the reader's mind instead of the colorful act—and our minds do prefer colorful acts to abstract commentary.

REPETITION

Despite what some of our teachers have told us, repetition is not only allowable; it is a very effective tool in the writer-reviser's kit. In addition to promoting coherence (as discussed in the preceding section), it can create emphasis. If it is to be effective, however, it must be deliberate, not accidental.

Repetition of Letter Sounds

At the first level, the repetition of letter sounds—*alliteration*—can create an attractive sentence that will therefore be remembered longer. Being careful not to step over the line into corniness, we can create emphasis through alliteration, as with the p's in the following:

> In a first draft, the writer usually attempts only to net the fleeting
> thought, and to put it in a bottle for safe keeping. During revision,
> the writer pins it down on paper with precision.

In corporate writing, alliteration has to be used with great caution. If it becomes too poetic, serious business people are turned off by it.

In a nonfiction article, however, a writer can employ alliteration within the limits imposed by the subject and its purpose. If he or she is writing about a midnight walk along Block Island's Corn Neck Beach, the reader will accept and enjoy alliteration: "There's but one source of sound, the sea and its surf." Later in the article the writer may use the repetition of another sound to achieve emphasis: ". . .quietly from behind a shadowed dune." In both examples, emphasis derives from the way the alliterative sounds echo the words' meaning: the *s*'s sound like the sea; the *h*'s and *d*'s reinforce the silent, soft atmosphere of the beach scene. Isak Dinesen, in *Out of Africa,* knew the power of alliteration when she wrote: "The geographical position, and the height of the land combined to create a landscape that had not its like in all the world" (listen to the *l*'s). In describing the plains, she wrote: ". . .in some places the scent was so strong that it smarted in the nostrils" (ten *s* sounds).

Repetition of Words and Phrases

Abraham Lincoln appreciated the power of repeated words to create emphasis when he wrote in his Gettysburg Address: ". . .who died *here* . . . *here* dedicated . . . that we *here* highly resolve. . ." The ungifted teacher would certainly have said to him, "Abraham, you've repeated *here* three times—in as many sentences!" There is nothing wrong with repeating a word or phrase, provided it is done to emphasize a point.

Repetition of an entire phrase and the intimately related *parallel construction* can be very emphatic, especially as tricolon (the division of a thought into three parts). Again, the Gettysburg Address provides a perfect example: "we cannot dedicate, we cannot consecrate, we cannot hallow this ground."

Like most techniques, repetition can easily be overused. Only your good sense will let you know when the line has been crossed.

Repetition of Ideas

Repeating letters, words, and phrases plays on one primitive facet of mind, the one that enjoys *rhythm,* which is simply the result of repeated accents and sounds. There is another level of repetition that plays upon the strings of the whole mind—the *repetition of an idea.*

We learn best when we "see" something from different angles. We understand and learn about something more effectively if we can first explore it physically, with as many senses as possible. The writer can therefore facilitate our comprehension if she writes to several senses. She is, in effect, describing her subject in different terms. If what she's describing is something intangible, she may wish to invent several different analogies or metaphors to help us understand.

I've coined the term *spiraling* to describe this business of repetition from different angles, different perspectives, different "heights." Spiraling occurs, or should occur, in all kinds of communication, because it takes advantage of how our brain-mind functions: It enjoys integrating related bits of information to create a meaningful whole.

A filmmaker spirals in several ways. He may give his viewer an establishing shot first. Using a wide-angle lens, he gives us an aerial shot that gives us a vertical perspective of the entire valley with the winding dirt road. Then he zooms to show a pub beside the winding road and our main character stumbling out the door. The filmmaker then shifts his camera's perspective to show the character from the rear, as he wends his wobbly way down the road. These shots tell us something about the character in his environment.

The camera may now "spiral" in on the character indirectly by showing his humble cottage down the road, then zooming slowly through the window to reveal his wife and children at the dinner table, an empty chair at the head of the table, and the wife looking anxiously toward the door. These increasingly specific "views" of the man tell us more and more about him.

A prose writer has the unique and wondrous advantage of having a verbal camera with an infinite zoom. A writer is able not only to present views very similar to those of the filmmaker, he can continue the zoom right into the minds of his characters—territory largely inaccessible to the filmmaker's camera. Through internal monologue, the prose writer will let us in on the wife's attitude toward her husband, her views about his drinking, her children's past reactions to his drinking.

If you find during the revision process that your point may not be getting across, consider repeating it several more times, but not in the Madison Avenue sense of hitting the reader repeatedly over the head. Instead, repeat it by spiraling in with new angles, new senses, new perspectives from other character's minds, and new metaphors.

We all recognize the importance of these techniques to oratory, sermons, and other forms of public speaking, but we should not limit our thinking to vocal speech. When we read, we "hear" a sort of subvocal speech in our minds. The better that subvocal speech is re-created in our minds, the more we believe—that is, become immersed in the story or topic of discussion. Psychologists tell us that people tend to believe more readily what they hear (and overhear) than what they read. Hence, the most effective writers (of both fiction and nonfiction) are those whose words make us *hear in our minds*.

DICTION

We'll get into definitional quicksand if we try to draw a tight distinction between achieving emphasis through the use of the best possible words and achieving emphasis through "style." I'm going to skirt this bog by talking about diction *(choice of words and phrases in speaking and writing)* in this chapter. In the next chapter I'll talk about style *(the mode or manner of expression, as distinct from content)*. Much of what is discussed here under emphasis is truly style, but it is style primarily in the service of emphasis.

In a first draft, the writer usually attempts only to net the fleeting thought and to put it in a bottle for safe keeping. During revision, the writer pins it down with precision, on paper.

One secret, of course, is to have the ability to recognize that what was first netted during the composition phase was not the *mot juste*—the just-right word that expresses the shade of meaning desired. The second secret is to have available in the mind a store of words from which to coin *les mots justes* when needed. I hesitate to summarize this by saying that one must improve one's vocabulary, because that usually gets translated into "building a powerful storehouse of words," implying that one needs a pile of polysyllabic, Latin-derived, *impressive* words.

A writer needs, rather, a store of *expressive* words, particularly verbs and nouns. This says nothing about their length or "impressive" appearance and is not to say that one does not need a solid base of Latin-derived words. Sometimes, *le mot juste* is French. More often, *le mot juste* is a simple Saxon word like *break, slam, scatter, glimmer,* or *shut.* Writing in English gains strength with these short, homely Saxon words because they are concrete and give us immediate sense impressions. We still need the Roman words when we need to deal with abstractions, generalizations, and concepts. A detailed analysis of President Lincoln's Gettysburg Address of 267 words, for example, reveals 222 of Anglo-Saxon origin. He was well aware of the power and clarity in the Saxon words, and of the dignity and beauty in the Latin. Like the man himself, his writing was a magnificent blend of the simple and the homey with the complex and the grand.

Part of America's writing problem comes from teachers and professors who tend to write prose that no one can read without nodding off. Even when what the professor writes about is something active, potentially exciting and persuasive, it comes out dull because he or she continues to use the Latin-derived language better reserved for abstract thoughts. Ironically, these same professors will tell their students to emulate Shakespeare, whose writing derives much of its energy from short, active, accurate, Saxon words, while they go on writing with the long, Latin-derived terms of academe. They should learn the lesson of moderation from the bard whose writing gained nobility by only occasional use of the just-right word of Latin origin. Latin words used with precision and in moderation add distinction to any writer's style, but enough is enough (or as they might say, sufficient).

Ironically, the uneducated and the pseudo-sophisticated are impressed by flowery, polysyllabic, Latin-derived writing. If you want to move the genuinely sophisticated, highly intelligent, and well-educated, write in plain English with only the occasional, carefully chosen Latinate amidst the otherwise Saxonate language.

Here are some examples of how prose can gain strength (emphasis) by replacing Latinate with Saxon words (especially verbs):
Original:

> If my eyes glance down from my window, I can see a parking lot
> with snow and ice. People carry packages by huddling over as they
> balance themselves carefully so as not to slip on the ice.

Revised:

> . . .I can see a parking lot with snow and ice. People huddle over their packages and shuffle cautiously across the ice.

Huddle and *shuffle* are concrete Saxon words that give us interesting mental images of the scene. It's true that the original had *huddling,* but that's not as active as *huddle.* It was only after coming up with *shuffle* that I saw the potential of the parallel *huddle. . .and shuffle.* I chose *shuffle* because it gave a better image than, *balance themselves so as not to slip.*

If you were writing for a Venezuelan audience, it might have been better to keep *huddling over as they balance themselves carefully so as not to slip on the ice.* The Venezuelans would not get the intended image because they have not danced from childhood on, the ice-crossing shuffle. For a North American audience, however, shuffle would be *le mot juste.* The careful reviser, of course, will note the alliteration in *shuffle cautiously across the ice.* (Can't you hear their boots sliding across the ice?) Again we see the close relationship of diction and style.

Original:

> Rose whimpered and leaned against the guardrail. Then without warning she lifted her head, stared at her husband, and tossed herself over the edge of the bridge.

Revised:

> Rose whimpered and leaned against the guardrail. She lifted her head, stared at her husband for a moment, and with an unexpected burst of strength, hurled herself over the rail.

This revision is a mixture of diction and style changes. "Tossed herself" lacked the drama that "hurled herself" presents to the reader. There's also a little gain in emphasis by the alliteration in "hurled herself," but the main purpose of the revision is to make more dramatic and energetic the act of her leaving. She might "toss" an empty popcorn box over the rail, but I think a body requires hurling (particularly when it combines alliteratively so well with *herself*).

We haven't discussed yet the emphatic potential of a pause, or dramatic delay, but the previous example provides us a perfect demonstration. The original had her stare at her husband and then toss herself over so quickly that there was no suspense built up. In the revision, the reviser has created a dramatic delay by inserting new information—that the staring was only for a moment. Then, to add to the suspense, the reviser inserts *and with an unexpected burst of strength* before she finally hurls herself over the rail. The original writer hadn't fully exploited the scene's potential for drama.

Original:

> Monica gasped as she raised her eyes to the bronzed stranger from the sloop, who posed now with his hands on his hips looking menacingly down at Ted's recumbent body.

Revised:

> . . . now poised, fists on hips, looking down at Ted's recumbent body.

Here *poised* is preferable to *posed*. A man may pose against a mantlepiece, but if he's standing on it, high above the unsuspecting burglar, he's poised, ready to leap—a much more suspenseful word in this context. *Fists on hips* makes him more menacing than *hands on hips*. Poised with fists on his hips, he is menacing enough, so we can drop "menacingly." Again, we are showing rather than telling.

Original:

> Monica's eyes were glued to this stranger, who she sensed was not a stranger at all. Consequently, she heard, rather than saw, Ted rise to his feet and walk away muttering under his breath.

Revised:

> . . . she heard, rather than saw, Ted rise to his feet and slap away in his flip-flop sandals, muttering under his breath.

The original tells us the mere fact that he walked away from the menacing, bronzed stranger; it does not tell us the more emphatic, dramatic point about *how* he walked away. The revision *shows* us, that he walked away slapping his flip-flops. This is better than "telling" us that he walked away petulantly. Let us see our actors acting; don't be forever telling us about our actors. (I may be reading too much petulance into his flip-flops, but the slapping of flip-flops does give us a more interesting aural picture.)

Original:

> She mounted the outside library steps, which were peppered with cigarette butts, careful to skirt the blue suits and brown paper lunch bags around her. Finding a space near the top, she scuffed at some debris and sat down.

Revised:

> She mounted the outside library steps, which were peppered with cigarette butts. Picking her way delicately through the blue suits and brown paper lunch bags, she found a space near the top. She scuffed away some debris and sat down, gingerly.

Aside from the original's unintended and unfortunate juxtaposition of *skirt* and *blue suits,* the verb *skirt* does not describe accurately her movement up the debris-laden steps. *Picking her way delicately* gives us a better image of *how* she moved up the steps. The original merely expresses the fact that she sat down. *Gingerly* likewise gives a feel for *how* she sat amidst debris. The comma after *sat down* makes us pause; the dramatic delay adds further emphasis to *gingerly,* already emphasized by its position at the end of sentence and paragraph.

The next example of how emphasis is achieved through careful diction also illustrates the use of *irony* to achieve further emphasis (see the subsequent section for more on the use of irony):

Original:

> A stale, thick layer of grass and cigarette smoke had formed and hovered at loft level, softening the lights and shadows. The polished hardwood floor was littered with party debris—paper cups, butts, dribbled caviar, and powdered crackers.

Revised:

> . . .softening the lights and shadows. The polished hardwood floor was littered with the debris of a sophisticated party—paper cups, butts, dribbled caviar, and shoe-ground crackers.

The revision adds a tiny note of irony by calling a party *sophisticated* that ends with such debris on the floor. The improved emphasis of *shoe-ground* over *powdered* crackers comes from its position as well as the irony it gathers from the likelihood that these "sophisticated" party-goers probably insist on *stone-*ground crackers for their tables. Even if all the readers don't "get it," the

phrase is more descriptive than the simple "powdered crackers."
Original:

> From the cafe's position at the head of a slope, anyone who sat in its privacy commanded a clear view of traffic which moved up and down this crowded section of Rome.

Revised:

> . . . commanded a clear view of traffic crawling up and down this crowded section of Rome.

Moved up and down gives no feeling of relative velocity. The writer probably thought he had *ex*pressed it by referring to *a crowded section of Rome*. The revised version *im*presses the image on the brain by personifying the traffic as *crawling*. Since, in a later description, the writer has the narrator dodging around in the traffic, it serves the careful writer to establish here that it is bumper-to-bumper slow.
Original:

> I moved swiftly to the little table Giuseppe had placed strategically for me. A pillar and two potted palms half concealed it from the body of the restaurant. From this vantage point I could see anyone who entered through the large glass doors of the cafe, as well as the piazza beyond.

Revised:

> . . . half concealed it from the body of the restaurant. From this post my eyes could sweep around the cafe, out through the large glass doors, and into the piazza beyond.

The major point of diction here is the change from the weak *vantage point* to the word *post*. I switched the diction because *post* is a word more likely to be associated with military matters (e.g., command post, forward observation post, military post). To the reader's surprise, this little table does become a sort of military observation post. The careful writer or reviser will plant words like this to prepare the reader for what comes next.
Original:

> Schneider tilted backward and crashed to the floor. I rose from my chair quickly and vaulted over the flowerpots and onto the sidewalk.

Revised:

> . . . and crashed to the floor. I leaped from my chair and vaulted
> over the flowerpots. . . .

I rose from my chair sounds like what Lazarus might have said. Any guy about
to vault over flowerpots and run out into Italian traffic is going to *leap* out of his
chair.

Original:

> Behind me, about twenty yards away, Café Brancusi erupted in
> pandemonium. I turned my head and looked straight ahead of me,
> and noticed a gendarme standing a little way off holding a sub-ma-
> hine gun.

Revised:

> . . . Café Brancusi erupted in pandemonium. I turned my head,
> and looked straight ahead. I spotted, a little way off, a gendarme
> holding a sub-machine gun.

In a situation like that, one doesn't *notice* a gendarme with a sub-machine gun.
"Saw a gendarme" would just barely do it; "spotted a gendarme" comes closer. You may find something even more accurate. One "notices" a piece of lint
on a tux.

Another revision was made by moving from where it was, the phrase *a little way off*—first because there was no sense separating the gendarme from his
sub-machine gun; second because it held off for a few words the punch line of
that sentence (that there was a gendarme in the way).

Original:

> . . . his polished black boots tapping out the rhythm softly on an
> Oriental rug. Brass cuspidors sat in convenient locations near up-
> holstered divans and settees.

Revised:

> . . . Brass cuspidors sat in strategic locations. . .

Strategic seemed to the reviser to have interesting overtones of artillery and the
geometry of trajectory. Yes—the writer/reviser has to consider everything, including the arcane art of tobacco spitting with its requisite accuracy of aim.

SENTENCE, PARAGRAPH AND CHAPTER LENGTH

One of the more effective ways to gain proper emphasis is through length—unusually long or unexpectedly short. Although there's no rule governing this, the rule-of-thumb might be: "shorter is better." The rule could be expressed as: "the shorter the better." Since shorter is better, perhaps *shorter is better* is better. In either case, the emphasis derives from the shortness.

Short (and Long) Sentences

When you're going over a manuscript, see whether you (or whoever the writer) might have made the point better (more emphatically) by using a shorter, punchier sentence. Even an incomplete sentence. See?

This technique will not be so useful, of course, if your writing tends to employ mostly short sentences. How could contrast (hence, emphasis) result from a short sentence set among other short sentences? If, however, you follow the advice of most professional writers and strive for variety of sentence length, short sentences will not only emphasize but also add valuable variety.

A one-word sentence is particularly emphatic, provided it's used only occasionally, and only for something deserving or requiring such great emphasis:

> The platoon of frightened young soldiers slithered under the barbed wire fence, rifles balanced across their arms. "Krauts!" They stopped moving and breathing.

The one-word sentence, *Krauts!* stops the reader in his tracks, as it did the soldiers. In a subsequent pass at revision, I broke up that final sentence into two dramatically short sentences: *They stopped moving. They stopped breathing.* The reader's breathing is almost required to skip a beat between the two sentences. The meaning does not change. The emphasis does.

Look at the final sentences of your paragraphs, where one would expect to find thoughts that are being emphasized, and ask yourself whether the thought can be expressed in a much shorter sentence—perhaps in a single word. It won't always be possible or, if possible, wise, but it's worth considering. Perhaps you'll find that a sentence cannot reasonably be shortened, but you may find it contains a word worth repeating as a single "sentence" immediately after the sentence in which it first appears. Here are two examples:

> (1) He rappelled down the vertical face of the building, his boots beating a rhythm against the bricks. Boots. They'd be the death of him one day. Him and his damned boots.
> (2) She told him that she felt toward him something she had never felt toward another person in her entire sixteen years. Sixteen. He

had children twice that age, but he felt something toward her that he had never felt before, even toward his wife. Lust. There it was. Out in the open. Pure lust.

Accuracy, or completeness, requires me to suggest that you can also achieve emphasis by occasionally using an unusually long sentence. It takes a gifted writer to pen an excellent sentence that is truly long (say, seventy words or so). William Faulkner wrote long but excellently crafted sentences. He was not usually seeking emphasis through length; long sentences were part of his style. Ernest Hemingway, known normally for short, punchy sentences, would occasionally create an emphatically long sentence. His long ones are emphatic because they contrasted so sharply with the shorter sentences surrounding them. His long sentences tend not to be intricately crafted. They are often a series of short sentences strung together with connecting *and's*. They achieve their emphasis by rolling on like surf running up on the beach and often provide a panoramic view of a scene. The beginning writer can easily achieve emphasis (and gain in style) by using the occasional, carefully considered, dramatically short sentence. Grow into longer sentences. How's that last one? Is it emphatic? Short? Yup.

Short Paragraphs

Everything I've said about gaining emphasis through short sentences can also be said about paragraphs. No one knows the proper length for a paragraph, but we know an extremely short one when we see it. We also know an excessively long one when we wade through it, but no one can give any very helpful guidelines for the length of an "average" paragraph.

Like short sentences, short paragraphs are emphatic only if used sparingly. A sentence of average length set off as a paragraph gains in emphasis over a sentence of equal length in the middle of a long paragraph. A dramatically short sentence set off as a dramatically short paragraph is doubly emphatic.

So, use one occasionally.

See how that stood out. Had it been surrounded by a number of short paragraphs full of short sentences, it would have been just another short sentence. Remember all that was said earlier about the relationship between white space, chemistry, and thinking time? White space = time = emphasis.

Short Chapters

What has just been said about unusually short sentences and paragraphs may also be said about chapters. In a long novel of, say, twenty-five chapters averaging about twenty pages each, one that is only five to ten pages long will stand out in the reader's mind. Since that is so, the author will probably use the device of a dramatically short chapter perhaps once in a book. Ordinarily, that chapter will be the pivotal chapter in which the plot suddenly takes the major twist that leads straight to the climax. I suppose someone more literarily minded than I could make a case for the emphasis inherent in an unusually *long* chapter. My fear is that all would be lost in the length. In my experience, shorter is better; longer is merely longer.

WORD ORDER

The careful, objective reviser will automatically consider many possible word orders for every sentence. He'll pay particular attention to how a revised word order may provide the needed emphasis. There are almost always at least two, if not many, different ways to order the words in an English sentence. The trouble is that the meaning may change with the order change; the emphasis will almost certainly change; the style will be different; and the rhythm will definitely change, for better or worse. Because a paragraph is an ecological system, a change in one part affects all other parts. One must revise with wide-open eyes and a mind alert to all possibilities. Let's consider changing word order only for the sake of emphasis, recognizing that we will have to assess what other effects the change in word order may have caused—and whether the change is, on balance, worth while.

Because we are all so used to the "normal" word order of English (subject-verb-object), anything that departs from that expected order is immediately noticed—hence, emphasized. A writer will use this knowledge to his or her advantage when attempting to create emphasis or ensure accuracy.

Let's consider some examples:

Normal word order:
Students who register late for classes this year are unfortunate.

For accurate emphasis:
Unfortunate are those students who register late for classes this year.

Even though the final position in a sentence lends emphasis to the word found there, the foregoing example shows how a change in word order can increase emphasis. *Unfortunate* is emphasized even more in the revision, since it is positioned where we least expect it in the normal course of the declarative English sentence.

Normal word order:
I took that test last year.

For accurate emphasis:
That test, I took last year.

In the normal order of English, the sentence emphasizes *last year*. If the writer wants in fact to emphasize *that test,* he must change the normal order. Notice that he realized after repositioning that there was now an incipient ambiguity ("the test *that* I took last year" versus "the test, *which* I took last year"), so he used a comma in the revised sentence to help the reader read it accurately.

Mislocated Modifiers

Word order can also mislead if modifiers are separated from their nouns where, in normal English word order, they would be found. How can we readers tell what the writer intends here, if we've noticed previously that he is not a careful writer:

If only he could climb the hill, she would love it.

What does *only* signify in this sentence? Does the writer really mean *only he* (as opposed to some other person), or:

If he could *only climb* the hill, she would love it.

or

If he could climb *only the hill,* she would love it.

Note too that *only* could take other positions that would alter meaning:

If he could climb the hill, *only she* would love it.

Only is a word particularly sensitive to proper positioning. Always ask yourself when revising whether *only* is properly positioned for your intended meaning.
Even is another word that should be watched carefully; it loves to mislead.

- Her father, a noted psychiatrist, was *even unable* to calm her.
- *Even her father,* a noted psychiatrist, was unable to calm her.
- Her father, a noted psychiatrist, was unable *even to calm* her.
- Her father, a noted psychiatrist, was unable to calm *even her.*

A recent, full-page promotional ad by a major corporation was intended to make the point that the firm's employees don't limit their giving to money donated at the office—that they help their communities by volunteering, for example, as Big Brothers and Big Sisters. The large headline read:

WE DON'T JUST GIVE AT THE OFFICE

One wonders what else they do at the office besides give. I imagine that this headline would have been more accurate as:

WE DON'T GIVE JUST AT THE OFFICE

The final line of the article makes it clear, at last, that the latter is, indeed, what was meant: ". . .our way of encouraging (our) people who want to do more than 'give at the office.' "

These examples demonstrate the close relationsip between *emphasis* and *accuracy of meaning*. By imparting a different emphasis to a word, whether by position or some other technique, we end up changing meaning. Writers and revisers must always stop and consider what damage (or improvement) they may cause by revising the word order.

Relocated Modifiers

In normal English word order, adjectives are placed immediately before the nouns they modify. When a writer wishes to put more emphasis on an adjective, he considers putting the adjective after the noun. Grammar requires, of course, that the modifiers be set off by commas, as in the following:

Original:

> The tundra is treeless and uninhabited and seems to go on and on forever.

Revised:

> The tundra, treeless and uninhabited, seems to go on and on forever.

Notice that the revision spotlights (emphasizes) *treeless and uninhabited,* and the writer was able also to eliminate an *is* and an *and*—worthwhile fringe benefits.

A reviser thinks it elegant when he or she makes a sentence more accurate, more properly emphasized, and shorter—all at one crack. Often, as in the preceding example, revising for one purpose can serendipitously yield other, unintended, improvements.

PAUSES

Possibly the simplest way to spotlight (emphasize) a phrase or an idea is to make the reader pause. The good public speaker and the clever comic know, usually intuitively, just when to pause, or skip a beat. The comic may even emphasize the emphatic pause by rolling his eyes to heaven, shrugging his shoulders, adjusting his tie, or staring silently into the wings. Meanwhile, the audience is busily filling in the gap with their own thoughts about what he's just said. This technique has been called the pregnant pause, because it's so filled with potential.

The writer is at a disadvantage; his readers can't see his eyebrows arching or his shoulders shrugging. But writers have their own techniques. In the second sentence of this section on pauses, for example, I wanted to emphasize slightly that the great speakers and comics probably don't theorize about pauses in their delivery—that they just know, intuitively. To throw a small spotlight, just a highlight, on that idea, all I did was put the idea in the middle of a sentence and surround it by commas. These commas made you slow *almost* to a stop before reading the two-word phrase. Read that first sentence again and you'll find that I've forced you to change your delivery rate to yourself. I'll bet you'll find yourself even lowering your internal voice when you say those two words. "The good public speaker and the clever comic know, *usually intuitively,* just when to pause, or skip a beat."

The same reasoning holds for embedding your *for examples* and *howevers* somewhere in the interior of a sentence. You want to reinforce (emphasize) that you are about to provide an example, or that what you're about to say is somehow contrary to what the first part of the sentence said. The words *for example* and *however* give their own message, of course, but by isolating them between commas we lend them emphasis.

Another effective way to provide emphasis or add emphasis is to position the word or idea at the very end of a sentence or paragraph (also suggested in the preceding discussion of positioning) and to precede it with a comma. Sometimes that single comma can be the difference between the bland and the emphatic. Like everything else, it should be used sparingly so that when it is used it's emphatic. Note that this emphatic use of a comma might be looked at askance by a strict grammarian. This is one of those cases where we must pay attention to effectiveness, not correctness:

> It's suddenly too hot, too bright, too glaring; everyone surrenders.
> The heat collects and thickens on the sidewalks and streets; it must
> be waded through, slowly.

The phrase *waded through slowly* is certainly emphatic, gaining its emphasis
through both diction and position, but listen to the added emphasis gained by
adding that simple little comma. Read it first without pausing between *through*
and *slowly.* Then read it again, emphasizing the pause at the comma. Dramatically improved.

My graduate student Phyllis Quiggley's very next sentence in her description of noon in Algiers shows the use of a semicolon to gain emphasis by a
change in rhythm:

> Since the sun refuses to retreat, we must; even the dogs seek shaded
> patches.

She felt, and I agree, that a period might have been too full a stop. Her next sentence is another good example of using a single comma for emphatic effect near
the end of a sentence:

> The streets are deserted now, abandoned.

A less thoughtful writer might easily have expressed the "same" thought, and
have been perfectly correct grammatically, with this sentence:

> The streets are now deserted and abandoned.

I think no one would say that this hypothetical version even approaches the real
one in style or in emphasis—yet, look how similar they are. One word, moved
ahead by one position, and a modest comma added. Of such small points is stylistic greatness made.

IRONY

Irony is a figure of speech used for humor and for emphasis, achieving its
effect by saying just the opposite of what is true. Because what it says is not to
be taken literally, it requires, like humor, an alert reader.

The contemporary writer E.B. White wrote a "letter" to the nineteenth-
century author Thoreau in an essay, "Walden." For the essay's gentle irony to
work, White's readers have to recall that in Thoreau's classic, *Walden,* he
wrote:

I went to the woods because I wished to live deliberately, to front only the essential facts of life, and see if I could not learn what it had to teach, and not, when I came to die, discover that I had not lived.

Mr. White, about a hundred years after Thoreau's time in the Concord woods, wrote:

I knew I must be nearing your woodland retreat when the Golden Pheasant came into view—Sealtest ice cream, toasted sandwiches, hot frankfurters, waffles, tonics and lunches. . . .

The Pheasant, incidentally, is for sale: a chance for some nature lover who wishes to set himself up beside a pond in the Concord atmosphere and live deliberately, fronting only the essential facts of life on [Route] Number 126.

Many of E.B. White's essays make their telling points through irony. One technique he uses to achieve irony is to list details, specific and concrete details (Sealtest, waffles, and tonics), leading the reader to create for himself the ironic statement he or she wishes. Another contemporary writer, John McPhee, has brought this technique of the telling detail to a creative high point.

Mr. McPhee uses the cumulative effect of details not just for ironic emphasis, but also for the feeling of authenticity they bring to his writing, for the atmosphere they construct, and for the universal truths the reader can see in the specific truths of detail. Readers from different regions may or may not read any irony into his description of riding through Georgia in *Pieces of the Frame:*

As we moved east, pine trees kept giving us messages—small, hand-painted signs nailed into loblollies. HAVE YOU WHAT IT TAKES TO MEET JESUS WHEN HE RETURNS? Sam said he was certain he did not. JESUS WILL NEVER FAIL YOU. City limits, Adrian, Georgia. Swainsboro, Georgia. Portal, Georgia.

Mr. McPhee, through this litany of signs, achieves something of all three objectives: the signs provide authenticity—we believe he really is driving through Georgia; at the same time, they help establish for the reader a feel for the environment along the long, straight roads of the coastal plain; and, if we care to notice, the signs make an ironic statement about a "backwoods community" by a "northern sophisticate."

In his *Survival of the Bark Canoe,* McPhee mentions the deer of New Jersey, especially around Princeton, where he lives and occasionally teaches at the university in town:

> Deer particularly gravitate to semi-rural research centers, of which there are many around Princeton, spaced like moons through the wooded countryside. The hunters know the size and special characteristics of each herd: the Squibb herd, the Dow Jones herd, the Western Electric herd, the Mobil Oil herd. The Institute for Advanced Study has extensive woodlots, and the smartest deer on earth are in the Institute herd.

We've been concentrating here on the continual use of irony that creates a tone for the entire piece, but irony can also be effective when used only occasionally in a generally more serious piece. The writer must be cautious about such infrequent use, because the reader may not be prepared for its reversal of logic in an otherwise straightforward composition. It may, on the other hand, make the piece.

Keep in mind that there are shades of irony all the way from gentle humor to bitter sarcasm. Each has its place. If doubt slinks into your mind at the time, better drop the use of irony. It could result in de-emphasis—or, as some prefer to say, it could be counterproductive.

TYPOGRAPHY

After we learned in our youth about the exclamation point as a device for spotlighting emphasis, we learned next to underline. The primary purpose of underlining is to inform the typesetter to set the underlined words in *italics*. Meanwhile, on typewritten manuscripts or in handwritten letters and memos, underlining serves to emphasize.

There's nothing very emphatic about italics in themselves; it's the *contrast* they provide that creates emphasis—the typeface is different and infrequently encountered. There's the key point about the use of italics—use them infrequently. Italics *lose* emphasis with *overuse*. The *more you use* them, the *less emphatic* your words become. If you look back over a page and find that you've underlined more than two or three phrases, reconsider your emphasis. Are you, by excessive underlining, looking down on your reader—afraid he or she can't figure out the emphasis from the context? If so, perhaps the fault is in your own failure to establish emphasis with the many other techniques available to you!

Other typographical techniques are available, and I've used them periodically in this book. They require no explanation, but they do require a caveat: Use them infrequently only. You should have heard the emphasis on *only* because of its position; I didn't need to italicize it.

Here, then, is a list of typographical devices for emphasis:

- all CAPS to emphasize a word
- *a different type style (font)*
- in rare instances, hand-lettered words
- outline letters
- simple indented blocks, especially for long quotations
- asterisks, lowercase o or degree signs, or bullets for lists (like this one)
- gray screens to highlight key words, sentences, or paragraphs
- **boldface type**
- parentheses to spotlight a (secondary) thought

I would like to put a non-rhetorical question here to the printers and editors of the world: Why is it that this many years after the invention of moveable type you have not yet provided writers with a piece of punctuation that will express the proper emphasis for a rhetorical question?! Or should that have been??!! Or more? Or must we continue providing no clue for the reader. The single question mark is inaccurate in that it has no exclamatory overtones. The single exclamation point is inaccurate because it has no interrogatory overtones. Isn't a more accurate punctuation mark called for—one more descriptive of intent— something more expressive than a stupid period?

I read somewhere a few years ago about a type foundry (in Cleveland?) that produces a new piece of punctuation that should solve the problem, but I never see it in print. It's a combined exclamation and interrogation point, the one superimposed on the other. It should be made available so we can accurately punctuate this sentence: This many years after Gutenberg, why can't we have such a handy mark?!!?!!

In the newspaper trade, they refer to the exclamation point as a SCREAMER, and in the typesetting trade as a BANG. The creator, Martin K. Spector, has named his new, greatly needed punctuation mark for a rhetorical question, the INTERROBANG.

LAYOUT

Admittedly, the writer does not always have control over how the words and type are designed for the printed page, but sometimes he does—especially if he is one of the thousands of writers who also act as editors or editor-publishers of organizational newsletters, brochures, or magazines.

In most situations, it is the art director who designs the pages, but it doesn't hurt for the writer, the writer-editor, or the writer-editor-publisher to know how words and ideas gain emphasis through their physical layout on the printed page.

As a general guideline, remember that words tend to lose emphasis to the degree they are surrounded by competing words or ideas. I suppose the exaggerated proof of this is the emphasis given the word that sits alone on a clean white page. Now picture that same word embedded in a page filled with five hundred or a thousand competing words.

The art director has only three major elements to work with on a page:
- Type
- Graphics
- White Space

Your words set in type (and also using the various techniques for gaining emphasis described earlier) can be made more (or less) emphatic by how well the art director does his or her job, as discussed in the foregoing section on typography.

Your words and ideas can be emphasized (or de-emphasized) by how the art director uses photographic and other artwork to illustrate your words. Illustration, as the word connotes, is intended to illuminate or throw light on the matter at hand. If we are able to write, edit, and publish under the new evidence from brain hemisphere research, we'll be certain to use good artwork and photography more frequently (and more thoughtfully). The research shows that many people with a dominant right hemisphere have a highly developed visual ability, but may have an underdeveloped verbal ability (a left hemisphere function). People with an oppositely organized brain (left hemisphere dominant) respond best to ideas that are well expressed and logically presented in words. They may be helped in their comprehension by illustrations or photographs. The highly visual people (right hemisphere dominant) may get most of their understanding from the illustrations and simply bog down if the accompanying words are at all complex or unusual. A well-illustrated article or book is effective across the broad range of human ability. Good writers genuinely appreciate good illustrators—a symbiotic relationship in the finest sense. We need each other.

This chapter has frequently stressed the electro-chemical significance of white space for emphasis, but usually in reference to small units of space. Here, we refer to large units of white space. Large areas of open space on a page are attractive to the eye-brain system. The brain does not wish to wade into a page black with type; it knows that it's in for rough sledding, that long periods of concentration will be required. The brain is so pleased when it comes upon a page that's light, airy, and relaxed in appearance that it walks willingly into the page.

White space *alone* makes a page enticing, but attractively designed blocks of type, white space, and illustrated space make the page irresistible. The writer's concern in all this is that the brain's chemical activity will have plenty of time to function because of the empty spaces. The writer also knows that the illustrations will massage the reader's more visually acute right brain hemisphere. That side will send supplementary, complementary ideas across to the left hemisphere for its logical processing of the writer's words and ideas. An apt analogy is that the writer-art director combination is a left hemisphere-right hemisphere team.

The De-Emphasizers

There may be no need for de-emphasizers, but there certainly are cases of unintentional de-emphasis. Ironically, most cases of de-emphasis occur in a misguided attempt to gain *extra* emphasis. The de-emphasizers include

- the exclamation point
- the passive voice
- abstractions
- euphemism
- intensives
- worn words
- hyperbole

THE EXCLAMATION POINT

The exclamation point has positive value, particularly after true exclamations: *Stop! Kill! Hands up!* However, it is frequently abused, as in sentences like: *Your new jogging outfit is simply dashing! He was so handsome!* Exclamation points in such sentences are fine for letters between friends, but they are inappropriate in most formal writing.

The *exclamation point* as a device for pointing up emphasis is the first method everyone learns. Some people "progress" from single to multiple exclamation points, reasoning that if one point adds emphasis, several will have a magnificent effect!!!!!! I would recommend eliminating the exclamation point entirely, except I'd likely be shot! How would the student make his summer vacation sound exciting in a September composition without a liberal sprinkling of these thought-savers.

They are thought-savers for the lazy writer, the writer who will not take the time to find the right words to express the excitement of summer. The right words usually provide enough emphasis without that little, period-tipped crutch at the end. This chapter has provided so many ways to achieve proper emphasis that you should seldom again need to lean on that frail crutch.

THE PASSIVE VOICE

A very common, unintentional de-emphasizer is the *passive voice*. Revisers should always look twice to see whether a passive expression is called for where it has been used. Many times the active voice is actually called for. If the passive is kept in the wrong place, even when grammatically correct, the result is de-emphasis. The reader may slide right over something important (i.e., something that she should read with emphasis) simply because it was expressed so weakly in the passive.

De-emphasized:

The returning heroes were cheered by the crowds.

Emphasized:

The crowds cheered the returning heroes.

De-emphasized:

The hymns were sung by the choir with enthusiasm.

Emphasized:

The choir sang the hymns enthusiastically.

The writer who wrote the original sentence about the choir unintentionally de-emphasized (made into mush) his point by using the passive voice when an active voice was obviously called for.

ABSTRACTION

Closely related to the inappropriate use of the passive is the inappropriate use of *abstractions.* I associate the two because they're both removed from what is real—active or concrete. There are occasions, of course, when abstractions are completely appropriate, but too often they are used unintentionally (i.e., without thought) and serve to de-emphasize. The abstract is the opposite of the concrete. If a concrete expression is available, it should be used, if not as a substitute for the abstract, then as a supportive, explanatory example:

- One should *vs.* you should
- Occupational opportunities *vs.* job openings
- Peacekeeper *vs.* nuclear-tipped missile
- By a narrow margin *vs.* within an inch of his life

EUPHEMISM

Closely related to abstractions is *euphemism,* another form that de-emphasizes. When a euphemism is deliberately used to soften a personal trauma, it is easily justified. When used under ordinary circumstances, it serves only to prevent our facing realities—it de-emphasizes what we should note clearly. If our military forces need our support in a time of trouble, we should not be told of their "defensive maneuver" when, in fact, they are retreating in disarray.

CIRCUMLOCUTION

Circumlocution, like euphemism, leads us down the garden path away from the concrete realities of life. Earlier in this book we've talked about deleting circumlocutions and other redundancies when revising our writing. Now we can see that we get two for one when we get rid of circumlocutions: we cut down on verbiage, and we make our writing more emphatic.

INTENSIVES

Another form of de-emphasis is the overuse of intensives. All of us are occasionally guilty of using some of the following words (intensives) in our well-intentioned but misguided attempts to emphasize our words (when we should, instead, look for better words or better techniques for gaining emphasis). When you think about each of these words for a minute, what do they mean as we use them:

- awfully — He was an awfully good frog.
- beautiful(ly) — Your frog did beautifully.
- certainly — Your frog is certainly beautiful!
- exciting — I find frog-keeping simply exciting.
- extremely — Frogs are extremely affectionate.
- fantastic — He was a fantastic frog!
- highly — A highly intelligent frog, too.
- perfectly — Hers was a perfectly charming frog!
- really — Frogs are really super pets.
- so — Frogs are so cute when in love.
- such — She was such a frog.
- super — She was a super frog.
- swell — His was a truly swell frog.
- too — Too bad about his frog.
- tremendous(ly) — He made a tremendous croak.
- very — He was a very nice frog.
- wonderful(ly) — His bulging eyes were wonderfully large.

These are all fine words. It's just that we frequently use them to add undue emphasis, only to learn that the reader found them excessive (and, thus, de-emphasizing). We make things worse by ending the sentence with one (or more) exclamation points! Because these are sixth-grade emphasizers, they become de-emphasizers in writing for adults. Delete them; they're tremendously childish. They really and truly are fantastically out of place! And I mean that sincerely!! And, while you're at it, have a good day!!!

WORN WORDS

Overuse of the worn is another common failing of us all. Worn-out words are called by many names, but they all belong to the ancient clan of the worn: *clichés, catchwords, hackneyed expressions, trite words* and *expressions, slang, colloquialisms,* and *obscenities.*

A more knowledgeable grammarian or lexicographer might not put all of these into the clan, but they are all worn, tired, shabby. They still have their good uses—say, to bring out character through their use in dialogue or to provide irony. Here, we're concerned with the likelihood that they will de-emphasize something of importance. An obscenity in a eulogy, for example, may well trivialize the other words, or even the person eulogized. Slang phrases used in the wrong place may de-emphasize what's being said. On occasion, of course, slang may be used to great ironic, humorous, or dramatic effect in the midst of an otherwise formal piece—but it must be intentional slang, not slang used for lack of an adequate vocabulary, or lack of thought.

Many of the same constraints should be placed on colloquialisms, clichés, and trite expressions. Each has its place in nonfiction and fiction, but the writer must use them deliberately (i.e., after deliberation). The problem, of course, is that all these worn expressions are readily at hand when we're writing. They roll easily out of the mind and through the pen without our thinking—yes, without thinking. In the interest of getting your thoughts on paper, let them flow out as you write the first draft, but only if you know that you're going to be serious enough to come back and revise time and again before going public.

My purpose in bringing up worn expressions in a book on revision is a serious one. Because worn-out words surface without much thought, they may reflect that lack. During the many routines of revision the writer will find again and again that these words and expressions are camouflaging inaccurate, imprecise, fuzzy thinking. A conscientious reviser will poke around and under each one as he or she comes upon it. There are two opportunities here for better writing. First, the reviser may dig deep and discover, now that he has a fresh chance to think it through, that he didn't know what he was talking about at the time of first drafting. Second, the reviser now has the time to focus on careful phrasing in substitution for the worn words.

During the first drafting, the writer's brain is working simultaneously on a paragraph, a chapter, and the whole book ahead, in addition to the words of the moment. In the revision mode, however, the brain can exercise all its electro-chemical magic on one particular idea, expression, or word. The reviser should thus look on worn words as helpful signals—they are rallying flags to better drafts. Flags of the worn are unique—they serve the reviser while they wave, and they serve the reader when they're lowered.

HYPERBOLE

Emphasis can also be gained through *hyperbole,* the use of overstatement or understatement. But, like the other devices we've been discussing, hyperbole can go overboard and become a de-emphasizer. Because hyperbole already has one leg over the rail through exaggeration, it doesn't take much more exaggeration to shove it overboard into the sea of the ludicrous. Exaggeration is one of the powerful tools in the wit's kit, thus sharing the danger of all humor—that someone with an underdeveloped sense of the absurd will not catch it. The literal-minded will not recognize it as a deliberate, hyperbolic, exaggerated statement, and will write the writer off as totally inaccurate—or worse, unserious.

Revision is the time to review your writing both for its proper emphasis and its unintended de-emphasis. Don't underestimate the power of the brain-mind when it is allowed to focus all its attention on small problems. Professional writers are fully aware of that power, and they'll readily admit that their very first drafts lack the punch and life that comes out after multiple revisions. It is only what is finally published that's important—nothing earlier matters. NOTHING EARLIER MATTERS.

CHAPTER III

Revise by Rewording

. . . a good style is bound to carry the impress of the writer's personality. Every tree in the forest has its own grain and the special quality of that tree—its unique grain pattern—will show through any honest piece of furniture made from its wood.

Brooks and Warren
Modern Rhetoric

. . .not the clothes a man wears, but the flesh, bone, and blood of his body. . .style is organic.

J. Middleton Murry
The Problem of Style

Le style est l'homme même.
[Style is the man himself.]

Buffon
Discours sur le style

. . .our personal appearance in print.

Charles W. Ferguson
Say It with Words

An author's style is his written voice, his spirit and mind caught in ink.

John Mason

When we speak of Fitzgerald's style, we don't mean his command of the relative pronoun, we mean the sound his words make on paper. Every writer, by the way he uses the language, reveals something of his spirit, his habits, his capacities, his bias. This is inevitable, as well as enjoyable. All writing is communication; creative writing is communication through revelation—it is the Self escaping into the open. No writer long remains incognito.

E. B. White
An Approach to Style

Style is not a method or system or even a decoration for one's writing, it is but the total impression the reader gets of the quality of the writer's mind, his depth or superficiality, his insight or lack of insight, and other qualities like wit, humor, biting sarcasm, genial understanding . . . and general attitude toward things.

Lin Yutang
The Importance of Living

For his style, the plain, undecorated language in which he addresses posterity is no mere knack with words. It is the manifestation of a mode of thought, of an outlook which colors every act of the writer's, and tells us how he rated life.

Jacques Barzun
Lincoln the Writer

It is not enough to use language that *may* be understood; he should use language that *must* be understood.

Quintilian

A good narrative style does not attract undue attention to itself. Its job is to keep the reader's mind on the story, on what's happening, the event, and not the writer.

Leon Surmelian
Techniques of Fiction Writing

"The fundamental rule of style is to keep solely in view the thought one wants to convey."

Jacques Barzun
Simple & Direct

An attractive style requires, of course, all kinds of further gifts (beyond clarity and brevity)—such as variety, good humor, good sense, vitality, imagination. Variety means avoiding monotony of rhythm, of language, of mood. One needs to vary one's sentence length; to amplify one's vocabulary; to diversify one's tone.

F. L. Lucas
"What Is Style?"
Contexts for Composition
by Clayes and Spencer

Here, then, we have three fairly distinct meanings of the word style disengaged: Style as personal idiosyncrasy; Style as technique of exposition; Style as the highest achievement of literature. The opportunities for confusion are great.

J. Middleton Murry
The Problem of Style

Style

Everything you do in your writing creates your style, but it is when you get down to revision by rewording that you come closest to creating what other people may eventually come to see as your "style." You'll be counseled in the following pages (as in some of the preceding quotations) not to consider consciously that you are rewording for style. You should reword only to make clearer for the reader what you had in mind when you wrote the first draft. At that time, you could not stop to improve what even then you knew was not the most accurate or beautiful expression of your thought. Now, in revision, you do have the time, and it's easier to do it at this advanced stage in the revision process. All the excess baggage has been removed in earlier revisions, so that the words stand out clear and unencumbered. The words may be clear, yet the idea remains vague. At least now you can see where the vagueness or inaccuracies are, and you can work on them.

The process is like renovating an old brick warehouse into a modern restaurant. The first stage in the revision is to decide which partitions have to be torn out, which sections of the ceiling have to be opened up to reveal the beauty of the beams, which floors must be refinished or ripped up. These early revisions do affect the eventual style of the restaurant, but the "style" of the renovator-architect is probably more clearly revealed by what he then does to express best the original concept he had in mind when he bought the run-down warehouse.

This is not to say that the architect's style (or the restaurant's style) consists of garnishes (artwork, brass shields, old sleighs, and copper tubs); rather, style reveals itself in an overall, total impression upon the mind of the viewer. If the same architect later designs an office building or a residence somewhere and someone recognizes his work from having eaten in the restaurant (even though the structure and decor of the two buildings are completely different), the architect can be said to have his own style.

Many people writing about the elusive topic of style finally resort to saying what it is *not,* and that is a helpful way to look at it. Their most significant point is that style is not what we are often led to believe it is. Style is definitely not garnishes sprinkled on our sentences to *impress* the reader. We should think of style, rather, as *all* the things we do to *express* our thoughts.

When considering a sentence with an eye to rewording it, do not consider *what people will think of you* if you elect to add a certain word, phrase, or metaphor. Think only and always about whether that particular word, phrase, or metaphor will conjure up in the reader's mind the image, feeling, or thought you, the writer, have in mind.

If you do this conscientiously, what will end up on paper will be your unique style—it will be you. You may or may not come off sounding like the greatest thinker since Plato. You will if you are; you will not if you are not. There are those of us, of course, who believe we can appear finer than we are by selecting words, phrases, metaphors, and so on that are grand. If such language does not come naturally to us, the truth will eventually out. In the long run, it's better to be ourselves—our *best* selves, but ourselves nonetheless.

One thought held in common by all those writers I read is an extremely useful one: Forget about your style when writing. Forget it! Since style is so deeply a part of you that, as Buffon said, it is the man [or woman] himself, it's going to be evident in your writing no matter what you do. Ironically, if you concentrate on your style, you'll inevitably come across as someone who thinks more about appearances than thoughts—superficial, egocentric, or a fake.

Just have a healthy self-confidence and try with every word, every sentence, every image to make an "impression" in your reader's brain cells that matches as closely as possible the impression in your own. What results, results—it will be you, beautiful and honest you.

I appreciate fully, nevertheless, that every writer, particularly in the early years, wonders, "Do I have a style?" "What is my style?" We've all experienced the intellectual joy of "spotting" an isolated passage as Hemingway's, Shakespeare's, or Churchill's, just by its style. It must be one of life's greatest intellectual thrills when someone says, "I read something yesterday that I just knew was your writing—I could tell by its style." That is a marvelous moment, a moment worth waiting for—but it will come only when your writing is "you."

The only way to ensure the possibility that such a moment will come is to think only of the thought being thought. What can you take out or add or modify that will express exactly—not just closely, but *exactly*—what you mean. Do that every day, year after year, and the great moment will come. Then your style will express itself over and over. Then you'll have the interesting new problem of trying not to analyze your writing to see how "they" can spot your writings. Fortunately, nature has a way of dealing with problems in life. By the time you have that problem, you'll also have a mature way of thinking about your writing and yourself—provided you continue to be honest in all things, especially with yourself and your reader.

As a way of demonstrating differences in style, I've collected a set of six descriptions having to do with a subject of particular interest to me, cabins.

> In a wilderness cabin there is always a need to set or hang things outside. My canoe paddles go up under the extended roof, and there are hooks where I can hang a pot of stew to cool, out of reach of pets, sled dogs, or forest creatures. It is not unusual to come upon a cabin of this protective roof style and see snowshoes, packsacks, saddles, and other gear hanging up. These are the items that give a wilderness flavor to a cabin. Under such a roof, firewood can be stacked against the wall where it will be fully protected from the elements.
>
> —Calvin Rutstrum
> *The Wilderness Cabin*

* * *

> Even the cabin was dismal and damp. I turned the gas mantle high, lit the kerosene lamp, and lighted two burners of my stove to drive loneliness away. The rain drummed on the metal roof. Nothing in my stock of foods looked edible. The darkness fell and the trees moved closer. Over the rain drums I seemed to hear voices, as though a crowd of people muttered and mumbled off-stage. Charley was restless. He didn't bark an alarm, but he growled and whined uneasily, which is very unlike him, and he didn't eat his

supper and left his water dish untouched—and that by a dog who drinks his weight in water every day and needs to because of the outgo. I succumbed utterly to my desolation, made two peanut-butter sandwiches, and went to bed and wrote letters home, passing the loneliness around.

—John Steinbeck
Travels With Charley

* * *

He was trying to farm stubborn ground and make a home in a cabin of logs he cut from timber nearby. The floor was packed-down dirt. One door, swung on leather hinges, let them in and out. One small window gave a lookout on the weather, the rain or snow, sun and trees, and the play of the rolling prairie and low hills. A stick-clay chimney carried the smoke up and away.

—Carl Sandberg
The Prairie Years

* * *

During the first week after moving into the cabin there was a lot of carpentry work to finish. Bunks had to be built of saplings set against the north wall, then covered with mattresses of sphagnum moss and caribou hides. Sleeping robes had to be made as well, and these consisted of deer hides placed with the fur side in, and sewed along three edges. Jamie built a table of flat rocks raised on stones to about two feet above the floor. Since there were no chairs, this was high enough. The boys crouched on two boulders, each of which had a cushion of caribou hides, and dined in style.

—Farley Mowat
Two Against the North

* * *

This was an airy and unplastered cabin, fit to entertain a traveling god, and where a goddess might trail her garments. The winds which passed over my dwelling were such as sweep over the ridges of the mountains, bearing the broken strains, or celestial parts only, of terrestrial music. The morning wind forever blows, the poem of creation is interrupted; but few are the ears that hear it. Olympus is but the outside of the earth everywhere.

—Henry David Thoreau
Walden

* * *

Serena Caudill heard a step outside and then the squeak of the cabin door and knew that John was coming in. She kept poking at the fireplace, in which a hen was browning.

"Where's Boone?"

"Around, I reckon." She looked up then and saw him shut the door against the rain, saw him shut it behind him without turning while his eyes took in the murky kitchen. He limped to the wall, making an uneven thump on the puncheon floor, started to hang his coat on its peg, thought better of it and hunched it back around his neck. In the warmth of the room the smells of cow and sweat and drink and wet woolens flowed from him.

—A. B. Guthrie
The Big Sky

We can see that these writers' styles are different, but we can also see that style is intimately related to meaning and purpose. Several of these writers are telling us about cabins because they want us to understand cabins. Others tell us something about cabins, to be sure, but they are more interested in having us understand the people who live in the cabins—the cabin is but a backdrop.

John Steinbeck's purpose in describing the cabin is to tell us about the loneliness he felt at the moment, rather than the details of his and Charley's cabin on wheels. A. B. Guthrie gives us a feeling for the Caudills' cabin, but he's more concerned that we see the relationship between Serena and John as they lived and survived on the frontier. Thoreau uses the cabin on Walden Pond as a platform from which to launch a philosophical discussion about Olympus being "but the outside of the earth everywhere."

One cannot, of course, decide from these short pieces whether the styles are generally representative of their authors or were created for the author's immediate purposes. From reading many other passages by these authors, however, it is my impression that each example does, indeed, represent its author's style.

Diction

Whatever you want to say, there is only one word that will express it; one verb to make it move; one adjective to qualify it. You must seek that word, that verb, and that adjective, and never be satisfied with approximations, never resort to tricks, even clever ones, or to verbal pirouettes to escape the difficulty.

—Flaubert to Maupassant

Although in the foregoing examples you may have seen other good techniques of writing that contributed to each writer's style, it must have been clear that the writer's choice of words—his diction—played a central role in creating what we recognize as his *style*.

Because no two people are going to come up with precisely the same word combinations to express a particular thought, no two people are going to have identical styles—similar, perhaps, but not identical.

When we do find numbers of people expressing a thought by almost identical word choices, as one tends to find among first-year college students, we say that they are trite writers—and that they have *no style*. When they finally realize that they're trying to express their own thoughts with other people's words, and begin to search for more precise words to express their inner selves, they are on the right track. The way may be long and tortuous, but they could never reach a personal style without at least taking that first step down the trail.

In the center of that trail lies diction—or diction lies at the *heart* of style—or should I say that good diction lies at the *root* of style? As I try to decide which metaphor expresses most closely my idea about the relationship between diction and style, I'm going through a process central to writing—careful thought. A writer doesn't make word choices by tossing a coin or playing thesaural roulette; he or she can do it well only by thinking, and sometimes only by prolonged thinking.

A child, with its necessarily limited vocabulary, will have little difficulty selecting words for a purpose. The mature writer, however, with his wider and deeper vocabulary, will have to do a lot more selecting, i.e., thinking. He'll be able to convey his ideas more clearly because of the great variety of words available, each communicating a distinction, a nuance, a shade of meaning.

It is this persistent search for the exact shade of meaning that makes the writer professional. If she feels that her ready vocabulary is not producing the just-right word, she doesn't hesitate to pore through the dictionary and the thesaurus until she finds it. Her style will be distinctive if the word or phrase finally selected was not one listed under an expected entry, but one brought in from another field (provided it works well) and used metaphorically, perhaps in connection with an unlikely word or in a context where it has never been seen before. One such phrase, now a tired cliché, must have been a stylistic gem when the word *glass* was wrenched from its traditional context and attached to an anatomical word: *From the way he fell, it was obvious that this giant had a glass jaw.* One can easily imagine the sportswriter rummaging desperately amidst his working words and flipping through his dog-eared dictionary for a term to express a jaw disastrously vulnerable to a sharp punch.

It is during this later revision routine that the writer makes a creative effort to improve the words that have survived the earlier routines. The experienced writer will usually forge on when writing a first draft, rather than stop his flow of thought to find the elusive words that will express more precisely what he wants to say. He uses a word that comes to mind readily, one that says more or less what he's aiming at. He may even place a question mark next to the word or in the margin, so he can move creatively forward, confident that he won't forget later to put some time into the hunt for a more accurate word. He is also confident enough that his diction has not permanently deserted him, that it's just out for coffee and will return when he calls.

As a demonstration of how the writer's mind works in its search for the right word, let's go back a few sentences and reproduce it just as it was in the manuscript (revisions added). Not that I'm claiming anything great for my final version; I simply want to show that I improved it by looking again at the individual words and asking myself just what I was trying to get across.

One can imagine *easily* the sports writer ~~searching~~ *rummaging desperately amidst* his ~~mind and~~ working words and *Flipping through* his dog-eared dictionary for a ~~suitable synonym for a~~ ~~weak jaw~~ term ~~that would~~ *to* express a jaw disastrously vulnerable to a

sharp punch.

If a person cannot take joy in shaping up a sentence like that, he or she might consider a less poetic existence. I can see right now that if I revise again, there are still some words I'd like to play around with. The sentence is long, but its style and diction, even as is, would carry the reader along without any trouble. I get a thrill, too, from the strength of the final two words. It's always nice to have a sentence end with a punch.

It's these small joys that keep a writer or editor happy with a job that can, at times, be toilsome.

Leon Surmelian had some useful things to say about diction in his excellent book, *Techniques of Fiction Writing*. Born in Turkey, he has great appreciation for our English language. I only wish I could use it as well as he:

> English has been the language of men of action, and probably no other European tongue has so many active verbs. Since drama means doing, English is naturally dramatic. *Strike, break, slam, smash, gash, shake, shut, shatter, scatter, batter, roll, trundle, thunder, blare, blow*—each arouses a mental image and the sound fits the sense. Or consider *shimmer, glimmer, rustle, tussle, sway, swoon, swing*—they sound right to our ears, and we can visualize them. With Saxon words, the writer is not likely to be precious and

> affected unless he goes to the other extreme and writes as a profes-
> sional Saxonist, a nativist diehard. . . . The sophisticated like the
> plain word better, while the uneducated are often impressed by fan-
> cy, flowery speech.

Mr. Surmelian adds that for good style we do need the words of Latin-French heritage to mix with the Anglo-Saxon. Latin words can act as uncommon, strange words, as lengthened forms, to give style distinction:

> The excessively domestic look of prose would make it homely, and
> Saxon needs the Roman mantle as it were to gain dignity and gran-
> deur. The strange words glamourize the language, and by balanc-
> ing Saxon words with Latin words the writer gets the characteristic
> swing and flavor of English prose, and avoids monotony in lan-
> guage.

> The Saxon word for sturdy peasant strength, the Latin word for ele-
> gance. The Saxon word for sensations, the Latin word for con-
> cepts. The Saxon word for the concrete and specific, the Latin
> word for the abstract and general. Exceptionally rich and varied in
> its vocabulary, English is the mighty hybrid among modern
> tongues.

Since a few years ago, when I first read those words by Mr. Surmelian, I've treasured my Anglo-Saxon English with its Latin-French additives. I took Mr. Surmelian's advice and applied it to a query letter for an article I planned to write on the great polar explorers:

> Captain Robert Falcon Scott operated as though he believed that a
> massive application of dedication, persistence, and pluck would
> enable one to muddle through to victory, come what might.

Following Surmelian's advice, I added to the noble-sounding *dedication* and *persistence* the short, homely word *pluck*. I can't swear that *pluck* and *muddle* are of Saxon origin, but they certainly sound it. Anyone familiar with the history of Scott's race to the South Pole would recognize that *muddle*, homely as it is, was the just-right word. Anyone familiar with Scott would agree on at least one point—the man certainly had pluck.

George Orwell, in his essay, "Politics and the English Language," warns us not to overuse pretentious, largely Latinate, diction:

> Words like *phenomenon, element, individual* (as noun), *objective,*

*categorical, effective, virtual, basic, primary, promote, consti-
tute, exhibit, exploit, utilize, eliminate, liquidate,* are used to dress
up simple statements and give an air of scientific impartiality to bi-
ased judgments.

Scrutinize the Verbs

Having come this far in your revision routines, it's important now to focus
on those few fortunate words that have survived. Look first at the verbs. Don't
merely look at them—scrutinize them, agonize over them. Time spent improving verbs will be repaid with interest—reader interest. The beginner is tempted
to look at the familiar verbs and see them as just fine. The writer knows the full
intent of the verbs (after all, they're his) and brings all his insider's knowledge
to bear subconsciously as he scans the verbs. Pity the poor reader. He doesn't
have all those supplemental, peripheral, helpful insider's thoughts to color the
verb used; he has only the printed words to go by. He needs help, and only the
writer (and reviser) can help. Discipline yourself to say (even aloud in the privacy of your work space), "O.K., let's settle down now. If so many professional
writers say that they scrutinize every verb, then I guess I should. Here I go; verb
number one . . ."

(1)   **If a form of the verb** *to be* **(e.g.** *is, am, are, will be, were, was, to
be***) eliminate it, or try hard to.**

I'm continually impressed by how my sentences improve by dropping these
weak-kneed forms of *to be.* I used to hear my professors talk about them,
and I've read over and again about how I must minimize them. Some time
ago I decided to discipline myself in this regard. Not an easy matter. I find
I can't get rid of them all. For example, I slipped one in on you in the first
sentence of this paragraph. It used to read . . . *how my sentences are improved* . . . How easy to solve that particular one: I simply deleted *are* and
added a "*d*" to *improve.* I consider the active *improve* an improvement. I
admit that you can drive yourself crazy trying to rid your writing of every
single form of *to be,* but you should make a firm effort to do so. **The Ted
Cheney rule-of-thumb: allow yourself no more than about one form of** *to be*
per one hundred words. Are you going to do it? Whoops.

The point: The search for a more active verb to substitute for the *to
be* form often leads serendipitously to a more accurate verb. An accurate,
active verb perks up any sentence. You may have to turn the sentence
around or inside out, but it comes out stronger, more effective.

Original:

> The wall on the side where I was sitting was semi-panelled. The panels were dark brown and the wall in between was light brown.

Revised:

> The wall along which my table leaned was semi-panelled, the panels a dark brown, the wall between, a light brown.

Surprisingly, *to be* forms can often be eliminated that easily; just delete and add commas where necessary. Admittedly, I had to insert a new verb, *leaned,* to make that one work. An editor could not do that; the original author could. He or she knows whether the table could be better described as "leaning" than as "being." The author might have elected to have the table merely "stand" by that semi-panelled wall. It all depends on the "facts" as he has invented them. Naturally, a nonfiction writer would not have invented "leaned." He might, in good conscience, have substituted "along which my table stood."

Let's see whether this advice holds up in another example:

Original:

> As he walked up to the bar, he quickly scanned the handful of customers who were scattered about the tavern. Reggie zeroed in on a blond who was sitting at the bar, and positioned himself next to her. Reggie was a sucker for blonds and he wanted this one.

Revised:

> As he walked up to the bar, he quickly scanned the handful of customers scattered about the tavern. Zeroing in on a blond sitting at the bar, Reggie positioned himself next to her. A sucker for blonds, he wanted this one.

In another example from the same story, note how the sentence comes to life with the dropping of the *to be* forms:

> Standing in the corner by the front window, Will Stiller ~~was~~ eyed eyeing
>
> the same blond ~~that was~~ sitting next to Reggie.

The sentence will still not win any prizes, but it ~~is~~'s certainly improved—see, it worked here, too. The next example becomes crisper and cleaner as the *was's* drop away:

Original:

> The beer was cold. The room was cool and the conversation was light and pleasant.

Revised:

> The beer was cold, the room cool, the conversation light and pleasant.

With some more thought, the writer would probably find a way to rid this sentence of the first *was,* but two out of three ain't bad.

Sometimes two sentences can be combined to get rid of an infestation of *being's, it's, was's,* and *were's:*

> The Corporate Psychologist is concerned and involved, ~~as opposed~~
> ~~to being~~ **not** detached and critical.

Original:

> His hair was black and his hairline was receding. His deep brown eyes were clear and thoughtful.

Revised:

> His hair was black, his hairline receding, his deep brown eyes clear and thoughtful.

The following example demonstrates again that you can often simply delete the offending (i.e., totally useless) *to be.*

> We found Baytown's Program ~~to be~~ very complete and well documented.

(2)   Is the verb accurate?

The careful reviser will not be content with gunfire *shattering* the valley. He or she will ask first whether it was from heavy artillery across the hills in a parallel valley. If so, the reviser will know from experience, intelligent speculation, or research that such distant and heavy gunfire would not shatter so much as *rumble* along the valley floor. If the story is about a peasant gone berserk and shooting his cattle, the gunfire might *crack* rather than rumble. The reviser can never rest in the pursuit of the accurate verb. Here are some examples of diligent pursuit:

Student Work   *Teacher Comments*

The young freshman does not seem to notice. He's ~~watching~~ *gazing at* the new faces entering the room. He's hoping someone will sit down with him.

> I see that you were not satisfied with *watching* and revised it to *gazing at*. You're on the right track, but I don't think you've found the right verb yet. It's worth worrying about, because it's central to what's going on. I haven't found the right verb yet, either, but it needs something like, *He's studying closely,* or *He's searching each face entreatingly,* or another that will get across more accurately that he's trying to lure someone to his table. Keep at it.

I had always liked the Cafe Brancusi. I liked the hum of vitality that always ~~surrounded~~ *filled* it.

> Technically speaking, I'd think the hum would not so much *surround* the cafe as *fill* it. A fine point, but that's the name of this game. If you intended to express the thought that one could hear a hum from outside the cafe, you were right, but I had the impression from the rest that you were referring only to the inside.

From its position at the top of a slope, anyone sitting in its privacy commanded a clear view of the traffic that ~~passed~~ *crawled* up and down this crowded section of Rome.

> *Passed up and down* gives us no feeling for relative velocity. You mention that this is a crowded section of Rome, so its traffic is probably *crawling*. Since later in the page, you have your character dodging around in this traffic, it would be careful and clever to establish in advance that it's bumper-to-bumper, crawling traffic.

The room is bustling with activity.

Cigarette smoke streams through the

air, ~~circling~~ **wrapping** around the statues of the

blessed saints.

Circling connotes, to me, that the smoke circles the saints and comes back. *Wrapping* connotes, to me, envelopment—and I believe that was your intent. Come to think of it, why not have the smoke enveloping the statues? And so it goes . . .

Mixed ~~odors~~ **wisps** of perspiration and per-

fume trail from person to person, ta-

ble to table.

Wisps and *waft* seem to carry your image of smoke flowing around the room, and the alliteration they present adds a bit of poetry to your prose—no?

Action stirs as adrenalin **spurts into** ~~soaks~~ the

minds of the participants. . .

Adrenalin might more accurately be said to *spurt* than to *soak*. Part of its miracle is the speed with which it works. Writers have to think of everything!

Creating ~~To create~~ a successful new venture

requires qualities that few individu-

als possess—imagination, drive,

and faith in oneself.

An infinitive like *to create* is usually rather weak, certainly not very active. *Creating* sounds more like something is happening.

Original:

Where we can assist in this high-risk

endeavor is in the selection of indi-

viduals who have these qualities

necessary to entrepreneurial suc-

cess.

I found your verb *(is)* rather far into the sentence—and not worth waiting for. This is a sales piece—come right out and tell them what you're going to do for them: *We assist.* . . Notice that the *-ion* attached to *select* tips us off about the passive. *Selecting* is more active than *selection*.

Revised:

We assist in this high-risk endeavor by carefully selecting individuals with these qualities so essential to entrepreneurial success.

Original:

My gaze swung to the right and there was another. I looked to the left and there was a man in an overcoat. There was something familiar about him, so I turned for a second glance.

Revised:

Another off to the right. To the left stood a familiar figure in a trenchcoat.

My gaze swung sounds too leisurely, even for Rome. Imagine having just vaulted over the pots and you're about to dash out into Italian traffic—would you *swing your gaze?* In cinematic terms, would you pan to the gendarme, or would you not speed it up by cutting to him? You can get a cut effect by using an incomplete sentence: *Another off to the right.* Look at the weak-kneed *was's* we're deleting. Things always grow more active without *was.* I've substituted *stood* as something at least a little more active than *there was.* Recall that *there* attached to a *to be* form spells trouble. I also changed his overcoat to a trenchcoat, both for the traditional symbolism and in the recognition that summer in Rome does not call for an overcoat. Possibly a trenchcoat.

It may be instructive, and certainly enjoyable, to read how some of our more famous authors have enlivened their work by selecting the perfect verb:

Author's Work

There was much to be said for Sarah, and he was glad to discover himself thinking so, to find himself remembering not the long hell of hours she had spent honing her tongue on his habits, supposed poker-playing, women-chasing vices, but gentler episodes: Sarah showing off her self-made hats, Sarah scattering crumbs on snowy window sills for winter pigeons: a tide of visions that towed to sea the junk of harsher recollections.

—Truman Capote

Among the Paths to Eden

We see the mark of the genius of diction— no reference to the cliché about a sharp-tongued woman; rather, a newly devised (and active) metaphor *(honing her tongue)* that echoes that familiar cliché. The author couldn't be content here to have her hone her tongue on his vices; he preferred to take advantage of the alliterative potential of *habits* and save vices for later in the sentence. Gentle, unintrusive alliteration like this contributes to the author's style.

Only a person of literary talent would have thought to speak of *a tide of visions that towed to sea the junk of harsher recollections.*

The peacock was following Mrs. Shortley up the road to the hill where she meant to stand. Moving one behind the other, they looked like a complete procession. Her arms were folded and as she mounted the prominence, she might have been the giant wife of the countryside, come out at some sign of danger to see what the trouble was.

—Flannery O'Connor

The Displaced Person

Miss O'Connor deliberately selects the unexpected *meant to stand* because it tells us something early on about that determined woman, Mrs. Shortley. The author reinforces it with the phrase, *she mounted the prominence*. What other verb would have served so well?

In front of the wheelchair was an ancient typewriter, and as he watched, an arm flung itself from the man's body, bending and winding as though it had more joints than it should. Arched at the wrist, rotating, flailing, it swung behind his head. Then the other arm appeared, flying up to meet its fellow, steering by the same incomprehensible stars. As they struggled in the air, the huge head tipped forward on its neck, lolling between the shoulders, and turned to face the right hand, squinting to get it in its sights. With a sudden violent jerk the hand was brought down on the typewriter and, pop, the index finger struck the key. His body slumped and the arms settled slowly, sinuously to his sides.

—Richard Selzer, M.D.

"Fairview" in *The Rituals of Surgery*

A master of description, author Selzer has used active verb forms here to perfection: *flung, bending, winding, rotating, flailing, swung, flying, steering, struggled, tipped, lolling, squinting, slumped,* and *settled.*

In addition to his excellent choice of active verb forms, Dr. Selzer has demonstrated further his talent for finding the best words and phrases with: *as though it had more joints than it should; arched at the wrist; steering by the same incomprehensible stars; squinting to get it in its sights;* and the alliteration that slowly ends the paragraph, *settled slowly, sinuously to his sides.* Our reading rate slows with his rhythm and stops when the arms stop.

Six weeks after I went back to my last year in high school the stock-market crashed, and tolled in modern times. It was this climate in which my head reared itself, beanlike on a pole, for suddenly, on my fifteenth birthday, I was the tallest of my schoolmates. I breathed in the world's ills, not saw them, my eye was enmeshed in the interstices of my own body and displeased with most of its cells, arranged now too vertically; my height was more foolish than my lack of it, and Minnie's calling me "a long drink of water" echoed too aptly my own sense that I was chronically in danger of collapse due to structural weakness. The elastic exerciser I bought to convert myself into a mass of muscles I could barely stretch out, and it dangled on my doorknob unused. I thought it better to die of thinness than of boredom.

—William Gibson

A Mass for the Dead

William Gibson, novelist and playwright of *The Miracle Worker* and *Two for the Seesaw,* is a master of diction. His use of *my head reared itself* echoes in our minds of the cliché *sex rears its ugly head,* with the meaning, "to bring up oneself as a child." At the same time it evokes the familiar image of the sprouting, gangling adolescent. By having this particular bean on a pole, the author leads us to the point that his character is the tallest kid in school. These common, everyday notions are presented to us in fresh ways—the mark of a writer who writes with style.

I can't imagine a more accurate phrase for the image Gibson wants to get across than *it dangled on my doorknob unused.* "Hung on my doorknob" wouldn't have worked. I can even hear the exerciser banging with every opening and closing (slamming) of the teenager's bedroom door.

(3)   Is the verb active?

If it's passive, look askance at it. Can it possibly be made active without ruining your intent? If so, change it.

This whole business becomes clear when we realize that it's not the verb but the *subject* that's active or passive. Almost everyone agrees that most sentences should be active; only rarely should a sentence be passive. When we cast a sentence in which the subject does something, we *see* the action. Our brains and minds work better when they have mental *images* with which to work. Our minds tend to bog down when presented with too many passives or too many abstractions. Abstract notions are most easily comprehended when the writer presents them metaphorically, because metaphors are images from "real life" that vivify (literally, bring to life) the lifeless abstraction. A sentence that speaks with an active voice is heard as well as seen.

As you examine your drafts, watch first for the "voice" of the sentence:

(1)   It bears repeating—pay attention first to the verb. Make sure it's the most accurate one you can find. Don't settle for the first one that comes tumbling out of your mind; keep searching by continually asking yourself just what it is you're trying to say.

(2)   Having found that perfect verb, make sure the *subject* does the acting described by the verb.

(3)   If, no matter how you twist and turn the sentence, the voice comes out passive, try throwing the sentence out and inventing an entirely new one that is active. Yes, it's that important. Many sentences die because they're so passive. If you care about your message (and about your growing reputation as a writer), you'll go to this trouble. After repeated self-discipline, you'll finally write in the active voice from the beginning.

(4)   If all effort fails, however, it probably means that the sentence indeed requires the passive voice. If it does, no amount of revising can make it active while retaining its meaning.

Let's consider a few examples of the difference voice makes:
Original:

> Service is provided to our clients in the form of custom-designed workshops, seminars, etc.

Revised:

> We serve our clients by custom-designing workshops, seminars, etc.

or:

> We custom-design workshops, seminars, etc. for our clients.

Original:

> It is clear that who the psychologist is, as a person, is tremendously significant to effective work with a client.

Revised:

> It is clear that who the psychologist is, as a person, greatly influences his effectiveness with a client.

This is still not a good sentence, and should be reworked totally, but it makes the point about having the subject *(psychologist)* do the acting *(influences)*.

Original:

> McClevy Park is about a block long by one block wide. Even with its small size, the attraction to the people is amazing. All kinds come to the park.

Revised:

> It's amazing how McClevy Park, only a half block long by a block wide, attracts so many kinds of people.

Original:

> Plunking pebbles cast idly by John and Simon broke the early morning stillness and rippled Lake Genesareth's becalmed surface.

Revised:

> John and Simon broke the early morning stillness, casting pebbles idly out into the calm surface of Lake Genesareth.

Original:

> The cattle were driven down the middle of Main Street by a cowboy on horseback.

Revised:

> A cowboy on horseback drove the cattle down the middle of Main
> Street.

A reviser must be aware that the meaning is changed by this revision to an active
subject. Does he want us to focus on the stupid, meandering cattle, or on the
cowboy slumping in his saddle, bored with babysitting the beasts? The writer-
reviser must not change meaning for the sake of creating an active voice.

> The prisoners were herded down the camp's main street by armed
> soldiers on horseback.

Depending on the meaning or mood intended, a reviser could either treat this
sentence the way he did the one about the cattle—*Armed soldiers on horseback
herded the prisoners down the camp's main street*—or, if the writer's intention
is to show how docilely the prisoners had to behave when confronted by armed
guards, the sentence should be left as is—in the passive voice. The subject
(prisoners) were being acted upon by someone else. The subjects were passive.

Notice how the innocent preposition *by* frequently signals the presence of
a passive construction: "Plunking pebbles cast idly *by* John and Simon."
". . .were driven down the middle of Main St. *by* a cowboy;" ". . .herded
. . .*by* armed soldiers."

This tiny "by" flag is not the only clue to passive construction. Unfortunately, other clues can easily elude the reviser. The following word-endings are
not passive in themselves, but they do attract weak verbs and passive constructions: *-ion, -tion, -ment, -ance, -ancy, -ization*. Those are perhaps the worst
culprits that lurk in the vicinity of passivity, showing up frequently in *authorization, determination, administration, implementation, realization, confron-
tation, negotiation, documentation, concession, quotation, announcement,
attention, legislation, cooperation, advancement, elimination, enrollment, development, compilation,* etc.

When you see a word like that on a draft, think first of the verb from which
it probably derived, and try to restore the verb in a reconstructed sentence. Let's
run through a few, just enough to give you the idea:

(a)   The authorization to proceed came from the President.
      The President authorized us to proceed.
(b)   The determination was made by the treasurer to proceed as planned.
      The treasurer determined that we should proceed as planned.

(c)   The concession was made by the union boss that the company was right.
The union boss conceded that the company was right.
(d)   The elimination of waste was suggested by the foreman.
The foreman suggested that we eliminate waste.

You can't tell out of context whether these revisions are appropriate and accurate; you'll have to accept my word that they don't change the meaning or mood. It is always possible that such editing would change the writer's intent, so the reviser must always examine the verbal environment of the sentence.

Original:

Gunfire was heard by the peasants on the floor of the valley.

Revised:

Peasants on the valley floor heard gunfire.

The revised version is more active in that we've made the peasants active subjects. Unless it changes the writer's intent too much, it might be even better to make the original subject (gunfire) do something instead of simply be heard *by* the peasants. When a subject has inherent possibilities for sound, let us hear it: *Gunfire shattered the quiet of the valley floor.* If it is important that the reader know that the peasants heard this shattering gunfire, the writer/reviser would have to work that fact into another sentence.

To wind up our consideration of verbs as the most important part of our diction, let's read what William Bayard Hale had to say about verbs and adjectives in his book, *The Story of Style:*

It is with true instinct that language calls the part of speech which represents action, "the verb"—THE word. The task of speech is to predict, not to paint. The advance of thought is just so swift as verbs carry it. Adjectives qualify, describe, limit. They are a brake, a drag, on the wheel—often necessary in order that advance may be kept in the right track—but not near so often as they are commonly and lazily deemed to be. They are popular, because easy; they eke out effortless poverty of idea. The man who has something to tell has little need, little time, for them; he snaps out his tale in words of action. The thought that pants for deliverance bursts out in verbs. A very little study will show that the world's great storytellers and thinkers have generally written in action-words, not quality-words; some by instinct, some on principle (as Stevenson, for one, confesses) eschewing mention of all but necessary attributes. The artist in language suspects approaching adjectives as he would suspect a possible rogue at the door.

Loren Eiseley, a scientist who wrote with great imagination and style, wrote the following in *The Immense Journey*. As proof that he was a man of careful diction, and a believer in the power of simple words used in the active voice, note that in the paragraph about flying birds he never once uses the expected verb *fly:*

> I saw the flight coming on. It was moving like a little close-knit body of black specks that *danced* and *darted* and *closed* again. It was *pouring* from the north and *heading* toward me with the undeviating relentlessness of a compass needle. It *streamed* through the shadows rising out of the monstrous gorges. It *rushed* over towering pinnacles in the red light of the sun, or momentarily *sank* from sight within their shade. Across that desert of eroding clay and wind-worn stone they *came* with a faint wild twittering that filled all the air about me as those tiny living bullets *hurtled* past into the night.

Nouns/Adjectives/Adverbs

All experienced writers agree that good prose is characterized not only by perfectly selected verbs but also by perfectly selected concrete nouns. Poor writers' and beginning writers' prose is often characterized by poorly selected *verbs* that must lean on adverbs to gain descriptive accuracy, and on poorly selected *nouns* that lean on adjectives for descriptive accuracy. The secret of good prose writing is to try first to express the thought with *only* verbs and nouns. Then, in revision, decide whether they absolutely must be modified to get across the meaning and mood.

One author writing about writing will advocate practically eliminating the use of adjectives; another will rant about excessive adverbs. I aim for a compromise and suggest trying first to write without, or with few, modifiers—and then to be willing to add modifiers only where necessary.

William Bayard Hale said that adjectives hold back the action of the verb the writer has tried so hard to find—and that we should approach each adjective with suspicion. Perhaps so, but we must at the same time view the adjective or adverb objectively. Check its credentials at the gate, but be perfectly willing to let it enter the sentence if it shows itself worthy and necessary to meaning and mood. The impressionist painter's secret is to let the reader fill in for himself, and not describe each tree down to the last leaf. Cultivate your diction so that you have at your command a series of related nouns that might be suitable.

From this collection you will be able to select the best noun, perhaps one so descriptive or accurate that no adjective is called for. You should also develop a store of related verbs, one of which you'll recognize as perfect for the situation of the moment—one that does not require an adverb for accuracy.

Having implied that adjectives and adverbs are second-class citizens, I must backtrack to make clear that accurate adjectives and adverbs, wisely used, can add sparkle and truth.

It is difficult to write interestingly at length about nouns, adjectives, and adverbs. Such a discussion is invariably abstract, and probably dull. It is more informative and interesting to watch these parts of speech as they try to do their work.

Many articles and books on building a powerful vocabulary might be useful, but I think the best advice is to take a keen and lifetime interest in words; listen to how people use words in their speech or writing; make your dictionary your friend and turn to it frequently (not just when you're in trouble); never let a new word go by without looking it up later that day; try using the new word several times during the following week until it comes naturally to mind; and read, read, read, always paying close attention to any words new to you or new uses for a word you already know (or thought you knew). Unless you become a word freak, you'll have trouble making it as a writer.

Appeal to the Senses

As you review a draft with the intention to reword where necessary, look closely at the attention paid to detail. Have you stimulated the reader's mind by including sensory details?

We humans, as much as we may like to ignore it, are animals—higher animals, perhaps, but animals that have survived eons by using our brains to process environmental data coming in through our sensory systems. That makes us sound more like modern machines than ancient animals, but the point is that our sensing apparati are at work twenty-four hours a day. As we became more "advanced" animals, we extended our sensing systems by inventing telescopes, microscopes, television cameras, infrared sensors, x-rays, microphones, robotics, and other means of scanning our environment to enable us to survive as a species. Although we may be evolving away from dependence on our five basic senses (as we have largely done with our sense of smell), we still depend on them for fundamental information about the outside world.

Our writing must reckon with our readers' dependence on sensory data for their thinking. When we read some philosophers and social scientists, we see how difficult it is to understand something new when that writer does nothing to stimulate vicariously any of our five senses. The best writers in those fields fill their writing with sensory data, even if they must employ metaphors.

We'll see later in this section how metaphors are used for this purpose, but let's look first at writing about subjects where sensory information is available. How well you insert this sensory data into your writing, of course, establishes your ability as a writer. If you select the most telling details and work them in well, you'll awaken in the reader the same, or very similar, emotions that you yourself experienced or imagined. That is your goal as a writer.

In the following passage from *Land of the Hibernating Rivers*, I tried to raise in the young reader the feeling of walking in this strange environment. I chose my verbs, nouns, adjectives, and adverbs carefully. Only you can decide whether I succeeded:

> The only break in the monotony of the taiga comes from an occasional, treeless bog or swamp. A stranger to the taiga might run out happily from the frightening forest into the openness of a bog, only to find that the forest had been safer. If the bog happened to be a quaking bog he would be in for a horrible surprise, if not a drowning. A quaking bog is a mat of grasses floating on water that is often deep. The mat looks wet, to be sure, but it looks like ordinary wet, swampy ground. A stranger might walk around for a while just thinking the ground terribly mushy, until he stepped on a weak spot and shot right down through the grassy, floating mat into the cold, black water below.

I appeal to the sense of hearing in the first paragraph—specifically, the *absence* of sound in the terrifyingly silent wood. After saying that the bog "looks" like ordinary wet, swampy ground (sense of sight), I appeal to the sense of touch by presenting the idea of walking around on "mushy" ground. Then I again trigger the sense of touch by mentioning that a person might step on a "weak spot" and shoot down "through the grass" into the "cold" water below. The reference to "black" water adds to the fear most people have of darkness combined with the general fear of drowning. "Quaking bog" happens also to be the technical term used in the area, but I use it deliberately to appeal to the sense of touch, knowing that almost no one wants to stand on moving ground. I use the phrase "shot right down through" to appeal to the kinesthetic sense, the feel of falling.

Let's listen in on the well-known author, Jesse Stuart, as he writes about a sensory experience in *Thanksgiving Hunter:*

> It was comfortable to sit on the rock since the sun was directly above me. It warmed me with a glow of autumn. I felt the sun's rays against my face and the sun was good to feel. But the good fresh au-

tumn air was no longer cool as the frost that covered the autumn grass that morning, nor could I feel it go deep into my lungs; the autumn air was warmer and it was flavored with the scent of pines.

Robert Penn Warren, one of our most distinguished contemporary writers, demonstrates in this paragraph from *The Cave* that he knows how to describe a sensory experience so that we can share it with him:

> Then the silence is over. The locusts begin again, for this is the year of the locust. In fact, there has not been silence at all, for the air has been full of a dry, grinding, metallic sound, so penetrating that it has seemed, paradoxically, to come from within the body, or from some little buzz saw working fiendishly away at the medulla oblongata. It is easy to forget that it is not from inside you, that glittering, jittering, remorseless whir so much part of you that you scarcely notice it, and perhaps love it, until the time when you will really notice it, and scream.

An author I'm coming again to appreciate as a poet of prose, Thornton Wilder, wrote of a Peruvian city in *The Bridge of San Luis Rey:*

> Thither the Marquesa was carried in her chair, crossing the bridge of San Luis Rey and ascending up into the hills toward that city of large-girdled women, a tranquil town, slow-moving and slow-smiling; a city of crystal air, cold as the springs that fed its many fountains; a city of bells, soft and musical, and tuned to carry on with one another the happiest quarrels. If anything turned out for disappointment in the town of Cluxambuqua the grief was somehow assimilated by the overwhelming imminence of the Andes and by the weather of quiet joy that flowered in and about the side-streets. No sooner did the Marquesa see from a distance the white walls of this town perched on the knees of the highest peaks than her fingers ceased turning the beads and the busy prayers of her fright were cut short on her lips.

Wilder demonstrates through this passage his excellent diction, but some phrases are particularly outstanding as examples for our present discussion: *crystal air; cold as the springs; carry on with one another the happiest quarrels; overwhelming imminence; weather of quiet joy that flowered; perched on the knees.* The verbs *flowered* and *perched* are so descriptive in themselves that they need no adverbs to modify them. The choice of *happiest quarrels* and *weather of quiet joy* shows us that we're in the presence of great style.

Dr. Richard Selzer of the Yale University Medical School writes (in his story, "Korea") with much sensorial detail about a young American doctor working in Korea and very much in love with a patient, Shin. She is leading him to her ill uncle's hut. The doctor is also ill:

> She did not turn to see if he followed. He was ablaze with fever. Shin turned off the road and into a path between water-filled rice paddies. A length of elevated footpaths separated the pools and wound toward the smoky village below. He could see the red sky reflected in the water, dotted by the sprouts of rice. The frogs were beginning their evening cacophony, belching richly in the paddies. The rotten overripe smells of kimchi and night soil were strangely stimulating. The path coiled and uncoiled before them, turning capriciously one way, then taking an agonizing backtrack, plunging boldly forward only to swing tauntingly in a new direction. He felt that he could not bear it, that tantalizing path, that solemn promenade; that he must run, take her hand, and lead her into the darkening fields before his strength left him and was too weak to go on.

The accurate verb *wound* gives us an immediate image, an overview of the scene with the village below wreathed in the smoke from the evening cooking fires. We are reminded of the time by the red reflections, and again by the early-evening sounds of frogs. Selzer's frogs *belch richly*. Even though we may not know what *kimchi* is, we are given a feel for it by Selzer's modifiers, *rotten* and *overripe*. The winding character of the path is described more accurately now as *coiling* and *uncoiling*. The young doctor's mood is described for us indirectly; we are given his attitude toward the path through the words *capricious, agonizing,* and *taunting*. There is also a case in which a highly descriptive noun, *promenade,* is deemed insufficient—solemn promenade is the result.

In my analyses of these passages I have referred to elements of good writing in addition to the sensory details the passages describe, because one element of good writing never stands alone. A piece of good, unified writing is always a fabric woven of many threads of technique. Woven tight, they are never discernible by the reader. He simply ends up with an emotional intellectual experience that approximates what the writer intended. This condition is explained much better by Morrison Philipson in his foreword to *Jacques Barzun on Writing, Editing, and Publishing:*

> The metaphor in the phrase "clarity of expression" names the condition that enables one to "see through" [the words] flawlessly to what is meant. Where transparency of the medium is coupled with density of thought or richness of feeling, Barzun argues, the contrast yields eloquence, the greatest power inherent in the artful use of language.

Concrete Details

Stendhal was the first novelist to specify that it's the little truth, *le petit fait vrai*, that makes for larger truth. His own prose was packed with *les petits faits vrais*, little truths. One means of presenting the little truths is to use concrete details. Whether you are writing fiction or nonfiction, this is good advice. Fiction requires concrete details to give an air of reality; nonfiction requires it for clarity and authority.

Even in pieces that are necessarily abstract, the wise writer will use concrete words that evoke images and breathe life into abstract concepts. Prefer the concrete, detailed "tattered rags," to the abstract, general "clothing"; "dregs of the city" to "men and women"; "ramshackled, windowless hovel" to "house." Concrete is real, specific, actual. Use concrete words to put us in *touch* with life. "Touch" is an apt metaphor because we can almost touch or "get the feel of" words that are concrete. Even the metaphor "concrete" is apt—what could be more solid, more real, more tactile, than concrete?

The advice to use concrete detail is implied also in the even clearer advice usually phrased as "show, don't tell." When editors, teachers, and other critics tell us to "be specific," they are usually telling us to use concrete detail. Someone else, usually a professor, might tell us to "develop our mimesis"—*mimic* life more closely, more accurately, more concretely. Few bits of literary advice are more valuable; follow them.

One flag to watch for when revising is the word *picturesque*. This is a perfect example of how easy it is to lean on abstractions. Stop and think about what *picturesque* means in this sentence:

> At one point on Route 138 she could see the bridge, and beyond that the picturesque city that was her destination.

If the reader has never seen that city, what is he or she to make of *picturesque?* The writer who put picturesque in this sentence had his own picture of the city in mind while writing, but forgot that *picturesque* doesn't begin to reproduce an image for the reader.

Even if the unique, visual characteristics of the city are not significant to the story and the writer wants merely to make a general point, he could (at least) have referred to the city's pattern of winding, narrow streets outlined by lights; to its geometrical pattern of straight streets accentuated by the sodium lights coming on; to the strings of yellow Christmas-tree lights looping along the roads; or to the rows of pink stucco houses surrounding the cathedral that was the character's destination in Lisbon. If it is truly not worth the thought necessary to describe the city, the reference to the city's "picturesque" appearance should be left out: *From a point on Route 138 she could see the bridge, and beyond that the city, her destination.* One kind of story would call for the latter; another story would benefit from some concrete description. *No* story calls for *picturesque.*

The reviser is not always alerted to the need for concrete detail by the *picturesque* flag; sometimes it is something left unsaid:

> "Have you ever been up here in the Skytop Lounge before?" "No," Kelly said quietly, "and I love it." "You know you can see the whole city of Boston from different points up here," Larry said, trying to sound knowledgeable.
> Larry turned around to pick up his drink, and noticed the other man next to Kelly.

When the writer writes that Larry tried to sound knowledgeable, he is setting up in the reader an anticipation that Larry will point out some Boston sights—then, nothing.

This is an example of two faults: Obviously, the writer should never create expectations in the reader's mind without following through. The fault of concern to us here, however, is the lack of concrete details. Don't *tell* us that we can see the whole city of Boston; *show* us the city. Have Larry take Kelly by her shoulders and face her toward the towering Prudential Building, the gold dome of the State House gleaming in the spotlights, and the blackness of the Commons and the Public Gardens criss-crossed by lighted paths. If such descriptive passages slow the story or are irrelevant to the story, don't let Larry make false promises in the first place.

Akin to *picturesque* is the summary phrase that is supposed to "describe" a scene for us:

> If I don't look down as I gaze out the window, I see a winter-woodsy scene that makes me feel lonely and cold and glad that I'm inside standing on my wooly rug.

Winter-woodsy is cutesy, and not much better than *picturesque.* The writer shows some promise with "standing on my wooly rug." That phrase could have been even more concrete had she been "curling her toes" in the wooly rug. The writer-reviser's job is to make us feel life as it is, if we're to believe what he or she is telling us (fiction and nonfiction). The most direct access to our emotions is through our senses. The visual sense, of course, is the human animal's preeminent sense, but the good writer will also find ways and words to vibrate our other senses vicariously.

> Dozens of chandeliers covered the ceiling. They were of modest size, but to Kelly they were awesome.

The first sentence "tells" us that there were chandeliers, and apparently many of them, on the ceiling, but the reader is not left with an image. The thought has been *ex*pressed, but the image has not been *im*pressed upon the cells of memory. Did the chandeliers literally or figuratively cover the ceiling? Were they all the same shape? Were they suspended on long chains? Did they have thousands of tiny bulbs, or several in the center whose images were magically multiplied by layers upon layers of refracting globules of glass? Were they in tiers? If they were awesome to Kelly, don't we the readers, deserve to see and feel that awesomeness? If the ceiling is not significant enough for the writer to describe, then he shouldn't lead us to great expectations by telling us the chandeliers are awesome—he might as well take the easy way out and call the room picturesque.

> "Let me help, Monica. Brooding won't do you any good. We can handle any problems together," Ted gushed.

Don't *tell* us that Ted gushed. *Show* us his gushing. Give us a gushing sentence or two and we'll discover for ourselves that he gushes. This advice just barely belongs in the category of concrete details, but it again makes a point that can hardly be made too often: *Use words that place us in the scene.* Don't make us observers only; make us participants with every technique you can muster.

If it's dialogue, give us real-people words; if it's a nervous girl at an Officer's Club party, don't have her "pick nervously at paper cups and Kleenex"; have her "scallop the rims of paper coffee cups or shred innocent Kleenex." If it's a freighter in the Arctic, don't have it "deliver to three Eskimo villages"; have the "*Baie du Nord* off-load annual supplies at Ivujivik, Inoudjouac, and Povungnituk." If the character falls onto a sandstone ledge, make it bruise *us* as well as the character: "The crystals of eroded-out quartz grind and abrade his knees and knuckles."

The writer's conscious and unconscious are forever interrupting and asking questions about what's going down on the paper. Here are several more questions the writer must continually ask—and answer:

(1)   Have I used the verb that comes as close as possible to giving the reader an "image" of the action—without requiring an adverb to make it work?

(2)   Have I used nouns that come as close as possible to describing the subject (or object) without requiring one or more adjectives? Do the nouns paint images, or are they merely vague abstractions?

(3)   Have I become so carried away in an attempt at accuracy that I've used too many parenthetical explanations, modifiers, and clauses— does my piece read like a legal brief? What can I safely leave to the reader's imagination? Is it crucial to what I'm saying that the reader know everything and that everything be known with precision?

(4)   Have I made my writing "live" by stimulating the reader's several senses, or have I relied too often on the visual—or have I not even done that?

Rhythm and Sound

When revising by rewording, revise for rhythm and sound, for these elements are central to our understanding and our enjoyment of words. Sound and rhythm are natural features of our language, yet some writers tend to ignore them.

Dr. S.I. Hayakawa wrote: "From the primitive beat of the tomtom to the most subtle delicacies of civilized poetry and music, there is a continuous development and refinement of man's responsiveness to rhythm." Rhythm has affected us from our earliest evolutionary beginnings. We feel the rhythms of the seasons; the rising and setting of the sun, moon, and other circadian rhythms; the tidal rhythms; and menstrual cycles. Even closer to us than these are the perpetual pulses of our own circulatory and respiratory systems.

Language has evolved with vocal rhythms, partly because the ancient storyteller found better audience responses to expressions that may, at first, have been accidentally rhythmical. He soon learned, as speakers and comics still do, to pace his presentations to gain certain effects. Stories told with the most "satisfying" sounds and rhythms were remembered easiest and longest.

What we fail largely to admit today is that the most satisfying words are the ones best understood, longest remembered, and most easily recalled. The earliest storytellers perfected their use of sound and rhythm over the centuries until, with the development of written language, oral storytellers became writers. At first, of course, the written word followed the forms of the spoken word—in rhythmic verse and poetry.

As society became more and more ''sophisticated,'' more and more business-oriented, it could no longer depend so heavily on oral communication. There were too many people to communicate with, making written communication essential. The older verse forms could not serve the needs of everyday business and commerce. Verse was not precise enough; it required too much time for reflection to allow its meaning to be interpreted efficently. It is the nature of poetry and verse to impart double or multiple meanings, quite deliberately; and life was beginning to require that words mean one thing and one thing only. We have yet to achieve this goal of efficiency, but today's "business English" tries hard to use unambiguous words.

As the need for precision and efficiency arose along with the increasing time pressures born of science and technology, written forms departed further and further from the natural forms of sound and rhythm. Rhythm and sound combine to form music—and it is music that is missing from our prose today (even from much of our poetry). It would be hopelessly romantic to plead for as much music in memo writing as there is in psalm writing, but there are ways you can write, or revise your writing, that will restore some of the satisfying sounds and rhythms. At least you can use the tomtom of old to overcome that drum of so much writing today, the humdrum.

If you write for business, you may be wondering how this discussion of sound and rhythm has anything to do with you. It has everything to do with you. It is so-called business writing (used in the business of education and politics as well as industry) that continues to beat away on the humdrum. Part of the solution lies in what is about to be said about rhythm and sound.

Not surprisingly, business people, educators, and politicians are, like everyone else, human animals. As such, their bodies and minds respond and react to what is fundamental, basic, human—sound and rhythm. They, too, felt on their mother's bosom the steady beat of the heart, and the gentle, soothing rise and fall of that bosom. The rocking rhythm of parental bodies or cradle motions continued the "satisfying" rhythms of the womb felt from the earliest stages of awareness. Is it any wonder that we are all affected, to one degree or another, by the rhythms of what we hear and read.

Much of what other writers and I lecture about business writing—that brevity and succinctness are requisite to clarity—misses the boat. Brevity may make for clarity; it does not make for music. Without at least a trace of music, words do not strike so deep. They glance off the surface. Short and concise as some writing is, it is not easily remembered. We all remember readily the phrase *quality versus quantity.* Have you noticed how frequently that duo comes up, even in the most boringly dull reports and journal articles? It's not just the idea behind them that accounts for their frequent appearances—it's also the combined effect of their alliterative sounds and identical rhythms (three syllables with the accent on the first). It's no surprise that this phrase, as cliché as it is, is used so often. It sounds too beautiful and is too wonderfully useful to die so soon.

There are not many such phrases in the language, so how can we get music into our work? Admittedly, there is a danger of putting too much music into our business prose, so we should proceed with our ears wide open. Prose should not be too poetic; neither should it be too prosaic.

The secret of making our writing less prosaic lies largely with repetition. Repetition is the basis of rhythm, whether in music, painting, or writing. It has been said that without repetition there is no art. Rhythm, rhyme, and alliteration work their magic through repetition. There are three main methods for achieving rhythm and satisfying sounds in our writing:

(1)   Vary your sentence lengths.
(2)   Vary your sentence forms.
(3)   Vary the sounds within your sentences.

(1) Vary your sentence length

Variation in sentence length is the fundamental rhythm of speech in all languages. Writing that does not resemble the rhythm of human speech will not succeed. That is why so much business, academic, and governmental writings go unread; if read, they go uncomprehended; if comprehended, they go unheeded, because such writing does not move us.

There are no firm rules for rhythm in writing. There is only one guideline: Vary the lengths of sentences. Everyone supposes he varies his sentence lengths—after all, he makes no attempt to keep them the same length, so they must be varied. The truth of the matter is that sentences written by untrained writers, regardless of the level of their formal education, tend to vary only slightly. The problem is intensified by the highly educated, who tend to write very long sentences, and they don't vary their sentence lengths enough. Two strikes against the writer (and the reader).

During the revising process, it is wise to keep checking variation in sentence length. If the variation is slight, take the trouble to dig in and improve it. Sometimes, it's simply a matter of changing a comma to a period and making an adjustment in the verb, or whatever is necessary, to end up with two shorter sentences in place of an ungainly long one. If sentences are getting too short and choppy, look for ways to change a period to a comma (or to a pair of commas) to convert one short sentence into a clause within a now longer, more graceful sentence.

How long is a "long sentence"; how short a short? After a lot of reading and analysis, I'm going to crawl out on a weak limb and say straight out that only a genius can write three forty-word sentences in a row without losing his reader totally. If you don't claim genius, don't write forty-word sentences. If a thought absolutely cries out for great length, do two things: (1) craft it carefully and test it carefully aloud (Do you run out of breath? Do you keep wanting to pause?); and (2) follow it up quickly with a short sentence, an emphatic one. By short, I mean a sentence that's perhaps a fourth or even an eighth as long. Follow up a forty-word beauty with a ten-word gem. Sometimes, an extremely short one will come to mind. Use it. See?

To illustrate several points about rhythm, I've graphed the varying sentence lengths of eighteen successive sentences from works by four very successful authors. The varied up-and-down undulations are apparent in these examples. In my experiences with business and education writers, their sentences cluster toward the top of the graph. There would be many forty- and fifty-word monstrosities leavened only slightly by an equal number of twenty- and thirty-word jobs.

WISE BLOOD
by Flannery O'Connor

Average length   15.3 words
Longest sentence   40 words
Shortest sentence   5 words

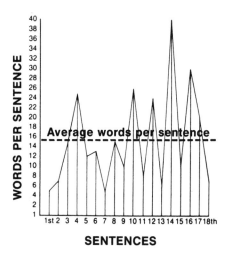

PYTHON
by William Braden

Average length   13.6 words
Longest sentence   39 words
Shortest sentence   1 word

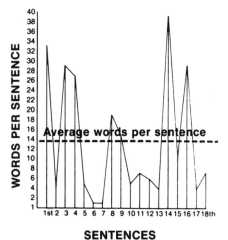

THE URBAN COWBOY
and THE STRANGER
by Herbert Gold

Average length   13 words
Longest sentence   40 words
Shortest sentence   1 word

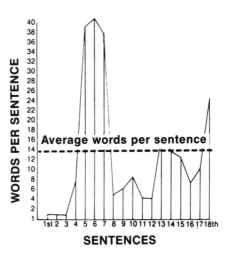

OF MICE AND MEN
by John Steinbeck

Average length   15.2 words
Longest sentence   35 words
Shortest sentence   6 words

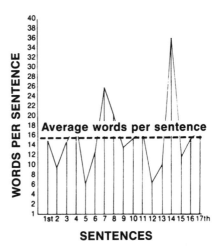

The average sentence length for educated writers (but ones *without* good training in writing) will run around twenty-five words. Notice, by way of contrast, that these four professional writers have averaged only about fifteen words per sentence. Not that they never have long sentences. They do, but they're always relieved, as soon as the subject allows, by one or more short to extremely short sentences. It's the average that's important—and the word-spread between the long and the short. The spread-ratios for these four are: 40 words in the longest sentence to five in the shortest, 39/1, 40/1, and 35/6. If as you spot-check your own writing in revision, you find your average above twenty (which is not too terribly long) but your word-spread ratio resembles 30/

20, take that as a warning. These numbers are all very imprecise measures of rhythm, but they are handy warning flags.

Do not presume, as many highly educated men and women seem to do, that fairly short average lengths indicate amateurish writing. I graphed articles and stories from *Atlantic, Harper's,* and *Saturday Review* to find what some of our most "literate" magazines thought was a reasonable average length. They all came close to averaging fifteen words per sentence. This, coupled with a good spread-ratio, yields rhythms resembling the four graphed here.

(2) Vary your sentence forms

Sample the pages of your first draft, and analyze five consecutive sentences from each of ten randomly selected pages. Do they tend to have the same form, varying only occasionally? Are they almost all "simple," "loose," or "periodic"? If one form totally predominates, you may have a problem.

A *simple sentence* is just that—there's nothing complex about it. A simple sentence is simply one that has one grammatically independent statement in it. The subject or the verb may be compound, but there must be no subordinated clause. Although simple sentences are frequently short, they need not be; e.g., "There was a lot of horsing around, fake fighting, and laughter—lots of laughter." Our writings would be a lot less interesting if no other sentence structures were available. Fortunately, there's a variety available beyond the simple.

The *periodic sentence* interrupts its basic point to add in details before ending the basic statement. Because of the delay between our reading the beginning of the sentence's basic point and its completion at the end of the sentence, and having to hold it in temporary memory storage while we wade through the interrupting details, there is an element of suspense until the end. Everyone enjoys a little suspense. Actually, we do not like the suspense itself so much as the relief of the long-awaited closure. The delay holds our attention and keeps us reading, so the periodic sentence does have its own value. The point is that it has the additional value of providing variety that contributes to rhythm in a paragraph. As with most good things, however, we can take only so much. Don't follow a suspenseful sentence with a suspenseful sentence, *ad infinitum.*

> The anonymous review, which suggests total judgment by an infallible institution, and in fact makes possible either cowardly assault or craven praise by the faceless keypuncher, has gradually slipped from favor with increasing sophistication.

The basic point of this sentence could be stated as: *The anonymous review has gradually slipped from favor with the increase in sophistication.* The writer

(Herbert Gold, writing in the *Atlantic*) chose to make the thought clearer and more emphatic by interrupting the basic statement with several explanatory thoughts before completing his basic point near the period (hence the *periodic* sentence).

A *loose sentence* makes its basic point early on, and then adds details, strung out like freight cars behind the locomotive. The majority of English sentences are of this loose variety, but your paragraphs should be relieved and made rhythmical by adding some other forms, such as the periodic sentence.

> The village appeared all but empty, for despite a diminishing salmon run, three-quarters of the families were away from home, working briefly in the canneries.

Paul Brooks's basic point here is stated in the first six words; the explanatory material is strung loosely after. In the same paragraph of his *Atlantic* article, "Warning: The Chain Saw Cometh," Paul Brooks used the following periodic sentence:

> The frame houses and even the white church on the hill—topped by the ancient cross of Russian orthodoxy—were built on piles.

Later in the same paragraph, contributing to its rhythm, he used the following sentence in a "loose" form. The basic point about the hope for the future lying with the school is followed "loosely" by details of the situation:

> What hope there is for the future seems to lie in the modern, well-run school, where talented young teachers from around the country seek to introduce these children from another age—many of whom have never been off the island—to the frighteningly complex world around them.

By varying his sentence lengths (11, 17, 17, 18, 18, 11, 8, 4, 17, 26, 22, 14, 10, 9, 32, 9, 7), by keeping the average sentence length reasonably short (14.7 words), and by having a good spread between longest and shortest sentences (32/4), Mr. Brooks made a rather long paragraph easily readable.

Fortunately we're not limited to only these three forms: simple, loose, and periodic. We can also combine the latter two as the ear demands—we can have "somewhat loose" sentences and sentences that are "a bit" periodic. These are not "official" sentence forms; they are simply examples of how flexible sentences can be—and how differently rhythmic, both in themselves and as they interact with others in a paragraph. Any sentence but the simplest has parts that can be (and should be) juggled around until they "sound" right to your interior ear. The best way to train your ear is to read aloud and listen to the rhythms—especially for the stumbling blocks. If you stumble, so will many of your readers.

> Miriam was suddenly, surprisingly antagonistic.

You might informally classify this sentence as "a bit periodic." The basic point is that Miriam was antagonistic, but by inserting *suddenly* and *surprisingly* in the midst of the point, the point is delayed—a tiny bit of "suspense" is created before the thought is completed at the period. The sentence qualifies, but just barely, as a periodic sentence (as does this one).

You could add rhythmic variety by adding to that sentence and making it more completely periodic:

> Miriam, a usually cooperative person, suddenly became increasingly antagonistic, so surprisingly antagonistic that we all worried about her mental health.

Further rhythmic variety could be achieved by reversing the sentence:

> We worried about Miriam's mental health as we watched this usually cooperative person become increasingly antagonistic.

A writer will not, of course, add irrelevant or inaccurate statements just to vary the rhythm. He will go to the trouble, however, of pulling some words or ideas out of another sentence to combine them for a better effect in a now more rhythmic, more periodic sentence.

(3) Vary the sounds within your sentences

Just as we are subconsciously satisfied by rhythm in what we read, we are additionally satisfied by sound. When we write prose we are not writing poetry, but poetry does not have territorial rights to rhythm and sound. I like to think that my phrase in the first sentence above, "subconsciously satisfied by rhythm in what we read," is more satisfying than if I had expressed the same thought more prosaically as "Rhythm satisfies our subconscious . . ."

It is important that a sentence not be so lovely as to make the reader stop, the way you might stop to admire a line in a poem. It should satisfy you subconsciously, not consciously.

In that same sentence there is some *alliteration* in the repetition of the initial consonant *s*'s; some *assonance* in the final vowel sounds of *satisfied* and *by;* some delayed alliteration in the initial *r* sounds of *rhythm* and *read;* an alliterative string in, "*what we* read, *we*"; some additional assonance in the long *e* sounds of "*we re*ad, *we*"; and some alliteration in the initial consonants of "*satisfied by sound*" is made even more musical by the consonance of the final consonants in "satisfie*d*" and "soun*d*." I deliberately inserted the word *additionally* ahead of *satisfied* to echo *subconsciously satisfied*, providing coherence to the sentence while contributing to its music. The repetition of *we are* also adds to coherence while providing a bit of rhythm (just as we are subconsciously satisifed by rhythm in what we read, we are additionally satisfied by sound).

It's time for a confession. I did not start out deliberately to compose the music that finally came to that first sentence. The first half of the sentence just came out of typewriter without any conscious effort to make it "beautiful to the ear." The point is that I recognized its potential as soon as I heard it, and began to worry about how to make the second half (after the comma) live up to the first half. My first attempt came out (following the comma) as *we are moved by sound*. When I read the entire sentence, *Just as we are subconsciously satisfied by rhythm in what we read, we are moved by sound,* I could hear the rhythm go to pieces as the comma was passed—and the sounds of the second half did nothing for me.

In my second attempt to repair (i.e., revise) the second half, I substituted *satisfied* for *moved*. I did that for the purpose of coherence, echoing back to the *satisfied* of the first half. When I heard it alliterate so well with the final word, *sound,* I knew it was the right word. It satisfied two elements of good writing—coherence and sound—but the rhythm was wrong.

In my third attempt at revision (and this was all before deciding to use the sentence as an example for you), I inserted *also: we are also satisfied by sound.* Not too bad, but my ear was not completely happy until I came up with *additionally satisfied.* When I realized that it not only patched up the rhythm but echoed attractively back to *subconsciously satisfied,* I knew I had a sentence that satisfied me and, I hoped, you.

I had written the second sentence of that initial paragraph before the thought came that I might use the first sentence as an example of what I intended to say about varying sounds within the sentence. I definitely did not go through all those analyses of alliteration, assonance, and consonance while I composed the sentence. I realized all that was going on within that sentence only in the process of explicating it for you.

I must emphasize, lest you throw up your hands in frustration, that I've gone into that long analysis only for those readers interested in the creative process itself. I don't intend to imply that a writer *consciously* goes through this complex process with each sentence he or she writes. There are times (like this) when a writer wants a sentence or paragraph to be as excellent as he can possibly make it. In this case, I wanted to give my readers a real example and what lay behind it. In the case of a query letter, for example, I would also go through that much analysis and conscious thought to impress the potential publishers with my abilty to handle words. A short query letter takes me days and days to write. Queries, it seems to me, are the most "important" things writers write. If they don't work, I don't work. Thousands of dollars and a reputation may well be at stake in a disarmingly short query letter. If you can move the editor, he or she will presume that you're going to move an audience—and an audience moves books.

You would develop terminal block, however, if you wrote every first draft with all these musical properties in the forefront of your mind. Rather, listen to the inner ear during the first draft and follow its suggestions. It may serve up too many alliterative phrases, but let 'em come, corny or not. By giving the natural, music-loving mind free rein, you enable it to come up with new and unanticipated words, simply through the associational paths lit by the lamps of alliteration. It's in the revision process that you can return to fully conscious control and eliminate any ludicrously long, though lovely, alliterations. Some will be saved, some modified, some deleted, but the result will have the touch of music that goes even in prose. Whoops, there goes one that would have to go, if I were writing an annual report for a conservative corporation. I'd keep other, more subtle touches of rhythm, rhyme, and sound in an annual report, but I know they'd never go for, *goes even in prose.*

Sometimes the rhythm of a sentence can be dramatically improved by a very small change:

Original:

> She was normally a shy person, but tonight she knew she couldn't afford to be.

Revised:

> Normally a shy person, she knew she couldn't afford to be, not to-
>
> night.

> "Then, if the sun was warm and the air lazy, and if the children were

off in the sandpile with their trucks and cars and shovels and pails
of water, she'd stay with him on the stoop."

The writer, Joan Johnson, had an enjoyable rhythm going with the list of toys (and I agreed that it was better for using the gramatically excess *ands*), but two words, *of water,* ruined it for me. It was not critical that the pails contain water; they were better empty and rhythmic. The writer was writing with her eye (she saw those pails with water sloshing around in them), but a writer must also write with the ear. If there had been no problem of rhythm, she might as well have let the water slosh. Writers must maintain continual dialogues between interior eye and ear.

The same writer shows in her drafts and revisions that her interior ear is acute:

Original:

> Just a series of events, a snarled, cluttered montage of feelings and
> a growing, not yet overwhelming sense of dread.

Look at the increased sense of dread she accomplishes by an ever-so-slight change in rhythm (a pause) in her revised draft:

Revised:

> Just a series of events, a snarled, cluttered montage of feelings and
> a growing, not yet overwhelming, fear.

Listen to how that final comma forces you to use a new rhythm, thus accentuating the final *fear.* An even smaller change in the next example improves the rhythm and, by so doing, enhances the mood the writer seeks to create:

> The subdued lighting gave an aura of elegance, graciousness, and
> tranquility.

The emphasis on tranquility is enhanced by the even, plodding rhythm forced by deleting *and.*

I wouldn't swear that my revised rhythm is an improvement in the next example, but there is a change of rhythm (and I believe of mood) brought about by the slight revision:

> She knew that he'd come each day, probably until late November
>
> when the last calf was scheduled for market. And then Robinhurst
>
> would ~~silently~~ await ∧ the winter snows.

(handwritten above "silently": in silence; caret inserted before "the")

Those small revisions improve the sentence's rhythm, and the sentence is made even more satisfying to the inner ear by the repetitive *s* sounds in *silence* and *snow*. Those two *s* sounds echo in our subconscious the sounds of snow and sleet against the shutters of Robinhurst.

Sometimes a sentence has a rhythm that's too choppy, too staccato, for the sense. In some cases, a writer deliberately writes in a staccato rhythm, but in the following example it serves only to induce hiccups:

Original:

> I exposed five to six rolls of film a week, on the average, and by the end of May, I had amassed 1500 negatives.

Revised:

> I exposed an average of five to six rolls of film a week, amassing by the end of May some 1500 negatives.

Sound

The second component of sentence music is sound. We tend to think that only poets worry about the sounds words make, but good prose writers are playing tunes in our minds all the time. They're usually so subtle, like carefully wrought rhythm, that we're not consciously aware of what the writer is doing to us. All we know is that we like reading one writer better than another. It may be that the ones we like are artfully playing on our interior strings, creating sounds that take us back to the happy days of childhood when everyone spoke in rhyming rhythms—and, some would say, all the way back to the ancient days when all writing was in the form of poetry, ballad, and verse.

The art today comes about by working in rhythms and sounds so that the reader-listener is not too consciously aware of it. Language too obviously musical is considered today suspect, unserious, unbusinesslike, childish.

Naturally, this does not hold true for writers creating children's books, songs, light verse, poetry, and other forms of what are usually (and not too accurately) lumped together as "creative writing." These forms rely for much of their beauty and effectiveness on artfully rendered rhythms and sounds.

Writers know, however, that musical language still contributes to the understanding, persuasion, and enjoyment of other forms, and therefore they find ways to produce subtly musical writing. We've discussed at length their techniques for working in rhythm. Now we will take a less extensive look (listen) at the methods available for working in the sounds that satisfy.

Like the truly musical writer, the poet, the prose writer may select words that sound (more or less) like what they describe: *blast, ping, hush, crunch, snap, crackle,* and *pop*. Since onomatopoetic words like these convey their sense by their very sound, the brain handles them more efficiently and effectively. They are the opposite of abstractions—they mimic reality closely. The brain has "real" concrete words filed under many different associational files, so finding them quickly is easy. If a word can also be filed by its sound as an aural metaphor of its sense, so much the better. I suggested the following revision strictly for sound, but the writer had to decide for himself whether the revision did for the interior ear what I thought it did.
Original:

> The house remained stubborn. After a moment, she closed and locked the windows, crunching dead fly bodies.

Revised:

> . . . After a moment, she closed and locked the windows, crunching the fly husks that littered the sills.

The writer was on the right trail with the use of "crunching," but the sound image is now amplified by the crispier, crunchier rasp of "husks." This revision did not make a more "beautiful" sentence—it did make for a more accurate, true-to-life sentence. Incidentally (but not accidentally), I tried to make my explanation of onomatopoeia more "satisfying" to your interior ear by using onomatopoeia myself—"the crispier, crunchier rasp of husks." Notice that it was not the use of sound for sound's sake, but to reinforce the aural image—and that must always be the case. I used "rasp" in that context because it added to the sounds surrounding it, and because "rasp" is itself onomatopoetic.

I think no one would object to the use of "husks" or "rasps of husks" in prose, yet it is deliberately "musical." The same people who might say that poetry, rhythm, and sound have little place in prose writing would probably prefer that revised version to:

... she closed and locked the windows, crunching dead fly bodies.

That latter sentence is an excellent example of one that *expresses* the thought but does not *impress* the thought on our brain cells so permanently as the more "poetic" one that crunches fly husks. Serious writers (as distinct from writers of serious stuff) know the value of rhythm married to sound—music. The writer must be wary of the possibility, however, that if the sentence is too powerful in its image-making, it may detract from the main point of the paragraph as a whole.

Figurative Writing

It seems to me a paradox, or at least an interesting realization, that the more important, the deeper, the more basic, the more truly essential a thought is, the less useful a dictionary becomes in trying to find words to express it. It's almost always true for the poet who usually seeks to express the essences of life; it's frequently true for the creative writer; and it is sometimes true even for the journalist. All writers need to "get beyond" literal writing and turn to more figurative writing.

Using figurative language comes natural to us humans. We use it in informal speech every day; it's only when some people turn to the written word that they put aside the figurative. They've been taught—if not explicitly, then implicitly by example—that you can only write accurately by using dictionary-correct words. It's true that most ordinary matters can be adequately described and discussed using words as defined in dictionaries, or as understood by the parties involved in the communication, but there will be times when these literal definitions will be inadequate. Before we go further, let's remind ourselves by some examples just what figurative language is:

- The hidden depths and unsuspected shallows were exactly what he loved her for: no one ever fell in love with a canal.
- He was a bull in a china shop.
- A dumpy, fat little steamer rolled itself along like a sailor on shore.
- This proposal is not yet chiseled in stone.
- My objections are not set in concrete.
- Lars squirreled away his leftover change.
- This was about to become her Watergate.
- He flew off the handle.
- The whole business was going down the drain.
- She's in music; he's in upholstery.
- He fell into the depths of depression.

It's easy to see from serious and trivial examples alike that everyone uses figurative language because it works—it makes the point without long, tedious explanations. Imagine how many words you'd have to use to describe the actions of a boy behaving like a bull in a china shop. Try using literal words to describe the attitude of the man in the first example toward the woman he loves.

Figurative language is perfectly natural to us because we think largely by figures, i.e., images. If you doubt that, try to imagine how people were able to think before language developed. We undoubtedly thought then much as we do now, through stored memories of images previously seen, smelled, felt, and heard. To understand some new, unprecedented thing, we had to tap our memories for old things the new things were like. As we learned more characteristics of this new thing, we filed them away in various brain cells—and we also crossed-filed them along with the old, similar things. If the new thing reminded us of some old thing that was opposite to, or in great contrast with it, we'd also cross-file the new along with the old, dissimilar object or idea. (I realize I'm covering in a very few words some very weighty and not totally agreed-upon theories of brain and mind evolution, but it must do for the moment.)

After language came along, we had little other than these stored images to work with to invent words, so we worked from the images (figures) stored in our collective brains. Today, most people have their language ability in their left brain hemisphere, while their imagery (imaginative) ability resides in the right. Electrical measurements of the two hemispheres show that when the brain is asked to solve a problem—any kind of problem—the right hemisphere becomes electrically active immediately; the left lags, checking first for solutions from the right—the older, intuitive hemisphere. If our earlier selves were used to thinking (solving problems) by the imagistic right, it doesn't seem surprising that we would continue to look hopefully to the right first—and then resort to asking the Johnny-come-lately left.

Brain research shows that people use both hemispheres cooperatively, allowing each to do what it does better. Research also shows that people seem to fall into three major categories: (1) those who depend for survival predominantly on the linear, logical, verbal machinations of the left hemisphere; (2) those who lean heavily for their problem-solving (survival in general) on the intuitive, imagistic, musical, poetic, pattern-recognizing right hemisphere; and (3) those who have a more balanced use of both hemispheres, neither one predominating.

That was a long (yet terribly abbreviated) way to explain why we should use more and better *figurative* language in our writing—even though this runs counter to what many writing counselors are saying today. They seem to think that writing—especially writing for corporations, governments, and educational institutions—should be clear and concise above all else. Those who go overboard in that direction are missing the boat. The point is that writing for those professions should not be merely clear and concise; rather, it should be designed to do the job intended.

It should be obvious that a great, long list of rules and regulations clearly and concisely presented in an organization's policy manual might not move employees to change their behavior—because the words are all literal, precise, unemotional, non-imagistic words. There was probably no attempt in the manual to inspire, to cajole, to explain in everyday figurative language how such a change in behavior could affect their paychecks.

Naturally, a corporate writer could not write so figurative a paragraph as the one quoted below, but it is one unified, coherent paragraph that exemplifies rather efficiently some of the main forms of figurative writing. The paragraph is from *The Immense Journey* by Loren Eiseley, the anthropologist so noted for his clear explanations of science and his philosophical speculations.

He wrote "The Flow of the River" for his readers to feel an experience he had—and that's the purpose of figurative writing. So relax and try to experience vicariously floating naked along a short, lonely stretch of the Platte River several hundred miles from its source high in the Rockies.

> . . . then I lay back in the floating position that left my face to the sky, and shoved off. The sky wheeled over me. For an instant, as I bobbed into the main channel, I had the sensation of sliding down the vast tilted face of the continent. It was then that I felt the cold needles of the alpine springs at my fingertips, and the warmth of the Gulf pulling me southward. Moving with me, leaving its taste upon my mouth and sprouting under me in dancing springs of sand, was the immense body of the continent itself, flowing like the river was flowing, grain by grain, mountain by mountain, down to the sea. I was streaming over ancient sea beds thrust aloft where giant reptiles had once sported; I was wearing down the face of time and trundling cloud-wreathed ranges into oblivion. I touched my margins with the delicacy of a crayfish's antennae, and felt great fishes glide about their work.

As a writer-teacher, I was pleased to find, just when I needed it, such a pregnant paragraph, one fertile paragraph full of figurative writing.

Simile/Metaphor/Analogy

I've grouped these three figures because they are so closely related. They could all be called *simile* because each tries to give us an improved understanding of something by telling us how it is *similar* to something generally unlike it, or something it's unlikely to be compared with.

A *simile* comes right out and says it is *like* (*as* or *so*) the other thing—it admits to being a figure of speech.

A *metaphor,* however, admits to no such thing—it uses deception. It tells us that one thing *is* the other thing—and trusts the intelligence of the reader to figure it out. This makes the metaphor a more powerful figure, because we are intellectually and emotionally satisfied when we see through the deception to the truth. The more novel yet readily understood the similarity, the more satisfying and the more memorable the point being made.

Whereas the simile and the metaphor usually point out only one similarity between the two items, an *analogy* points out a number of similarities—a sort of extended metaphor.

Let's sample how Eiseley used these basic figures of speech:

> . . . cold needles

He's telling us here that the cold water is striking him like cold, metallic needles. His metaphor sort of overlaps the next one, in which he says that these cold needles are

> . . . alpine springs at my fingertips

The next figure is the only *simile* used:

> . . . flowing like the river was flowing . . .

By this he was saying that the continent itself was flowing like a river down to the sea. This would have been a metaphor, rather than a simile, had he written that the continent *was a river* flowing down to the sea. Similes and metaphors are like that—each can be readily converted to the other if, in the revision process, you decide that one is more appropriate than the other.

> I touched my margins with the delicacy of a crayfish's antennae.

The reader can picture Eiseley floating along, arms and fingers outstretched, and when they touch land or bushes he kicks or otherwise adjusts his direction. The basic metaphor here is that his fingers (and toes?) are the antennae that sense the margins of his traverse. His use of the word "delicacy" gave me the definite impression of a slow, luxurious, quiet float. If he were floating rapidly through a riff or a rapid, I can't imagine that a writer of his sensitivity would then use the word "delicacy." Without that excellent word choice, we'd not have any feel for the velocity of this naked anthropologist afloat on the Platte.

Before leaving this brief discussion of metaphors and their friends, it is interesting to note that the word metaphor derives from a Greek word meaning "to transfer" or "to carry over." The word "ferry" derived perhaps from the "phor" part, a ferry being a vehicle that transfers or carries things over: a metaphor carries over a meaning from one context to a different one. The cargo stays the same, but it's put to a new (and perhaps unexpected) use on the other side.

When plastic jugs are on the mainland their "meaning" is that they contain *Clorox,* but when they are unloaded from a metaferry out at the fishing village, the "meaning" of the jugs is that they are inexpensive floating marker buoys for lobster pots. Nothing changes but the meaning.

Personification

One of the most effective and frequently used figures of speech is *personification*—attributing life to the lifeless. Properly used, personification stimulates greatly the reader's imagination. Like a metaphor, it transfers meaning from one (frequently unexpected) source to another:

- Genius is always impatient of its harness; its wild blood makes it hard to train. (Oliver Wendell Holmes)
- . . . On his crest sat horror plumed. (Milton)
- . . . while justice sheathed her claw. (Browning)

We don't have to go to the famous writers of the past for this; we find that in the quoted paragraph Loren Eiseley used personification makes a number of points:

- body of the continent
- wearing down the face of time
- the vast tilted face of the continent
- reptiles had once sported
- fishes glide about their work

Metonymy

One of the main reasons figurative language works is that the mind takes delight in recognizing the sudden leap the writer has made from one object or idea to an object or idea normally considered unlike it. The previously unheralded similarity is suddenly seen. These figures of speech massage our imagination, and because so much writing does not, we are doubly delighted — we like it because we are active partners with the writer in this creative act. If we do not make these leaps with the writer, the thought is lost, of course. Our role as readers of figurative writing is a significant one, we are no longer passive observers.

Some of the most imaginative images come when the writer (and the participating reader) uses a part of an object or an idea to stand for the whole object or idea — *metonymy*. The writer may also use a species to stand for a genus, an individual for a species, the abstract for the concrete — or vice versa. A creative writer may also use the sign for the thing signified, the instrument for the user — or vice versa. The force of these metonymies lies in their singling out a quality of an object and focusing attention upon it, e.g., the *bench*, the *bar*, and the *pulpit* standing for the men or women occupying them; *the pen is mightier than the sword* standing for the thought, "the instruments of peace are mightier than those of war."

Loren Eiseley, in that paragraph I felt so fortunate to find, used several metonymies in addition to all the other figures we've discussed:

> . . . its taste upon my mouth

He was using the taste of the water coming down from the Rockies to stand for all the materials eroded from ancient mountains and everything else of which the continent was made.

> . . . giant reptiles

Here he used the reptiles of the past to stand for all the life forms that lived in prehistoric eras, and for the eras with all they had within them.

> . . . cloud-wreathed ranges

This poetic image of mountains with layers of clouds hanging low on them like wreaths was used to stand for all the continental detritus he felt he was helping trundle (wheel) to the sea.

Hyperbole

Hyperbole is the name for the figure of speech that gets its strength through exaggeration — *overstatement*. This kind of overstatement is not intended to deceive; this is exaggeration used in the search for truth. Since it is used for emphasis, there is also some discussion of it in a previous section of this book (see *Emphasis*).

We all use overstatement every day, especially in informal or colloquial ways. The most erudite professor may be heard saying to his assistant, "Go ahead, Dr. Smith, I'm all ears." We might hear a learned woman say to her dean, "I won't be able to give that speech in Hartford; I'm dead on my feet." Although overstatement must be used with more caution in writing, it can be a better way of making a point than a more accurate, precise, literal description. The receiver, of course, must be aware of its exaggerated nature, or unintentional deception occurs.

The other end of the exaggeration scale is *understatement.* As mentioned earlier (under *Emphasis*), this form can be very effective, but it does presume an alert mind in the receiver. So quiet and unassuming, it may slip right by, or, to use another figure of speech, it may go right over the head of the receiver. Understatement is often not far from irony—both devices are apt to say something more or less opposite to what is really meant. Its strength lies in the psychology of the receiver, who is pleased to have played a role in the figure and is thus more easily persuaded to follow whatever the originator wishes.

Allusion

Writers, in their attempts to get across some point or other, will frequently allude to something in literature, someone from history, or some happening of the recent or distant past. The word allusion is deliberately used because these references by the writer are casual, brief, incidental—they are not detailed, lengthy explanations or elucidations. They are made briefly in the belief that this small clue will trigger associations in all the necessary detail.

A writer might want to get across, for example, a particular typewriter's high level of dependability by referring to it as the "C-47 of the typing war." If he were writing today with young secretaries in mind, the allusion would go right over their heads. The error lies with the writer, not the secretary born twenty years after the heyday of World War II's greatest all-purpose cargo plane. If he were writing for fifty-year-old veterans, the allusion would clearly conjure up an image of a piece of equipment that can be depended upon at all times, under trying conditions, and with low maintenance costs.

Allusions that work delight the reader; he or she is pleased to be sufficiently aware of life that allusions do not fly by but sink in (see *Danger of Mixed Metaphors*). Frequently, allusions are made by single words, sometimes coined from the metal of a famous person's name. "He was definitely Freudian in outlook." "He's an Archie Bunker if ever I saw one."

As you revise a piece of writing, watch for opportunities to insert one of these various figures of speech, as they will frequently have multiple benefits: they'll enliven your work in general; they may, in some cases, add some beauty; they may add emphasis; and they will certainly help make your point. Because they are so close to human talk, figures of speech are more enjoyable and more effective than the predictable words that predominate in so much writing.

The Dangers of Figurative Writing

The importance of metaphors to our language can hardly be overstated. Authors George Lakoff and Mark Johnson wrote in the afterword of their book, *Metaphors We Live By:*

> But metaphors are not merely things to be seen beyond. In fact, one can see beyond them only by using other metaphors. It is as though the ability to comprehend experience through metaphor were a sense, like seeing or touching, or hearing, with metaphors providing the only ways to perceive and experience much of the world. Metaphor is as much a part of our functioning as our sense of touch, and as precious.

In that excellent philosophical book they go much further than saying metaphors are central to language. They prove, it seems to me, that metaphors are central to thought itself. Anything that effective, that central, that significant, must be used in writing of all kinds. Unfortunately, there are dangers in using these powerful implements.

When revising, look carefully at each figure of speech: you may think up a better, fresher, more apt figure. You may also discover by this second look that you should never have used it at all. It's easier to see during revision than during the moments of masterly creation. The dangers are easily understood; we just need to remind our revising selves to remain alert.

THE DANGER OF MISINTERPRETATION BY THE LITERAL

The overriding, central problem is that figurative writing is figurative, not literal. Its power comes from the very fact that it is not literal—not precisely true to the facts. Since your readers vary in psychological make-up, all the way from the very fanciful, poetic, fey types to straight-ahead, A-through-Z, logical, precise types—someone somewhere in that range may take as literally true what you said with tongue in cheek. You may decide, of course, that it's worth the risk, but you must take the possible danger seriously.

Don't use a figure of speech simply because it comes to mind; don't use one simply because it's extremely clever; don't insist on retaining one merely because it's beautiful, musical, philosophical. Be as objective as possible; ask yourself whether you're including it because it will demonstrate your intelligence, your educated background, your sensitive soul—or whether you are leaving it in because it's the most effective way to make the particular point for a specific audience.

THE DANGER OF COMBINING THE FIGURATIVE AND THE LITERAL

There's a danger in combining both a literal and a figurative meaning in the same thought:

- Johnson, the father of outboard motors, was brother to the head of The Chamber of Commerce.
- He went deep in the cave searching for bats. Luckily, he found one right off the bat.

THE DANGERS IN MIXED METAPHORS

This may be the best-known (and most-committed) fault in the use of figurative language. Sometimes the fault can be humorous, so humorous that the writer or speaker loses much of his credibility. You must keep your humor glands open and your sense of the absurd sharp when revising—especially when revising your own work. If you had realized how ludicrous sounding your mixed(up) metaphor was when you created it, you wouldn't have written it down—so it's difficult to recognize your own error during revision.

We see now that old war-horse of the Democracy waving his hand from the deck of the sinking ship.

"That's horrible," she said, "diluting the best blood of the country to pave the way to revolution."

While Moscow is thus stoking up the cold war, however, Peiping is playing it pianissimo.

Whenever the chips are down, I'll back you to the hilt.

The lesson in all this, I suppose, is not to switch metaphorses in mid-stream. And be wary of puns.

DANGER IN THE CONFUSED METAPHOR

The danger in using an inaccurate or confused metaphor is that the whole idea of a metaphor is to enable the reader to create in his or her brain a *visualization* of the metaphor. Look at the trouble you get into, for example, if you intend to say that the Marine sergeant spoke candidly, straight from the shoulder, but in a careless moment you write, *The burly sergeant let his hair down in the barracks, and talked candidly with the nervous young boot.*

Your point may get lost and you may lose some credibility as a serious writer when the reader almost certainly plays with the mental image of a burly Marine coyly removing his broad-brimmed hat, letting his tresses fall across his shoulders, and talking with a frightened young fellow in the barracks.

DANGER IN THE SUSTAINED METAPHOR

Metaphors usually compare two things that are unlike, separating out one similarity that does exist. Metaphor gets part of its strength from pointing out this unexpected, not usually noticed similarity. A writer is often tempted (and sometimes gives in) to extend the metaphor, pointing out a number of other similarities between the two objects. One danger lies with the overextension of similarities, pushing them further than the comparison can sustain.

Figures of speech, in general, have their value in the compression they allow. The imaginative author can sometimes, with the perfect metaphor, make his point in just a very few words. To make the same point by straight explanation, compilation of irrefutable facts, and impeccable logic might take many paragraphs. The poet's great strength is in the tight compression he can bring about, and his most powerful tool is the metaphor. The danger thus lies in stretching a sustained or extended metaphor too far—until it is no longer concentrated, focused, pointed. It becomes diffuse, spread out, lost.

Metaphor also works wonders by its potential for emotional intensity. If one similarity between the two parts of a metaphor slams home a point, a stringing-out of other similarities is apt instead to cool that emotion. As soon as the writer is seen slipping in more than two similarities, she is seen as "stretching a point" or "milking a metaphor." What may have been effective and profound ends up diffuse and silly. Her credibility begins to melt away.

DANGER IN THE MORIBUND METAPHOR

I have deliberately coined the phrase *moribund metaphor* because of the connotative load it bears: something in a dying state, on its deathbed, on the verge of extinction, something going nowhere, stagnant. Therein lies the danger of a moribund metaphor—it's been around too long (although not yet dead) and it's stagnant.

When a metaphor is clinically dead, it's buried in the language as an ordinary word or phrase—indeed, most language is a collection of dead metaphors. They started out as clever, insightful images created by generations of past "poets." Then the metaphors became senile, creeping quietly around the house in soft slippers for years as boring clichés, finally becoming moribund metaphors in nursing homes where no one appreciates or even understands how fresh, youthful, and active they once were.

Once dead and buried within the language, they are relatively harmless; they are dangerous only during the nursing home stage when writers are using them to provide a mental image—yet when readers are no longer familiar with the elements of the metaphor. How many young men and women today, for example, have ever experienced for themselves the uncontrollable action of an axhead flying off the handle in mid-swing? The trajectory of that steel missile is totally unpredictable, just as apt to cleave the head of the wielder as the spectator. From this visual description, you can see some of the original force of the metaphor about the unpredictable, uncontrollable action of a person who's flying off the handle.

The power of that image was still strong in the 1800s, weaker in the early 1900s, weaker still now at the end of the 1900s. In the 2000s, it will have little visual power; it will retain its "meaning" as a phrase in the language, but its day as an effective, powerful metaphor will have passed.

"Flying off the handle" has been a *cliché* for some years now, much of its effectiveness blunted; it's beginning to smell like a *moribund metaphor* unable to raise its intended visual image in the average reader's mind, and before too long it'll be a *dead metaphor* safely interred in the tongue of the tribe.

DANGER IN THE MISUSED ANALOGY

An analogy is, in effect, a sustained metaphor. As we've seen in the previous paragraph, it's inherently dangerous. Analogy is particularly dangerous when used as "proof" of something. Many have tried to argue, in court and elsewhere, by analogy. Some have won; many have failed, because the analogy's real purpose is not argumentation but explanation.

Let's think of a misused analogy in a commonly known context—an egg and an acorn. The hen's egg and the oak's seed are not in themselves alike, but they do bear like relationships: to the parent in each case and to the young chick and the young sapling—the *relationship* being the genus that each falls under.

Philosophers have claimed that analogy is more than a resemblance between relationships. An analogy implies a preponderating resemblance between two things that makes us infer that the resemblance *extends even further*.

No harm is done, provided the reader (and writer) understand that an analogy is being used only for explanation, exposition, or description—and not as an attempt at proof by illegitimate extension.

The danger, of course, is that you may try to support your argument with a resemblance insufficient for the job. For example, years ago many Frenchmen were persuaded to invest money in building a canal across the jungled isthmus of Panama. The argument put forth was that this was analogous to the digging of the canal across the isthmus of Suez that had been successfully managed by the same engineer now to slash the isthmus in Panama—Ferdinand de Lesseps. But the only resemblance between the two projects was the presence of a narrow neck of land separating two large bodies of water. Suez had no giant jungle trees, no giant rocky cliffs, and no giant mosquitos bearing yellow fever. The Frenchmen were persuaded, nevertheless, to part with millions of francs and innumerable lives in the process of digging an insufficient analogy.

DANGER IN PERSONIFICATION

The main danger with personification is its overuse: that temptation is strong with a language like English, because it is so easy to personify an inanimate object. You need only refer to it by a masculine or feminine pronoun—or simply spell it with an initial capital letter.

When used to excess, personification leads to what has been called "fine" writing. If you would write well, avoid fine writing, i.e., don't always display the best in your verbal wardrobe. Back in 1750, Lord Chesterton wrote to his son, "It is by being well drest, not finely drest, that a gentleman should be distinguished."

The perpetrator of "fine" writing sees every crowd as "a sea of faces"; every clapping of two hands as "an ovation"; his breakfast as "his morning repast"; his going to dinner as "his repairing to the festive board"; the opening of a sewage treatment plant as "its inauguration"; and he finds many occasions to refer to himself as "we." These are not so much examples of personification but of the bad habit of fine, overly elegant writing into which people tend to fall when they also use personification at every turn. Such "fine" writers always see Virtue (capitalized) sitting on a mountain summit serene, and Religion (capitalized) comes down from the skies bearing Truth (capitalized) in one hand. This type of writer usually fails ever to see religion or virtue as it really exists in the helping hand of a black man saving a white child from the flames, or a stranger leaping into the icy Potomac to save a half-frozen woman swimming from a downed aircraft.

Personification is a valued figure for the writer; only its inaccurate use, its inappropriate use, and its excessive use are to be avoided—like the Plague (capitalized).

DANGERS IN THE USE OF ALLUSION

Danger hovers ominously over the use of allusion. In the past, it was reasonable for a writer to presume that his or her college-educated readers, at least, would have a common background in literature, history, general science, etc. A writer today cannot presume the same similarity of cultural background; he's perhaps only completely safe with allusions to television shows.

The danger thus lies in ignorance. If the writer has alluded to a Greek goddess by name, presuming the reader would understand that this goddess was noted for leaping through the woods, bow and arrow at the ready, but the reader has no knowledge of her, the visual image the writer planned to conjure in the reader's mind remains unconjured chemicals. (A reader ignorant of the chemical component of memory would not appreciate my allusion here to unconjured chemicals.) I have to run the risk that most of my readers will appreciate the connotative allusion to the almost magic ability of the human brain to produce internal images, triggered by the mere mention of goddesses and conjurers. Have no illusions about the potential of allusion to make a point—or lose it. Use it as you would the gift of magic—cautiously and with forethought.

A section on figurative writing shouldn't just stop cold. It could just wind down, I suppose, but it's considered better form to have a wind-up paragraph. Imagine how blah those two sentences would be without "stop cold," "wind down," and "wind-up." Figurative language keeps us in "touch" with the world we "feel" around us. To the extent we avoid the abstract and stay near the concrete, we'll succeed as writers who are read. To the extent we create new, unexpected, accurate figures that simulate our world in words that stimulate our readers' senses, we'll be writers who are remembered. If you want to be read and remembered, remember what you've just read.

Distractors and Detractors

There are words and phrases not necessarily wrong, bad, ungrammatical, or totally unacceptable that nevertheless should be avoided (or used very consciously) because they can both distract and detract.

When you're writing a first draft, you're so busy trying to figure out just what it is you want to say that you hardly have the time or energy to decide on the best possible way to express the myriad thoughts you're dealing with. In the passion of those early moments, you may use words, phrases, constructions that come naturally to speech (and that would be acceptable in casual conversation among friends) but, upon sober reflection, you realize they should be modified, moderated, or deleted. Some words and phrases can distract the careful reader, diverting his attention from your message. To the degree that he or she is distracted, something is detracted from your reputation as a writer.

I have commented elsewhere in this book on some of the following examples of words and phrases that may both distract and detract, but the point may be more tellingly made by putting all of them here under one rubrical roof:

- obscenities
- sexisms
- dialects
- clichés
- jargons
- misspellings & misuses

Obscenities

Obscenities these days seem to be in the ear of the beholder, so I enter this short discussion rather timidly. Having been in the U.S. Navy for several years, I can't say that I never use obscenities, and I've certainly heard them all. My point here is not a moral point; it's a practical point. An obscenity in the wrong place can be both a distractor and a detractor.

We're all witnesses to the fact that obscenities were seen by most people as out of place in the White House Oval Office. Hearing the President of the United States of America using coarse and obscene language on tape certainly detracted from the dignity of the man, the office of the presidency, and even of the nation itself.

The White House tapes provide an admittedly extreme example, but they do make the point that there are places where obscenity is out of place. In contrast, are there places where it's perfectly acceptable? Referring to the use of written obscenities only, there are several places where most people will accept it today.

Normally, it's inappropriate for the narrator or the author to use obscenities very often, but story characters may include the occasional obscenity when the author considers it essential to characterization. Students claim, of course, that that's exactly how the character would talk. The fun of writing all those f_____ing obscenities makes them forget what they've been taught about writing dialogue: the character's speech is supposed to have the ring of truth about it, and not be a *verbatim* recording. Some students fail to realize that the ring of truth can be accomplished just as well with only the occasional obscene expression. Even with today's permissive attitude, an obscenity in a book is still enough of a shock that the point is made without laying it on thick. In fact, too much obscenity blunts its own effectiveness, and it distracts the reader from the important message. If the reader perceives that the writer is leaning on obscenities for lack of a full vocabulary, the obscenities' presence detracts from the writer's reputation. Most readers resent the author's use of obscene expressions simply to shock; something is thereby detracted from the author.

So as not to be accused of failing to practice what I preach, I'll only use one example from a student's writing that should sharpen the point and send it home (if you are easily offended, please jump over this example).

The scene is aboard a jet plane heading for Orlando; a young man is making a play for one of the stewardesses:

> "I'll bet you're a wild woman in the sack," Ben said, giving her his best, big, put-on smile that his periodontist had been laboring on for five years now. "How about meeting me in the head during lunch?" The stewardess's mouth went slack for an instant, and then the smile returned. "Fuck you, honey," she whispered in his ear; and smiled sweetly as she moved to the next row . . . The old man sitting behind them hadn't missed a word. With the stewardess's answer, he'd dropped half his drink into his lap. Ben heard him gasp and turned around: "Shithouse is in the back," he said, glancing at the old man's crotch. Turning back around, he picked up his book and started to read.

I don't deny that some young man just might be that crude, and some stewardess, sick and tired of all the male passengers' moves, just might respond that way, but was it necessary for the telling of this particular story? That, of course, is the final (or first) question—is it essential to the story I'm writing at this moment? The question is not whether these are bad, dirty, unacceptable words, but whether they're absolutely appropriate for this particular character in this particular scene in this particular book aimed at this particular audience. The audience is at the core of the decision. Who are they and what will they accept? My philosophy is to write honestly about life. It is not my job to make over the world by forcing everyone to accept obscenities, simply because there's a lot of that going around. The acceptance of obscenity is a rather ridiculous *cause célèbre*.

Sexisms

There's nothing more pathetic today than reading a writer out of touch with the realities of his time—women are equal partners with men. The male within me wants to add that they are certainly not identical, but they most certainly are equal. There's another little (and increasing in volume) voice within me that says women may finally be shown to be superior; for now, however, they'll have to be content with equal.

Since women are equal, writers must be careful not to write things that imply inequality. Part of the problem lies in the tendency for old ideas and expressions to hang on long after they're dead and should have been buried. Some of the great humor that came out of "All in the Family" grew out of the disparity between Archie's old attitudes and expressions, and Meathead's usually modern attitudes toward women. Archie's wonderfully male chauvinistic comments would not have received even a chuckle thirty years ago—they would have been perceived simply as "the truth about women." The writer who allows old sexist expressions to creep into his (or her) work will be laughed at—but not with the good-natured laughs given Archie and Meathead. The use of sexisms (anything that implies or connotes that one gender is or ought to be inferior or subservient to the other) distracts the sensitive, perceptive reader from the writer's main thought—and it detracts from the writer's reputation.

It's perfectly all right, of course, to put sexist words into a character's mouth, either to establish his or her character, or to help establish the mood of the time when the story took place. It is irresponsible of a writer to drop all such references in a story that takes place many years ago, or that takes place today in a more primitive society. A writer must tell the truth as he or she sees it. To deny that America used to have slaves, or that women have been in a position of semi-servitude, is to practice revisionism, something we're incensed about when practiced by totalitarian governments. It may even be good for us to remind ourselves periodically of our less-than-perfect past, so as to see more clearly our present as we look to our future and the betterment of our society. The truth shall make us free, and the truth shall keep us free. Our writers are responsible for telling us what they see as the truth. If we have enough writers giving us enough of their truths, however imperfect and incomplete, we'll be able to piece together what for us is "the truth."

Dialect

Don't write in dialect unless you're absolutely steeped in it, preferably from birth. Part of dialect is a regional or local accent that sounds different from the rest of a country's accents. It's extremely difficult to approximate the pronunciation by misspelling the words, so don't try it—certainly don't try to spell every word phonetically to simulate the local pronunciation. Just do it occasionally with some word that's pronounced so totally different in the region that it will help give the reader a feel for the area.

Dialect also has to do with how people structure sentences, and their special grammar. If your story must be told with some dialect, do it with the occasional bit of idiosyncratic grammar. Well done, dialect can add greatly to the realism of the story; done poorly, dialect distracts the reader from the story. (Some writers get so caught up in the accuracy of their dialect that the reader forgets what the story is all about.) Badly written or overdone dialect not only can distract the reader, it can detract from his enjoyment—and detract something from the reader's evaluation of the writer. This is especially true today with the greater concern we feel for ethnic groups. Dialect may be used to establish their ethnic background, but not to the extent that it mocks. Flannery O'Connor, for example, handles dialect so that it neither distracts nor detracts but is central to the regional feel of the story. The example here is from her short story "A Circle in the Fire."

> "You done angered them now," Mrs. Pritchard said, "and it ain't any telling what they'll do."
>
> "They'll be gone when we get back," Mrs. Cope said.
>
> Mrs. Pritchard could not stand an anticlimax. She required the taste of blood from time to time to keep her equilibrium. "I known a man oncet that his wife was poisoned by a child she had adopted out of pure kindness," she said. When they returned from town, the boys were not on the embankment and she said, "I would rather to see them than not to see them. When you see them you know what they're doing."
>
> "Ridiculous," Mrs. Cope muttered. "I've scared them and they've gone and now we can forget them."
>
> "I ain't forgetting them," Mrs. Pritchard said.
>
> "I wouldn't be none surprised if they didn't have a gun in that there suitcase."

Another writer who has an ear for regional dialect is John Sayles. The following example of this ability is from a 1976 story in *Atlantic*, "Breed":

> "Many of these people around here Indian?" Brian asked it noncommittally, fishing. The drillrigger the night before had gone on and on about how the Indians and the coyotes should have been wiped out long ago.
>
> "Oh sure," said Shangreau, "Most of 'em. Not many purebred though, things being what they are. Most of these boys I'm af-

ter is at least half or more Indian. You got your Ogalala around here, your Hunkpapa and the rest. I'm a good quarter Sioux myself. Old Jim Crow who we're headin after now is maybe seven-eights, fifteen-sixteenths, something like that. It's hard to keep count. Jim has got three or four tribes to start with, his mother was part Flathead as I recall, and then he's got white and I wouldn't be surprised if one of them buffalo soldiers didn't slip in a little black blood way back when. But you won't see too many purebred, less we catch Bad Heart at home, and he's another story altogether. What are you?"

"Irish."

"Me too, a good quarter, Monaghans."

If you can write dialect as accurately and cleverly as these two authors, then use it. If not, don't.

Clichés

Clichés and trite expressions are worn-out words. They probably began their life in language as innovative, clever, insightful, accurate, and lively; today they drag.

George Orwell said in *Politics and the English Language* that he was not so worried that thought corrupts language as that language corrupts thought. He referred to debased language as being unfortunately convenient—thus its fast-spreading use. It is the ready-made, the pre-packaged phrase that entraps us: *leaves much to be desired; would serve no good purpose; which we would do well to bear in mind; history tells us; like a bolt from the blue; a land flowing with milk and honey* (there's one whose antiquity is familiar to us all); *oh, home is anywhere I hang my hat; a poet at heart; he ekes out a precarious existence* (have you ever read of a precarious existence that was anything *but* eked out); *I was taken aback; generous to a fault; come one, come all* (I hope someday to receive an invitation that does not summon me along with the herd: COME ONE, COME ALL (always in ALL CAPS—and followed by at least three!!!).

Some of my students have fallen into this trap of ease:

- She looked familiar, but he wasn't sure whether it was the girl—*still, the resemblance was uncanny.*
- She *exchanged pleasantries* with some of the people on the balcony.
- She *looked vaguely familiar* to him, but he couldn't be sure.
- Finally, Bob *broke the silence* with an answer to her question.
- The mysteriousness of the whole incident, *not to mention* Bob's good looks, kept her coming back.
- Blazing beacons *high atop* ultra-modern structures lure the *weary trav-*

eler . . . (why are objects on tall buildings always *high atop;* and the people inside hotel rooms always *weary travelers*).
● They eked out their precarious existence (there it is again) in a *weather-beaten* shack *in dire need of* paint and repair.
● Along the Rue Royale, rows of *quaint antique shops* . . . (oh, to read some day of an antique shop that's not quaint).

Anyway you look at it, these ready-made phrases, expressions, and words are distracting to the intelligent reader—and they detract from you, the writer. As a way to summarize, here's a beginner's sentence that's not only trite, it's wrong:

The silence was so sharp you could cut it with a knife.

Apparently, both the knife and the silence were sharper than the writer.

Jargons

A jargon is a language, especially the vocabulary part of a language, peculiar to a particular trade, profession, or other group. As such, it's a valuable language—in the appropriate place.

At one end of the jargon spectrum is the highly specialized vocabulary of the scientist for whom no ordinary words express his specialized knowledge—

jarosite — a yellowish or brownish mineral of a specific chemical make-up.
infundibulum — a funnel-shaped organ or part.
infrastructure — the basic, underlying framework or features of something, e.g., the communication infrastructure of the USA is considerably more complex than that for Namibia.
horst — a portion of earth's crust, bounded on at least two sides by faults, that has been moved upward.
swizzle stick — a small rod for stirring drinks.

Specialists need this accurate short-hand to communicate efficiently with others in the same specialty. Imagine the inefficiency of two geologists conversing about a highly faulted region if they had to say something like: "George, what about that block of sandstone that's been moved upward relative to the rocks on either side—you know, the block that has faults bounding at least two sides?" They might have to refer to that or other similar blocks many times per day. How much easier and efficient to say: "George, what about that sandstone horst?" And pity the harried bartender on a Saturday night being asked by ten waitresses to please hand over some of those small rods with the fuzzy cellophane used for stirring drinks. How much more efficient to say: "Hey, Harry—gimme a coupla swizzle sticks."

Thus are born the jargons of the day, especially during these days of increasing specialization. Jargon is not bad of itself; the problem arises when the writer writes for people outside the specialty. He or she may unknowingly use the jargon of the trade too much, just through long familiarity with it. That would be an understandable and forgivable error, but what is unforgivable is when the writer tries to impress someone by the deliberately heavy use of jargon. That someone may be within the specialty, and the writer is trying to impress him or her with his own intimate understanding of the profession. Or that someone may be outside the specialty—someone like a reporter. We've all heard the police detective suddenly finding himself in front of the TV camera referring jargonistically, pseudo-legalistically, to the alleged perpetrators.

What is most inexcusable—and it happens all the time—is to hide one's ignorance behind a verbal barricade of jargonistic babble. With that, we've left the world of the acceptably technical, highly specialized vocabulary and entered the world of obfuscation where people try deliberately to make matters obscure, confusing, bewildering—for their own peculiar purposes.

Sociology has taken a lot of ribbing (much of it justified) for its elegant obscurantism, largely born of a desire to appear as a hard science, rather than a soft one. Business and industry are often guilty of similarly obscure writings:

- ABC Inc. can provide single-problem program recommendations, concepts, finished written speeches, and other communication method analyses designed to accomplish particular results.
- One thing they can work on is involving contractor supervisors more in permit procedure safety verification.
- Implement a comprehensive dock inspection program such as the one in the recent acid barge handling course.
- Near miss accident and unusual occurrence investigation deserves more stress.
- Like precipitation measurements, temperature is probably measured within the present accuracy of our knowledge of temperature effects on resource utilization, and provides us with a standard measurement which can be linked empirically or theoretically to specific environmental applications.
- The VGPO jammer can present a wide variety of ECM situations by varying other parameters such as the J/S ratio.
- To 'see the forest for the trees' a fresh look often enables a composite view—an objective understanding of your needs.
- The main functions of the university security department are the preservation of community peace and order, the prevention and detection of crime, the apprehension of offenders, the protection of

persons and property, and the enforcement of the rules and regulations of the university and the laws of the state. For these purposes security personnel are endowed with unique authority. In the exercise of this authority, justice and equity should be the actuating motives at all times.

- This coupled with a proven capability in the area of corporate communications helps assure a meaningful 'description of the view' and positive interpretation of the need translated into the exact language of the audience.
- When you visited our plant and gave your presentation, there was considerable discussion in regard to the subject problem. In recent weeks, it has been brought to my attention that we are experiencing a severe and continuing contamination problem in controls being shipped from your facility. Pieces of lockwire found in fuel controls suggest careless workmanship and lack of pride in the product.
- Our ability to quickly identify needs and recommend continuance, modification or change of existing programs as well as consideration for and implementation of new methods and programs assures timely and economical results.
- The County's recreational facilities appear to be not inadequate to present needs and its untapped resources are strong. There is a question, however, whether in the light of changing characteristics of its residents, concepts for the future have been creatively examined in comprehensive terms.
- We have made significant steps, however, in delineating the informal organization and assessing the impact of its variance from the formal organization on such output variables as productivity and quality of organizational life.
- The public expects (AETNA) to do good. But first, it expects us to do our job. Recently, that's been difficult in some areas as inflation, the need for more and better health care, and the desire for compensation for any untoward happening have combined to drive up the cost of many products and services insurance companies must pay for.
- You have been selected to attend (Professor Cheney's in-house course) because of the amount of correspondence you generate in the execution of day-to-day functions and we feel the course will be helpful to you in your communications with business associates.
- It's a long yardage passing situation out there.

If you are writing within a specialty, perhaps one in which you're uncomfortable with your ignorance, and are revising your writing, be honest with yourself and your readers. Find the truth somewhere, and rewrite as clearly as you can—don't hide behind some bits of jargon that will sound to the reader as though you're up on that specialty. Such obscurantism is easily practiced by an intelligent, well-educated person working too close to the edge of his knowledge, whether within or without his specialized field. A writer must be honest about what he knows, and accurate in his expression of it.

If, during the process of revision, you discover that you have fallen, deliberately or unintentionally, into this ethical bog, dig deeper and fill it in with words of more substance.

In other words, each of us, whether in education, business, government, security, or sports, uses a specialized jargon every day, and we use it effectively. We get into trouble, however, when we use it outside our specialty to try (usually in vain) to impress someone with our clever use of jargon—or when we use it to put ourselves forward as experts in fields we are actually only beginners in. As some of these examples demonstrate, we make matters infinitely worse when we combine obscure jargon with sloppy writing habits. This book has tried to give you ways to overcome these poor habits by approaching the process of revision as an art in itself.

Fiction writers, of course, are encouraged to use some of the jargon within which a character lives. If the character works every day deep within the Pentagon, military and bureaucratic jargons make a mix that a good writer will use to set the tone, establish the man's character, and give the reader a look into the possible effects these jargons may have on the man's thought processes, the way he sees the world, and how he treats his teen-age son. The clever writer will still use only enough jargon and specialized technical language to make the point. His writing should probably not sound like a bureaucrat's internal memorandum, but it should make us understand how people talk within the pentagonal wings of war.

Misspellings and Misuses

In my work with students and clients over the years—not to mention what I've witnessed on television, radio, and in the print media—I've found that there is a relatively small number of words misused at every turn. There are entire books published that purport to help everyone over the hurdles of misspelled, misused, and mispronounced words. These books are valuable tools or research resources for the full-time writer, but this section is for the more typical, reasonably well-educated person who simply doesn't want to fluff in public on words that are in common use (or misuse).

An author's misspellings can be corrected by various secretaries, editors, and proofreaders along the way, and not much is detracted from the author (everyone happily recalling that Ernest Hemingway and other masters were notoriously creative in their spelling efforts). But when an author misspells or misuses words constantly in query letters, proposal outlines, and sample chapters, his or her chances of getting to a contract are greatly reduced.

If the first reader or editor at a publishing house finds himself distracted from the story by the constant misuse of language, the writer's true talent may never be discovered. An editor knows, certainly, that spelling and fine grammar are not the name of the game, that it's ideas and style that are of central significance. Still, he or she is definitely distracted. (I suppose readers didn't see Hemingway's poor spelling until they had already seen his talent and style.) Someone said that misspellings and misuses are like flies buzzing around your head: as long as you're caught up deeply in the reading, you'll not notice the flies—but at some point you throw up your hands in frustration and discover that it's the little flies that are driving you crazy.

I've selected those few words that seem to show up most often in my reading—words that detract from the author and drive me to distraction:

Affect/Effect/Effect

Your red flag should automatically run up the halyard when you see any of these words on the horizon. *Affect* is usually the verb you're looking for. Television is said to *affect* children's minds, and the *effect* is often said to be negative. Your problem all along, presuming you have a problem, is that you knew that one was the verb and one the noun—it's just a matter of remembering which is which (and how to remember it from one time to the next). I have a red flag memory device that is embarrassingly simplistic but one hundred percent effective for me.

First, let's concentrate on only the noun; if you get that straight, the other one *has* to be the verb. (My high school English teacher is going to hate me for this.) When you're momentarily confused about which to use (*effect* or *affect*), ask yourself whether the sentence calls for a noun or a verb. If it calls for a noun, remind yourself that only a noun could have the word *the* inserted in front of it, and still make sense. Then remember that since *the* ends with an *e*, the word you want is the one that begins with an *e*—*effect*. If that seems like an awfully long way around the barn to remember that the noun begins with an *e*, then use your own infallible system. (I told you it was embarrassing to admit that that's how I learned, but now I never make that particular mistake.) What I've just said will keep you out of trouble ninety percent of the time, but there is that other use of *effect* as a verb, e.g., she *effected* the changes suggested. This use is limited to the idea of: she *brought about* the changes suggested. The average person does not use this word very often, so if you need a verb, it is probably *affect*.

Anxious/Eager

You might say that I'm *anxious* about how people more and more say *anxious* when they mean *eager,* e.g., "I'm *anxious* to see The Stones at Madison Square Garden." If I've had my expensive tickets for weeks or months, my sentence probably means that I'm *eager* to see them—so I should have said, "I'm eager to see The Stones at Madison Square Garden." If, on the other hand, I'm a bit worried that there may be a violent mob scene that night, my sentence was correct—I'm *anxious*—i.e., there's a little gnawing *anxiety* inside me. There's the key—if there's *anx*iety involved, *anx*ious is the word.

The careful writer will preserve this distinction, even though we hear it said incorrectly around us every day. Why in the world should we use the same word (anxious) to mean either: *to look forward to something with fear:* and *to look forward with pleasant anticipation.* Use *anxious* for the meaning that has *anx*iety lurking within it; use *eager* for the meaning that has *eager*ness in it. (Seems straightforward and logical enough.) Dictionaries allow that eager is a secondary meaning for *anxious,* but I recommend that you maintain the distinction between *anxious* and *eager.*

Bad/Badly

Nine times out of ten you should probably say or write *bad.* You might as well drop *badly* from your active vocabulary because it is so rarely correct. Think of the parallel case, *goodly.* Would you ever say, "I feel goodly about what I just said." No, you'd say that you felt *good* about what you just said. Some people, however, feel a compulsion to say that they feel *badly* about this or that. You either feel good about it or bad about it; you never feel badly or goodly about it.

Bring/Take

These words are used too often as synonyms, which they are not. You select the proper word on the basis of whether the object under discussion is moving *toward* or *away from* the speaker. If the general direction is toward, *bring* is the correct word.

"Please *bring* that here."

"Please *take* this over there."

In the sentence, "(Take/Bring) your lunch to school with you," there is no way for you to know which word is correct. You must first know who is speaking and from where—e.g., if the teacher said to the children as they were leaving school in the afternoon, "*Bring* your lunch to school with you tomorrow," *bring* would be correct. If it were a case, however, of a mother at home in the morning, she'd be correct if she said, "*Take* your lunch to school with you." In the first case, the *Star Wars* lunch box with the peanut butter sandwiches would be moving toward the speaker (teacher); in the second case, it would be moving away from the speaker (Mom).

Center on/Center around

The meaning would probably be clear if we wrote, "The town's intellectual life centered *around* the schoolhouse," but we could provide a more accurate picture of what we meant by writing instead, "The town's intellectual life centered *on* the schoolhouse." We can almost see the radii of influence converging on or spreading out from this dynamic school. Since the goal of most writing is to paint a clearer picture in the receiver's mind, why not practice what we preach in that little red schoolhouse on which our intellectual life is centered? Probably the difficulty comes from the closely allied thought, "The town's intellectual life *revolved around* the schoolhouse." That is correct usage, and the meaning may be the same as *centered on,* but we can't mix the parts and say *centered around.*

I may be overly sensitive, but I have a different picture drawn for me by each expression. If I felt that these were the kinds of intellectual activities going on all around town, inspired perhaps by the presence of the schoolhouse, I'd use the expression *revolved around.* If, on the other hand, I wanted to express the thought that everything intellectual in the town happened *at or in* the schoolhouse, I'd say *centered on.*

You might say that that was a rather fine distinction—and it is. That's what good writing (good thinking) is about—finer and finer distinctions. I admit that in this case, your reader would not be thrown very far off the track by your using the less accurate expression, but it is worth pointing up again and again that a writer should be a person of distinctions.

Oh, yes, then there's the parallel matter of *focus.* Don't fall into the trap of saying that these chapters *focus around* the requirements of good, effective communication. *Focus* should always preserve its image of rays converging on a spot or small area. Your writing will have a blurred effect if your words and thoughts are not focussed.

Your communications will provide clear meaning to the extent that your thoughts are focussed on making fine distinctions. *Focussed around* gives me a blurry impression; *focussed on* gives me a clearer picture of what you mean.

Have you noticed that I've spelled *focussed* with two *s*'s—and I'd do the same with *focussing*. The usual dictionary will report that you may use *focused* and *focusing*. I recommend that you use the doubled *s*. Otherwise it seems, to my eyes and ears, we'd have to pronounce them as *foke-used* and *foke-using*. It is truly optional, but not when you write to me.

Continual/Continuous

These are very similar-sounding words with a similar meaning, but there is a distinction to be made. *Continual* refers to something that is always going on, although there are discernible intervals—e.g., The *continual* ticking of the alarm clock drove him mad. *Continuous* refers, rather, to something that continues without any significant intervals in between—e.g., The *continuous* hum of the refrigerator drove him madder still. The *continual* snowstorms made that the winter of his discontent. There was that winter a *continuous* belt of snow from Vermont to Maine. There were intervals between the snowstorms, and it must have seemed to him that no sooner had one stopped than the next began, but use *continual*. There were possibly patches where there was no snow between Vermont and Maine, but one could reasonably describe it as a belt in which there was snow everywhere—hence, *continuous*. If there are periodic, but humanly discernible interva*ls*, the word is continu*al*. If there are no discernible intervals, use *continuous*.

Disinterested/Uninterested

These words are vaguely related, but they are not the synonyms so many people seem to believe. Unless you happen to work within the legal field, the word you usually want is *uninterested,* e.g., He was *uninterested* in what was being said, and was bored by it. In another situation the same man might be interested in what was being said, but he might at the same time be disinterested—i.e., he was impartial and his opinion was not influenced by any personal advantage. A financial manager, for example, might be interested in hearing two men discuss the relative merits of two stocks in which he had no money invested. They could ask his financial advice because they would see him as knowledgeable and interested but *disinterested*.

I should think that the average person would only rarely find the need to use *disinterested,* so if you find yourself starting to write or say it, raise the red flag. If it's simply a lack of interest, use *uninterested*.

Enthusiasm/Enthusiastic/Enthuse

No one misuses enthusiasm or enthusiastic; the problem (admittedly one of life's minor problems) comes with the verb coined from them, i.e., *enthuse*. Enthuse is a non-word, so you should not use it in formal writing. Although a non-word today, I expect it will soon be accepted into the language; it has such an enthusiastic sound to it. *She was one of those who enthuse* (enthooooze) *over everything.* Until it becomes officially accepted, work around it—*she was one of those whose enthusiasms include the entire world*—or, *she was enthusiastic over flea-jump records, flea markets, and the latest in flea collars.*

Enhance/Improve

There's too great a tendency today to use *enhance* as a supposedly fancy variation of *improve*. It should not be used to express simple improvement; it has higher ambitions, e.g., The factory *improved* its cold cream; the cold cream *enhanced* her appearance. The factory *improved* its lens; the new lens *enhanced* the microscopic image. (I believe this vogue use of "enhance" began with the technology of "image enhancement," first with "edge enhancement" on the U-2's aerial photographs. Then everyone heard about the "computer-enhanced" photographs coming back from probes to Luna, Mars, and Saturn.)

Some examples may clarify the sometimes subtle shades of distinction.

- They *improved* the fields, barns, and outbuildings, greatly *enhancing* the farm's value.
- The editor *improved* upon this book, greatly *enhancing* my reputation as a writer, and hers as an editor.
- A good product will *improve* profits; the improved profits will *enhance* the value of the stock. One should not say that the profits were enhanced by the activities of the sales staff. The sales staff's reputation, however, was enhanced by its improved sales record.
- Keep in mind also that *a person cannot be enhanced.* His or her appearance may be enhanced, but not the person.
- A person's prosperity might be enhanced, but a person can't be enhanced in the matter of his prosperity. She might have her beauty enhanced by eye shadow, but she could not be said to be enhanced by the addition of eye shadow.

Envious/Jealous

A man could be *envious* of another man who has a gorgeous wife; he could not be *jealous* about it. The husband, on the other hand, could feel *jealous* about his wife's interest in the other chap. He might *envy* the bachelor his freedom, but he could not be *jealous* of him. *Envy* has to do with being discontent, and wanting what someone else has. *Jealousy* has to do with a fear of rivalry, or suspicion that someone wants and may try to get what you rightfully have. Although most dictionaries will say that you can be jealous both about a man's job and a man's wife, I prefer to save *jealousy* for affairs of the heart and *envy* for all else.

> He was *envious* of his partner's good looks.
> He was *jealous* when his wife glowed in the presence of his partner's good looks.
> She was *envious* of her friend's abilities.
> She was *jealous* when her husband showed keen interest in her friend's abilities.

Those are examples of my preferred uses. The learned lexicographers would have you relax; I won't.

Farther/Further

When writing about comparative distances, distances that you could imagine measuring, use the word *farther.* Some of the more liberal dictionaries state that these two distressingly similar words are synonyms, but I prefer to use them for distinct purposes. If writing of measurable distances, use *farther;* if of abstract, impossible-to-measure distances, use *further.* The painter climbed *farther* up the ladder against the house. His son, the artist, climbed *further* up the ladder of success. A *further* example of this distinction might be that as the son thought *further* about his success, he moved *farther* and *farther* from his dad's house (while moving *further* and *further* away from his dad's heart).

Fewer/Less

Somewhere there must be one little ol' signmaker who paints the signs for all supermarket "fast checkout lines"—*Six or less items only.* You'd think that at least one store somewhere would break the mold and put up a correct sign that reads—*Six or fewer items.* Would that be so difficult? The rule is that you use *few* and *fewer* for things you can imagine *counting;* use *less* for quantities that one doesn't count, e.g., It takes *less* time for them to go through the line because there are *fewer* people in the fast line. You could imagine yourself counting the people in the line; you couldn't imagine yourself counting the time. Another example to sink home the point: It takes *fewer* seconds for them to go through the line because the clerks are *less* busy. You could imagine counting the seconds; you couldn't imagine counting the "busy."

A *few* bottles (count them) have *less* liquid in them than their labels claim. (You could imagine measuring the liquid, but you couldn't *count* the liquid.) Don't buy those items on television commercials that claim to have *less* calories; they're contributing to our national delinquency of language. Why don't they simply claim to have *fewer* calories (count them). Perhaps they've hired that less-than-literate supermarket sign painter to moonlight on Madison Avenue.

In/Into

One would think that these two well-known words would not be misused, but I see it every day. It wouldn't surprise me to find this sentence—*the minister leaped in the church and preached his sermon.* This paints a different image of the minister for us than would this corrected version—*the minister leaped into the church and preached his sermon.* In the latter case he was merely late; in the first, he was carried away by his work.

In means *in*clusion with*in* space, a place, or limits. *Into* means, *to* the inside of, or *in to*ward; direction is implied. He stumbled *into* the cave. While walking *in* the dark for about a quarter mile, he fell *into* a pool of water. He swam *in* the pool for awhile, staring up at the vaulted ceiling with its pendant stalactites. He finally climbed out on the far side and walked *into* a low passageway. It was impossible to walk upright *in* it, but it was possible to get through. Suddenly, *in* the darkness, he fell *into* a grammatical error. He hadn't realized what he was getting *into*.

Insure/Ensure/Assure

Dictionaries and usage books sometimes leave the reader confused as to how to use these temptingly similar words. Some of the more liberal books almost give permission to use the three interchangeably—certainly we find people using them as synonyms. In my own writing I prefer, especially in the case of any two words that are as close in spelling and sound as *insure* and *ensure,* that each have its own meaning. First, I limit myself to using *insure* for financial matters, especially concerning payments in the event of loss or harm. "Hartford, Connecticut, home of the *insurance* industry." I use *ensure* only to express an idea about how something is to be made certain. "My job is to *ensure* that all goes off on schedule." "Can your company *insure* us against the possibility that everything does not go off as scheduled?"

I save *assure* for cases where someone or an organization is guaranteeing someone, or declaring earnestly, that such and such is true, or promising sincerely that a certain thing will go off as scheduled. "He definitely *assured* me that we were insured against unmet schedules." I *assure* you, the reader, that if you can remember the following cooked-up sentence, you'll be able to keep these three distinctions straight. He was overheard at a cocktail party saying to a fellow in the corner, "I *assure* you that if you'll *insure* yourself with my company, you'll *ensure* that your family will be adequately cared for, should you . . . ahh . . not be around." To drive home the point: After he told his family that he was now *insured,* they felt greatly *reassured.* They saw how his selfless act had *ensured* their future comfort, even if he were . . . ahh . . . no longer around.

Nauseous/Nauseated

I hear these words misused all the time on television and in everyday conversation. Once you know the true meaning of *nauseous,* you'll find yourself laughing aloud at the next person who says she's nauseous. This expression means that she is *making others feel nausea and creating their desire to vomit.* If you feel nausea, say, "I'm nauseated." It's almost impossible to invent a situation in which one would properly use, "I'm nauseous." (How often does anyone cause others to vomit?) In that unlikely case, however, say something like, "I'm apparently being nauseous and making you ill; I'd better leave." (Please do.) In other words, 99 times out of 100, the word you need is *nauseated* (to feel nausea). A correct use of nauseous would be: *The ship's stove was nauseous,* causing the seasick to feel even more *nauseated.* To sink home my point, *ad nauseam,* here are some synonyms for nauseous: *revolting, repellent, abhorrent, offensive, despicable.* So, the next time you're tempted to say that you're nauseous, recall that you are saying, in effect, that you're either revolting, repellent, abhorrent, offensive, or despicable. If you're none of these, but simply ill, say that you're nauseated.

Use/Utilize

It would be difficult to find a page of governmental, military, or academic writing that doesn't have on it the word *utilize.* It must be one of the most over-utilized words in the world. It seems as though people out to impress people with the significance of what they're doing use *utilize* when they should use *use.*

Utilize is not an elegant variation of the word *use;* it has its own distinct meaning. When you utilize something, you *make do with something not nor-*

mally used for the purpose, e.g., you *utilize* a dime when the bloody screwdriver is nowhere to be found. If the screwdriver were there, you'd *use* it, not *utilize* a stupid dime for the purpose. Use *use* when you mean *use,* and *utilize* only when it's properly used to mean—*to use something not normally used.* The computer went off-line, so they *utilized* Mr. Wang's abacus, the one he liked to *use.* Despite the temporary breakdown, the computer's *use*-rate was up (not its *utilization*-rate).

Whether/If

When you want to introduce two or more alternatives in a sentence, use *whether* (*or not* is the implied alternative), e.g., The Governor said that he didn't yet know *whether* he'd run. The Governor also said that *if* he ran, he'd win. He claimed he'd be equally happy *whether* he wins, ties, or loses. *If* is usually *setting up a condition of the future,* not preparing us for the *consideration of several alternatives,* as *whether* does. Since they have these totally different meanings, I prefer to use each for its intended purpose. I don't know *whether* you'll follow my advice on this, but *if* you do, I'll appreciate it.

A F T E R W O R D

I've often lectured on how difficult any author finds the writing of a satisfying ending. I was right.

If you've read this entire book, you probably have the perseverance required to *write* a book—and it does take that. Even if you've read only parts, you'll have discovered that it's impossible to tell revision from writing. Whoever first said that "writing is rewriting" must have been a writer; those three words came close to being the title of this book.

I had best repeat what I said at the outset and reiterated periodically—the long-experienced writer does not follow closely the sequence of revision routines as set forth between these covers. Since revision is such a complex intellectual process, it seemed to me that the learning writer (and aren't we all) would not be helped much by a book that suggested he go about revising the same way the professional may—everything simultaneously—and then do it all again several times. Rather, this book recommends a reasonable sequence to follow until you just naturally begin doing it all simultaneously.

My other purpose in writing a book about revision rather than about writing was to throw a much-needed spotlight on the art of revision. Revision is too often treated as craft, not art. There certainly are many elements of craft involved, as there are in painting, piano playing, and sculpting, but good writers, like good painters, make of revision an art. Writing and its revision boil down to the not-so-simple art of getting the words right.

RECOMMENDED READING

Throughout the years, I've collected a great number of books about writing, some of which referred me to other books as models of excellent writing. Every book taught me something; some books changed my writing quality, and occasionally, one changed my life. I would like to share many more with you, but I've limited myself to selecting those most useful to a consideration of revision.

I worry about the strict distinction made between fiction and nonfiction, but I've perpetuated the practice by so dividing the twenty-four, even though the books in each category have much to offer people primarily concerned with the other. Who could say seriously that studying John McPhee's articles or E.B. White's essays would not in the long run help the writing of our fiction, our writing in general? Wordsmithing is wordsmithing.

FICTION

- *Techniques to Apply*

   The Lively Art of Writing (3 vol.) Lucile Vaughan Payne; Follett Publishing Company, 1982. I'm sure that if I were to meet this author, I'd like her right away. Her writing about writing is so easily conversational, so witty, so understanding in its attitude toward young writers, and so practical in its advice that I recommend it for anyone, but especially for those who teach students of any age. Each of its three paperback volumes stands well on its own two feet, but I recommend having all three (Understanding Forms; Effecting Style; Developing Structure). I also recommend an earlier (1965) paperback volume of the same title, published by New American Library.

   Short Story Writing; Wilson R. Thornley; Bantam Books; 1979. I've found this book that Mr. Thornley presumably wrote for his high school students very useful for graduate students and for myself. Particularly well done is the final section wherein he analyzes a series of short stories to show what the author was up to in a scene, or even in his use of a particular word. Thornley makes it informative and enjoyable by a two-column layout of text and anlaysis. I like to learn in this way.

Techniques of Fiction Writing: Measure and Madness; Leon Surmelian; Anchor Books (Doubleday) (a549). It's impossible for me to say how important this book has been for me in learning about fiction. If I were allowed only one book on fiction writing on a desert isle where I'd be allowed to write as much fiction as I'd like, this would be that single book. Leon Surmelian has thought it all out and put it all down. There are so may underlinings, so many exclamation points in the margins, and so much "Hi-liting" from my many readings and appreciatings that it looks like a case of severe book abuse. It is not; these are marks of love.

Writing the Natural Way; Gabriele Lusser Rico; J.P. Tarcher, Inc.; 1983. Dr. Rico has produced a unique book that will be around for a long time. Like Bob Baker (*Newsthinking*) and me, she's fascinated by the implications of brain research data for writers. She's developed some teaching and learning techniques from her knowledge of how the two brain hemispheres work in the creative process. Her ideas about clustering, remindful of Tony Buzan's "brain patterns" (*Use Both Sides of Your Brain*), provide help to thinking and writing far beyond what might at first be seen as something simple or gimmicky. I think she and Buzan have a tentative grip on Truth.

A Writer Teaches Writing; Donald M. Murray; Houghton Mifflin Co. A professor of English and a Pulitzer Prize winning writer of newspaper editorials, Don Murray decided to help the cause of better writing in elementary and secondary schools by finding out how professional writers and teachers felt about learning the writing process. He put all the results in this book. I found it extremely enjoyable to read and it helped me learn how people can best be taught to write in the classroom. There are excellent chapters on how to edit and advise students.

● *Techniques As Applied*

The Bridge of San Luis Rey; Thornton Wilder; TIME Inc. Book Division. I don't know whether the literati have said that this is an American classic, but I so declare it. If you enjoy the style of the following quote, you'll love the book. "With great effort Dona Maria tried to fix her mind on what was being said to her. Twice she lay back, refusing to seize the meaning, but at last, like a general calling together in a rain and by night the dispersed division of his army she assembled memory and attention and a few other faculties and painfully pressing her hand to her forehead she asked for a bowl of snow." Here is a writer of high style who writes with the clarity of a mountain stream.

The Complete Stories of Flannery O'Connor; Introduction by Robert Giroux; Farrar, Straus & Giroux (Sunburst Books). What can I say that has not already been written in appreciation of this great writer of short stories? Others may admire her for the symbolism they find in her works, but I like her best for the characters she creates so well—and all within the tight limits of the short story.

Furious Seasons; Raymond Carver; CAPRA PRESS (A Noel Young Book); 1977. My brother-in-law writer, Alan L. Bates, gave this book to me as a birthday gift. He had no idea how pleased I would be to discover the writings of a relatively unknown (at the time) writer. Carver is a wonder with words. I marvel at his ability to say so much with so few. His newer book, *Fires* (CAPRA PRESS 1983) is equally good and gives us a fine taste of Raymond Carver, poet.

Mrs. Bridge; Evan S. Connell, Jr. (Fawcett Premier Book); Fawcett Publications, Inc. Don Murray, in *A Writer Teaches Writing,* told his readers they had to read *Mrs. Bridge* if they wanted to see how a novel ought to be written. He was right, so I'm exhorting my readers to go and do likewise. Evan Connell has discovered the secret sought by so many of us—clarity. It's really transparency, a quality that makes the reader see not the words but right through them to the ideas behind them. It all seems so easy in the hands of this master. Simple ideas expressed by simple words in short, straightforward sentences that accumulate quietly to create in the reader a deep understanding of this woman.

Of Mice and Men; John Steinbeck; Easton Press (Special Collectors Edition) but also available through Viking Press. One class of students must have heard me say so often what a wonderful piece of work this book is that they presented me with this leather-bound edition at the end of the course. Perhaps I did go overboard, but I do consider this small book an American gem. How many novels of far greater length have given us two characters who echo in our minds so well and so long as do George and Lennie? This should be required reading for all aspiring writers.

Rituals of Surgery; Richard Selzer: Simon and Schuster (A Touchstone Book); 1974. Although many of Dr. Selzer's stories grow out of his special knowledge and understanding of the human body, the title of this book must mislead the bookstore browser. This is a collection of highly imaginative short stories having little to do with medicine or surgery. His imagination is complemented by the skill of a poet. His words are as accurately aimed and precisely ground as his scalpels. These stories deserve a wider audience and should be used to teach short story writing.

NONFICTION

● *Techniques to Apply*

The Elements of Style (third edition); William Strunk, Jr. and E.B. White; Macmillan Publishing Company. Never has a nation so large been so conquered by a book so small. Almost every book about writing recommends that it be read; almost every teacher suggests that it belongs on every educated person's shelf. Prof. Strunk taught enough students to know where they were most apt to falter, and he continues to keep us out of harm's way today. E.B. White's addition of a new section, "An Approach to Style," is a list of twenty-one reminders about what to do and not do as we attempt to develop a style as graceful as his.

The Golden Book on Writing; David Lambuth; Viking Press. Similar in content and intent to *The Elements of Style,* this book is just as useful. The title may turn some browsers away, if they mistakenly believe it one of a well-known series of books for children. It is not; it's a book for every person who must write during the course of the average day. I get perverse enjoyment out of listing this book title for my graduate classes, but I find more value in its eighty pages than in many "academic" books many times longer. There's gold in more than the title.

Modern Rhetoric; Cleanth Brooks and Robert Penn Warren; Harcourt Brace Jovanovich. A typical college textbook in the breadth of its coverage, but I believe atypical in the quality of its writing. So often we find texts on writing that are, in themselves, examples of how not to teach someone. It contains almost nine hundred pages of useful information on how to write beautifully and persuasively—too much information, if there can truly be such a thing.

On Writing Well (second edition); William Zinsser; Harper and Row. The enormous success of this book attests to its utility. Everyone who reads it recommends it. It appears on just about every list of Recommended Readings I've come across. Its success must be the result of the writing itself, because it's so strangely organized. Somehow, its 175 pages cover the expected topics related to style and usage, but it also addresses such specialized topics as science writing, sports, criticism, humor, interviewing, and writing in your job. It's a definite tribute to Bill Zinsser's wordsmithery that people come away from the book talking about how useful, practical, and enjoyable it is—and they're right.

Newsthinking: The Secret of Great Newswriting; Bob Baker; Writer's Digest Books, Inc.; 1981. Bob Baker has written a book I planned to write, and he's done it better. He's interpreted much of the brain research about the varied competence of the two hemispheres and applied it to the practical world of thinking about and writing up the news. Almost everything he discusses is useful for any writer, especially the writer of nonfiction.

Say It with Words; Charles W. Ferguson; University of Nebraska Press. Mr. Ferguson says many interesting things in this enjoyable, informative, inspiring book. He thinks that writing is nine-tenths rewriting, but says it's not all drudgery. "Revision, properly undertaken, can be as imaginative and satisfying as the original creation. Here a man's skill with words really shows itself. Improvement from draft to draft is the dearest reward of the writer." A fine book that I recommend to anyone in love with words.

Simple and Direct: A Rhetoric for Writers; Jacques Barzun; Harper & Row. This is a book for writers (and teachers) intending to become excellent. It's refreshing to find a bona fide scholar writing with evident joy about what he obviously cares deeply about—the expression of ideas with effect. His explanations and instructions throughout are simple and direct.

Writing with Style (The News Story and the Feature); Peter Jacobi; Lawrence Ragan Communications, Inc.; 1982. Jacobi enjoys words—not the super-fancy words but the words of our everyday language—and he wants us to write our nonfiction more creatively. He instructs with his own fine words, but he works in quotes, unexpected quotes from sources not usually seen in books on journalistic writing. He wants to bring art to nonfiction and shows us how in this easily read book with its admirably extravagant white space.

● *Techniques as Applied*

Essays of E.B. White; Harper & Row; 1977. The essayist himself says that he chose which essays to include on the basis of whether they amused him in the rereading. They have certainly amused (and instructed) me in the rereading)—and I reread E.B. White's writing over and over again. It never fails to uplift me.

The John McPhee Reader; Editor, William L. Howarth (Second Vintage Book Edition); Random House; 1978. My son Ralph introduced me to the writing of John McPhee, and I'm forever grateful. Nonfiction (and fiction) writers should read McPhee's articles and books to learn the value of research and the use of concrete details to provide an aura of authority to their writing. I've found William Howarth's introduction to the book highly instructive. I reread it several times a year.

The Medusa and the Snail (More Notes of a Biology Watcher); Lewis Thomas (Bantam New Age Books); Viking Press; 1979. Warts. If I should need to devise a foolproof test of a writer's ability to write interestingly about science, I should ask for an essay on warts. As I began reading the essay on warts, I planned to give the author a paragraph or two to win my reading time investment; he had me with the first four words. These short essays on everything from warts to committees to punctuation are models of clear, witty, concise writing about science, or should I say, life. Equally good is his National Book Award winner, *The Lives of a Cell.*

The Night Country; Loren Eiseley; Charles Scribner's Sons; 1971. I hope it will compliment each man to say that what Lewis Thomas is to biology, and what Richard Selzer is to medicine, Loren Eiseley is to anthropology. The trouble with that comparison is that it comes nowhere near capturing these men, their talents, and their message. They each make us see ourselves from different angles, different times— and we go away eager to write well and exhilarated to be human.

On Writing, Editing and Publishing (Essays Explicative and Hortatory); Jacques Barzun; University of Chicago Press; 1971. An unusual collection of some nine pieces by Jacques Barzun, one of the best writers of clear prose I've ever come across. Three of them are worth the price of this slim paperback: "A Writer's Discipline"; "English As She's Not Taught"; and "Lincoln the Writer."

119 Years of the Atlantic (Atlantic Subscriber's Edition); Editor: Louise Desaulniers; The Atlantic Monthly Company; 1977. One selection from each of the magazine's years between 1857 and 1976 gives us a rare cross-section of American thoughts in nonfiction, fiction, and poetic forms in one book.

This is a highly personal list. I paid no attention to what authorities might say should be included in a bibliography to help writers. This is an honest list of what I believe have been the most useful, and at the same time, enjoyable books I've worked with. My readers deserve to know what I read and think, not what someone else reads and thinks.

INDEX